Tips for Teaching CULTURE

Practical Approaches to Intercultural Communication

PEARSON
Longman

Ann C. Wintergerst
Joe McVeigh

Series Editor: H. Douglas Brown

Tips for Teaching Culture: Practical Approaches to Intercultural Communication

Pearson Education, 10 Bank Street, White Plains, NY 10606

Staff credits: The people who made up the *Tips for Teaching Culture* team, representing editorial, production, design, and manufacturing, are Pietro Alongi, Rhea Banker, Maretta Callahan, Nancy Flaggman, Jaime Lieber, Lise Minovitz, Linda Moser, Barbara Sabella, Jennifer Stem, Katherine Sullivan, and Paula Van Ells.
Cover design: Barbara Sabella
Text design: Barbara Sabella
Text composition: Rainbow Graphics
Text font: ITC Garamond
Illustration credits: Illustrations on the following pages are by Don Martinetti: 20, 41, 65, 110, 129. All other illustrations are by Rainbow Graphics.
Photo credits: : viii (top), Luci Geraci, St. John's University; viii (bottom), Tad Merrick; 1, Jon Feingersh/Blend Images/Corbis; 4, Christopher Futcher/iStockphoto.com; 9, Jurgen Ziewe/Shutterstock; 13, grafica/Shutterstock; 25, Gale S. Hanratty/Alamy; 28, Petr Vaclavek/Shutterstock; 34, Monkey Business Images/Shutterstock; 48, argo/Shutterstock; 53, Fancy/Alamy; 56, Photo by David M. Goehring courtesy of Lindsey Blackhurst; 68, Valentyn Volkov/Shutterstock; 77, Bernd Vogel/Corbis; 79, AVAVA/Shutterstock; 83 (top), Vyacheslav Osokin/Shutterstock; 83 (bottom), Ingrid Balabanova/Shutterstock; 90, Steve Skjold/Alamy; 99, cloki/Shutterstock; 107, Jose AS Reyes/Shutterstock; 119 Monkey Business Images/Shutterstock; 123, michaeljung/Shutterstock; 135, Michael Newman/Photo Edit; 140, Photo by Jonathan Blake courtesy of Leila McVeigh; 143, AVAVA/Shutterstock; 153, El Greco/Shutterstock; 157, Michael Newman/Photo Edit; 163, Laurence Gough/Shutterstock; 167, Jeff Greenberg/Photo Edit; 170, Photo by Joe McVeigh courtesy of Zeynep Ayasli; 177, Andresr/Shutterstock; 186, Photo by Katie Bartlett.
Text credits: 171, Wink, *Critical Pedagogy*, pp. 134-135, © 2005. Reproduced by permission of Pearson Education, Inc.; 186-187, "Thinking Peace/Doing Peace" adapted by permission of the author, Anna S. Ochoa-Becker.

Library of Congress Cataloging-in-Publication Data
Wintergerst, Ann C.
  Tips for teaching culture : practical approaches to intercultural communication / Ann C. Wintergerst, Joe McVeigh ; series editor, H. Douglas Brown.
      p. cm.
  Includes bibliographical references and index.
  ISBN-13: 978-0-13-245822-1
  ISBN-10: 0-13-245822-5
  1. English language—Study and teaching—Foreign speakers. 2. English language—Social aspects—United States. 3. Language arts—United States. 4. Multicultural education—United States. 5. Children—Language.
I. McVeigh, Joe. II. Title.
  LB1576.W493 2010
  428.2'4—dc22

                                                                                              2010015283

ISBN-10: 0-13-245822-5
ISBN-13: 978-0-13-245822-1

PEARSON LONGMAN ON THE WEB

Pearsonlongman.com offers online resources for teachers and students. Access our Companion Websites, our online catalog, and our local offices around the world.

Visit us at **www.pearsonlongman.com**.

1 2 3 4 5 6 7 8 9 10—V056—15 14 13 12 11 10

Contents

About the Series

English language teachers always appreciate and enjoy professional reference books with practical classroom approaches that are firmly grounded in current pedagogical research. *Tips for Teaching* is a response to this demand in the form of a series of books on a variety of topics of practical classroom-centered interest.

Designed for teachers of English in native English-speaking countries as well as in non-native English-speaking countries, *Tips for Teaching* addresses audiences in secondary schools, colleges, and adult education courses with students at varying levels of proficiency. Users may be novice teachers seeking practical guidelines for instruction in a specified area or experienced teachers in need of refreshing new ideas. Each book in the series provides teachers with clearly described procedures, tasks, activities, and techniques, all based on communicative and/or task-based language teaching foundations.

*　*　*　*　*

In *Tips for Teaching Culture*, Ann Wintergerst and Joe McVeigh have addressed an issue that has both fascinated and bewildered language teachers for decades—ever since Robert Lado's *Linguistics Across Cultures* (1957) stimulated teachers to consider the intertwining nature of culture and language in their classrooms. Today, as we speed into this second decade of the millennium, the cultural nature of human language is perhaps too often swept under the rug. The allure of new technologies, the fascination with communicative task-based methodology, and the rise of English as a world *lingua franca* have possibly contributed to a blurring of the centrality of language as a sociocultural tool for communication.

Wintergerst and McVeigh's book goes a long way toward refocusing teachers on this all-important aspect of our language teaching craft. *Tips for Teaching Culture* offers refreshing attributes: simplicity, conciseness, and practicality. Each chapter is carefully constructed to provide readers with a set of "tips" for exploring and teaching various aspects of culture, which are then systematically treated in terms of what research says and what the teacher can do in the classroom.

Virtually all of the classic subtopics about teaching culture in the language classroom—the language-culture connection, language and one's (cultural) identity, cross-cultural differences in education, the cultural nature of nonverbal communication, and more—are treated with a spectrum of activities and techniques. Not to be overlooked are the so-called "hot topics" in treating culture— that is, sensitive issues on which students may have deeply rooted feelings that disagree with those of their classmates. Examples in this book include: recognizing cultural stereotypes, especially as linguistically expressed in words and phrases; politely disagreeing (within cultural norms) with others; and debating political and religious beliefs. The final two chapters of *Tips for Teaching Culture* provide a stimulating treatment of culturally-based assumptions about education and the moral dilemmas involved in assuming one's social responsibility as a language teacher.

Best wishes as you use the tips in this book to help your learners achieve their goals.

Dr. H. Douglas Brown
Professor Emeritus, San Francisco State University
Series Editor

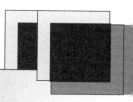

Preface

What comes to mind when you hear the word *culture*? Some people envision visiting exotic places and trying interesting new foods. Others think about the challenges of communicating with someone from a different cultural background. What comes to mind when you hear the words *teaching culture*? Some teachers may picture teaching about a country's holidays, its foods, and its famous people. Other teachers think about the importance of giving their students the needed skills and strategies to perform everyday tasks in a new country with a new language. While writing this book, we thought carefully about how best to convey the concepts and implications of culture for language learners and for teachers. Our goals are to equip you with an understanding of the basic concepts of culture and intercultural communication, to give you explicit ideas on how you can introduce these concepts to your students, and to provide activities that effectively promote discussion in the classroom.

The purpose of *Tips for Teaching Culture* is to provide teachers of English to speakers of other languages with a practical overview of culture and intercultural communication. It is the end product of our collaborative work as classroom teachers, teacher-trainers, workshop presenters, authors, editors, and consultants. Our material links theory, research, practice, and experience with specific activities that teachers can use to help learners develop intercultural awareness. In other words, the book explains in concrete terms what teachers can do to help students benefit from learning about intercultural communication and what learners can do to demonstrate their understanding.

In this book we use the terms *intercultural* and *cross-cultural* interchangeably. We feel that both terms equally address the concepts of learning about how people from different cultures communicate amongst themselves and with others, as well as how people perceive their own culture and the world around them. Discussions of intercultural and cross-cultural issues offer fruitful and essential realms of exploration for language teachers and learners. In this book, we hope to communicate our enthusiasm about these issues to you.

INTENDED AUDIENCE

Tips for Teaching Culture is intended for teachers of English to speakers of other languages, and for their students who aspire to function effectively in their new culture and language. The book is designed to be helpful for teachers working with adults or young adults. The classroom activities can be used with a range of language levels, from low-intermediate to advanced proficiency levels. We have also offered ideas for lower level language learners. We encourage you to adapt the materials so that they are most suitable for the students in your own classroom.

About the Authors

The authors have over 50 years of combined experience in the field of English language teaching. In this book they have shared some of the stories from their lives as classroom teachers and as travelers. The authors have also included interesting and informative experiences of other English teachers around the world. You will find them in the sections titled "Voices from the Classroom."

Dr. Ann C. Wintergerst has taught English as a Second Language students for three decades. She is professor of TESOL at St. John's University in New York City, where she established and directed the university's first English as a Second Language Program. Ann has trained teachers and presents annually at conferences. She has published books and articles on culture, the maintenance of heritage language, learning styles, classroom discourse, writing assessment, and English language programs. Additionally, she serves as an ESL and German language consultant and editor. Ann holds a B.A. in German from St. John's University; an M.A. in TESOL, an Ed.M. in Applied Linguistics, and an Ed.D. in TESOL, all from Teachers College, Columbia University in New York. Born in Germany, Ann is bilingual in German and English.

Joe McVeigh has taught English for over 20 years at Middlebury College, the University of Southern California, the California Institute of Technology, and

California State University, Los Angeles. His classrooms have included students from more than fifty countries. Joe has also lived and worked overseas in the United Kingdom, Hungary, China, India, and Chile. He works independently as a consultant, teacher-trainer, workshop presenter, author, and editor. Joe has a B.A. in English and American Literature from Brown University in Rhode Island and an M.A. in TESOL from Biola University in southern California. You can visit Joe's Web site and blog at http://www.joemcveigh.com, where he offers ongoing perspectives on the teaching of culture and on English language teaching.

WE'D LIKE TO HEAR FROM YOU

We invite you to share your experiences of teaching and learning inter-culturally or to ask questions about the teaching of culture and intercultural communication. You can email us at Culture@Pearson.com.

ACKNOWLEDGMENTS

We would like to acknowledge the following reviewers who offered valuable insights at various stages of development: **Andrea DeCapua,** College of New Rochelle, New Rochelle, New York; **Alvino Fantini,** School for International Training, Brattleboro, Vermont; **Steven Humphries,** Shenandoah University, Winchester, Virginia; **Gerard Krzic,** Ohio University, Athens, Ohio; **Piper (Margaret) McNulty,** Foothill-De Anza Community College, Cupertino, California; and **Suzanne Medina,** California State University, Dominguez Hills, California.

We would like to express our gratitude to the many people who contributed useful ideas and gave support throughout the development of this project. Doug Brown provided thoughtful comments on drafts of the manuscript and, in particular, suggested the addition of Chapter 8 on Culture and Social Responsibility. Lise Minovitz launched the project, assisted us in formulating the framework for the book, and kept us on target. Maretta Callahan skillfully helped develop the manuscript, refined our writing, and worked tirelessly to bring the whole book together. We are grateful to the members of TESOL's Intercultural Communication Interest Section who contributed their ideas for useful films for teaching culture. We would like to thank all of the teachers who sent us their experiences for the Voices from the Classroom stories—we're sorry that we could not include all of them. We thank, too, our friends and families who supported us throughout the writing period.

DEDICATION

In memory of my parents, Martin and Charlotte, whose personal sacrifices inspired me and my brother, Walter, to follow our dreams.

Ann C. Wintergerst, Ed.D.
New York, New York

With thanks to the professors who started me on my professional journey in TESOL many years ago: Don Dorr, Betty Chastain, Herb Purnell, and Kitty Purgason.

Joe McVeigh
Middlebury, Vermont

Overview of Tips and Activities

CHAPTER 1

EXPLORING CULTURE

Consider these questions:
- What do you think about when you hear the word *culture*?
- What experiences have you had interacting with people from other cultures?
- Have you spent time living in another culture? What do you remember about your experience?

Many English language teachers have experienced cross-cultural interaction. We may have traveled, lived, worked, or come from overseas. Perhaps we have studied about other languages and cultures. Although we have had these experiences, we may not always remember the extent to which culture plays an important role in our lives and in the lives of our students. In

1

this chapter we hope to raise awareness of what culture is, the unexpected effects culture has on our lives, and the way we communicate with people from cultures different from our own.

The English language classroom is a place where different cultures interact. Students are learning a new language and learning about a new culture. When students arrive in language classrooms, they bring with them their own cultural background and experiences, which may differ from those of their teachers and classmates. Often students don't realize the importance culture plays in language teaching and learning. As teachers we not only have the responsibility to acquaint students with their new target culture and language, but we also have an obligation to be aware of the impact culture has on our students' daily lives.

TIPS FOR EXPLORING CULTURE

The six tips in this chapter offer specific suggestions about how teachers can encourage language learners to build an awareness of culture—their own as well as that of others. With each tip, we provide a summary of the research related to the tip and offer practical ideas for what teachers can do in the classroom. Some of the activities include photocopiable handouts. These are located in Appendix A on pages 192–194.

 **TIPS**

1. Have students articulate their own definition of culture.
2. Raise culture to a conscious level.
3. Point out the hidden aspects of culture.
4. Show how cultures may value the same thing differently.
5. Help students understand how culture works.
6. Build awareness about stress caused by cultural adjustment.

In this chapter we introduce the concept of culture and its many facets. We raise issues related to culture and introduce basic concepts to help students avoid cross-cultural and intercultural misunderstandings. The activities heighten student awareness of culture, present situations to help avoid miscommunication, highlight varied aspects of culture, and provide alternative ideas on how to present culture. Our goal is to equip you with research-based knowledge about culture and to suggest classroom practices that will allow you to serve as a facilitator and in turn help students in their cultural development.

1 Have students articulate their own definition of culture.

Students will have different ways of explaining what culture means to them. To discuss culture in a meaningful way as a group, it is helpful to have students describe what they think culture is.

Ann, one of the authors, teaches an advanced English as a second language (ESL) speaking and listening class. Donkor, a student from Togo, told Ann that it was his grandmother's stories that allowed him to understand his African culture. As an international student in the United States, he turned to television and listened to music on the radio to try to learn about and understand American culture. He said, "I learned about my culture from the oral tradition of my grandmother and now that I am here in the United States, the media contributes to my understanding of American culture." Ultimately, he thought that his personal definition of culture applied to him and him alone. But Donkor's situation is not unique. Our students often share more cultural commonalities than they think with their classmates.

What the research says

Culture is a far-reaching dynamic concept and an elaborate, ever-changing phenomenon. There are many ways to look at it. The sister disciplines of anthropology, sociology, psychology, linguistics, and communication have each contributed significantly to our understanding of culture, intercultural communication, and cross-cultural awareness. Each discipline has brought its own perspective to the way that we think about culture. While anthropologists view culture from the perspective of the study of human beings, sociologists view culture from the standpoint of the study of social relationships between people and groups. Psychologists consider culture from the perspective of the mind and behavior, whereas linguists consider it from the standpoint of human language. Communication specialists look at culture from the perspective of interactions or the exchange of information.

In 1952, two anthropologists surveyed the work of existing researchers in some 300 studies in an attempt to come up with a unified definition of culture. They failed in their attempt. Through their investigation, however, they did uncover three general characteristics of culture: its historical dimension, its interdependency of components, and its complex nature (Kroeber and Kluckhohn, 1952).

In 1999 the National Standards in Foreign Language Education Project issued standards for foreign language teaching in the United States. This project based its definition of culture on three interrelated components: products, practices, and perspectives—which can also be described as artifacts, actions, and meanings (Moran 2001, p. 23). Other researchers define culture as a set of basic ideas, practices, and experiences that a group of people share. DeCapua and Wintergerst (2004, p. 11) describe culture as shared beliefs, norms, and attitudes that guide a group of people's behavior and help explain their world.

Communication scholar Stella Ting-Toomey (1999, p. 10) defines culture as "a complex frame of reference that consists of patterns of traditions, beliefs, values, norms, symbols, and meanings that are shared to varying degrees by interacting members of a community." Just like Peterson (2004), Ting-Toomey compares culture to an iceberg. In this analogy, the deeper layers of culture consisting of traditions, beliefs, and values are hidden from our view below the surface. The uppermost layers of culture consist of fashion, trends, and pop music, as well as verbal and nonverbal cues which can be easily observed.

Cross-cultural communication trainer Robert Kohls (1996, p. 23) offers the following comprehensive definition:

> Culture = an integrated system of learned behavior patterns that are characteristic of the members of any given society. Culture refers to the total way of life of particular groups of people. It includes everything that a group of people thinks, says, does and makes—its systems of attitudes and feelings. Culture is learned and transmitted from generation to generation.

Within the context of the classroom, Kramsch (1993, p. 1) states that "Culture in language learning is not an expendable fifth skill, tacked on, so to speak, to the teaching of speaking, listening, reading, and writing. It is always in the background, right from day one." In other words, culture is an integral part of language learning and affects all aspects of learning.

Damen (1987) cautions that when learning about a new culture, we have to consciously observe and be aware of events, behaviors, or situations without making judgments. We have to seek out information and ask questions. As we do this, we bring our own cultural patterns and those of others to a conscious level of awareness. This awareness can pave the way to our understanding of the

unfamiliar. As you can see, there is no firm agreement on a definition of culture. However, students can begin to understand culture as they explore and discuss its different aspects.

What the teacher can do

Teachers can help students by talking about how we have come to define culture and how it relates to our own lives. Ann, one of the authors, is originally from Germany. She often reminds her students that, as a nonnative speaker of English, she has had to adapt to her new American culture from her German culture, but she identifies with both. She points out that she does not exist in one culture at the expense of the other but that she exists fully in both cultures and enjoys the advantages of being not only bilingual but also bicultural.

Teachers can further help students develop their own understanding of what culture means by using classroom activities that encourage students to articulate their own ideas. Activity 1.1 asks students to work together to create their own definitions of culture. Discussing the concept of culture at the beginning of a course can be beneficial to students as it equips them to better comprehend what a significant role culture plays in their daily lives.

Activity 1.1	*What is culture?*
Level	Intermediate – Advanced
Handout	None
Tip	Have students articulate their own definition of culture.

Steps:

1. Write the following on the board: "Culture is _____."
2. Form small groups. Have students talk about how to fill in the blank. One student should take notes about the group's ideas.
3. Have groups share some of their ideas with the class. You may want to write them on the board.
4. Ask the same groups to work together again. This time they need to fill in the blank for "Culture is _____." but with only one idea as a group.
5. Ask each group to tell the class their sentence. Write the sentences on the board.
6. Ask the class to notice the similarities or differences in the sentences. Ask: "What made this exercise challenging?"
7. Continue the exploration of culture by having students create an analogy. Write on the board: "Culture is like a/an _____."
8. Ask students to work individually to write their ideas for completing the sentence.

(continued on next page)

9. Form new groups of 3-4. Have students discuss the analogies that they wrote. Students should try to explain why they chose their particular image.
10. Ask volunteer students to share their analogies with the class.

Teaching notes:
- It is helpful to point out to students that you are not talking about culture in the sense of music, art, literature, and history.
- If students can't think of an analogy for step 7, suggest creative responses such as a melting pot, salad bowl, mosaic, tapestry, pizza, spider web, or clouds.

 ## Raise culture to a conscious level.

Often students are not conscious of how culture affects their daily lives. When students make mistakes in language, they are usually corrected and then they try to improve. But errors in appropriate cultural behavior can often pass without comment, and students then miss a chance to increase their cultural knowledge.

When Raul, an Argentine student in the United States, wanted to answer a question in class, he simply called out the answer and did not wait for the ESL teacher to call on him. Although he understood it was important in an American classroom to show his knowledge of the subject, Raul did not know that just calling out answers violated acceptable classroom behavior norms. The teacher explained to Raul and others in the class that in many classrooms in the United States it is expected that students first raise their hands to show they would like to speak and then wait for the teacher to acknowledge them. By bringing these characteristics of culture to a conscious level, we can start students on the road to intercultural awareness.

What the research says

Atkinson (1999) conducted a survey of the academic literature and concluded that culture had not been adequately addressed by the TESOL profession in the fifteen-year period leading up to his study. In his opinion, "Except for language, learning, and teaching, there is perhaps no more important concept in the field of TESOL than *culture*. Implicitly or explicitly, ESL teachers face it in everything they do" (p. 625).

There are many characteristics of culture, and different academic disciplines view culture through different lenses. From the perspective of the pragmatic **ethnographer**—who deals with the systematic recording of human cultures— Damen (1987, pp. 88-89) sets forth six significant, observable characteristics of culture and their individual interpretations as shown in the following chart. To bring learning about culture to a conscious level, she proposes that teachers and students assume the role of an ethnographer and explore, describe, and understand the new culture by engaging in ethnographic inquiry.

CHARACTERISTIC	INTERPRETATION
Culture is learned.	Culture can be taught.
Cultures and cultural patterns change.	It is vital to adapt to a culture rather than merely learn facts about culture.
Culture is a universal fact of human life.	No human group exists without culture. Cultural patterns are closely aligned to human needs.
Culture offers a set of blueprints for living and values and beliefs to support this way of life.	Values and beliefs are linked through strong networks of relationships. Values and beliefs support the way in which we live.
Language and culture are closely related and interactive.	Culture is conveyed through language. Cultural patterns are manifested in language.
Culture functions as a filter between its possessor and the environment.	Intercultural communicators need to be able to go beyond their own filters.

What the teacher can do

Teachers can introduce Damen's six characteristics of culture and use them as a springboard for discussion. This discussion can help raise culture to a conscious level. Teachers can also share their own stories about experiencing new cultures.

Teachers can use Activity 1.2, which encourages students to play the role of cultural explorer—or ethnographer—to investigate and discuss cultural differences. This activity gives students the opportunity to engage with a native speaker and make direct contact with an expert on the culture they are investigating.

Activity 1.2	*Exploring culture*
Level	Beginning – Advanced
Handout	None
Tip	Raise culture to a conscious level.

Steps:

1. Tell students that they are going to assume the role of an ethnographer— a person who explores human culture.

(continued on next page)

2. Have students choose a cultural or ethnic group they would like to know more about and form small research groups. As part of their exploration, they need to work with a native informant of the target culture. If it isn't possible for students to find native informants, use the alternative suggestion at the end of this activity.

3. Have students choose a topic of interest to explore within the selected culture. You can brainstorm possible topics with the class and write them on the board. Examples are raising children, the place of the elderly, the role of women in society, government, holidays, etc.

4. Have students prepare 5 to 10 open-ended questions to ask the informant about the topic. For example: "Did you attend school? What memories do you have about school? Did your race/ethnicity play a role in your school life?"

5. Have students meet with the informant. Students should ask the interview questions and take notes.

6. Have student groups prepare an oral report using the following format:
    a. Name and location of target group
    b. Major ideas and findings from the interview
    c. Student experiences in interviewing the informant
    d. Student feelings about assuming the role of ethnographer

7. Have student groups present their oral reports to the entire class.

Teaching notes:

*   It can be helpful for students if you are able to locate the informants.
*   *Alternative:* If you are teaching beginning level students, use the following version of the activity. Choose the culture/ethnic group. Ask the class to pick one or two topics and have the class create the list of questions. Invite an informant to class. Assign each student a question to ask. Write the informant's answers on the board. Then review and discuss the information together with the class.

 Point out the hidden aspects of culture.

Many aspects of culture are hidden below the surface and therefore not visible or observable. A teacher can play an important role by bringing these hidden features to the surface. Abdullah, from Saudi Arabia, is in Ann's advanced ESL listening/speaking class. When asked to speak about the way his culture influences him, Abdulla talked about how his religion, his education, and his family's business influenced him. As he spoke, it did not occur to him to mention the underlying values of his culture, namely honesty, integrity, and esteem.

While some aspects of culture are clearly observable, many of the key aspects of a culture are less easily seen. In this section we explore some of the hidden aspects of culture. These aspects are often somewhat neglected precisely because they are less visible.

What the research says

One distinction that can help our students understand the concept of culture is the distinction between **big *C* culture** and **little *c* culture**. Peterson (2004, p. 25) categorizes big *C* culture as "classic or grand themes" and little *c* culture as "minor or common themes." He further organizes these two types of culture as visible culture—imagine the tip of an iceberg—and invisible culture—imagine the bottom of an iceberg.

Big *C* culture is often described as objective or highbrow culture, or as the institutions that people have created. Big *C visible* culture includes a culture's literature, classical music, architecture, historical figures, and geography, whereas big *C invisible* culture includes core values, attitudes or beliefs, society's norms, legal foundations, assumptions, history, and cognitive processes, according to Peterson.

Little *c* culture, on the other hand, is often described as subjective culture, as people's everyday thinking and behavior, or as the common traditions, practices, and customs of people. Little *c invisible* culture, according to Peterson, includes popular issues, opinions, viewpoints, preferences or tastes, and certain knowledge such as trivia and facts, whereas little *c visible* culture includes gestures, body posture, use of space, clothing styles, food, hobbies, music, and artwork. Understanding our own culture and that of others will help us achieve intercultural competence, or the skills, knowledge, attitudes, and cultural awareness we need to interact successfully with someone from another culture.

To help her students better understand visible and invisible culture, Ann, one of the authors, talks about her trips during semester breaks. She has visited various parts of the world. For example, when she traveled to Australia and New Zealand, she immediately recognized visible concepts of culture in the geography and in the architecture of the large cities. Invisible or hidden aspects of the cultures that Ann learned about were how people lived. In Australia, she observed the living conditions of the Aborigines and noted their difficulty in becoming integrated with mainstream society. In New Zealand, Ann learned about the complex culture of the Maori derived from their Pacific Island heritage where singing and dancing are integral and vital parts of Maori life. Ann's discovery of both sides of culture reflects our students' experiences. Only after learning about the core values and norms of a culture can our students understand the invisible part of their new culture.

What the teacher can do

Teachers can point out the hidden aspects of culture to students by helping them understand that many parts of culture may not be initially evident and it takes time to fully realize and understand them. These invisible aspects of culture can be better understood if students connect their personal experiences to them. A case in point is Abdullah, from Saudi Arabia, who found that his view of culture expanded when he realized that the invisible aspects of culture are as much a part of his culture as are the visible aspects.

Teachers can use Activity 1.3 to help students build awareness of the aspects of culture that are normally less visible. In this activity students are asked to focus on the less obvious manifestations of culture as articulated in the idea of little *c* culture. Students can then use this new level of awareness as they try to navigate the culture of their new surroundings.

Activity 1.3	*Exploring the iceberg*
Level	Intermediate – Advanced
Handout	None
Tip	Point out the hidden aspects of culture.

Steps:

1. Draw an iceberg on the board like the one on page 9 or bring in a picture from a book or magazine.
2. Ask students what they know about icebergs.

3. Write the following chart on the board, including the empty spaces:

Big *C* culture	Little *c* culture
architecture	gestures and posture
literature	use of physical space
historical and political figures	food and cooking
classical music and composers	clothing and style
geography	popular music

4. Present and explain the concepts of big *C* culture and little *c* culture. Big *C* culture consists of large classical themes from the culture. Little *c* culture consists of smaller everyday types of culture. Point to the chart to show examples of big *C* culture and little *c* culture.
5. Ask students to brainstorm some new ideas to add to the chart. Discuss them and then add them to the chart.
6. Discuss the following concepts. Refer to the image of the iceberg during the discussion.
   a. Which aspects of a culture are easily visible to those from another culture?
   b. Which aspects seem hidden or more difficult to see?
   c. Which aspects do you think would be most challenging for an international visitor to understand?

(continued on next page)

Teaching notes:

- *Alternative:* If you are teaching lower-level students, use the following version of the activity. Draw the chart on the board without extra spaces. Show a picture of an iceberg or draw one on the board. Ask the class to say which items in the chart are at the top of the iceberg (visible) and which are at the bottom of the iceberg (invisible). Ask students to explain why. Label the iceberg. Then ask students to think about other big *C* or little *c* culture items they can add to the iceberg.

 ## Show how cultures may value the same thing differently.

Many of us believe that the behavior of our own family provides the definition of normal behavior. Likewise, individuals assume that their own cultures' values are the norm and that other ways of doing things are strange or different. The underlying values of a culture have a particularly strong influence on behavior, yet these values are often not obvious or clear to someone experiencing a new culture for the first time.

When Makoto, a Japanese graduate student in business, was asked what he thought about the economic problems in Japan in his economics class, he responded that it wasn't his place to suggest causes and responsible parties because Japan had excellent economic advisors who formulate his country's policies. Paul, an American graduate student, insisted that the economic problems in Japan were the result of poor advice. He wondered why Makoto wouldn't go into more detail as the class discussed this issue. Paul and Makoto were unaware that their disagreement about this topic was compounded by their unspoken ideas about attitudes towards authority and of being critical of superiors. In Japan it is considered inappropriate to question authority or to speak against it, whereas in the United States it is considered part of a healthy discussion to voice one's opinion even if it is critical of authority.

What the research says

Beliefs, values, norms, and attitudes are fundamental elements of any culture. These elements influence and affect people's behavior. Each element is distinct and has its own meaning. Knowing the definition of each element helps us understand how these beliefs, values, norms and attitudes affect our daily lives.

Beliefs are convictions of the truth of something or the reality of some phenomena based on an examination of the evidence. In other words, beliefs are specific statements that people hold as true. The more convinced we are of a belief, the greater its intensity. Beliefs sometimes vary not only from culture to culture but also within a culture.

Examples
- the religious belief in the power of prayer
- the belief in alternative medicine, such as acupuncture or homeopathy, rather than surgery as a means to alleviate pain or cure disease
- the belief that humans can improve or change their lives by taking action

Values describe our feelings about the worth, usefulness, or importance of something. Our standards about what is right or wrong are steered by moral guidelines and bring emotional vigor to beliefs. Peterson (2004, p. 22) defines cultural values as "principles or qualities that a group of people will tend to see as good or right or worthwhile." In short, they are the standards by which people measure such things as goodness and beauty.

Examples
- constitutionally guaranteed rights
- one's work ethic
- the importance of group membership

Norms are principles of appropriate behavior that are binding to the members of a culture. They guide and regulate proper and acceptable behavior in terms of what members should and should not do. Norms include **mores** or morally binding behavior that distinguishes right from wrong, as well as **taboos** or banned actions.

Examples
- showing respect by bowing to elders
- refraining from plagiarism when writing a college or university assignment
- not eating pork in a culture where it is prohibited

Attitudes are mental stances that we take in regard to a fact or a state of something. Attitudes are also feelings or emotions that we show toward something. Attitudes shape our cultural behavior.

Examples
- the German concept of *Gemuetlichkeit*, which characterizes a social gathering and reflects a feeling of comfortableness, contentment, and a *joie de vivre*.
- people's instant dislike of others who "look like foreigners"
- a positive identification with the target language that can increase motivation and enhance language proficiency

Attribution is how we interpret the behavior of others using our own cultural lens. Our beliefs, values, norms, and attitudes are used to impose our worldview or point of view when we attempt to explain what we "see."

Examples

- In some cultures it is unacceptable for a male and female to go out together in public unless they are accompanied by an elder or are married. In other cultures, it is acceptable for single males and females to spend time together in public.
- In some cultures people get a job or receive a promotion because they are the most qualified candidates. In other cultures, people may get a job or receive a promotion because they are related to the boss or their families have some kind of connection with the boss.

Ethnocentrism also influences our perspective on culture. Ethnocentrism refers to "our tendency to consider our own cultural practices as superior and consider other cultural practices as inferior" (Ting-Toomey 1999, p. 14). In many instances, we are unaware of our own cultural prejudices and emotional, subjective tendencies and are inclined to view our cultural practices as better than those of others.

Examples

- Americans that regard themselves as better entrepreneurs than Latin Americans
- Religious groups that consider their particular religion superior to all others

Enculturation refers to the act of learning a primary culture and becoming socialized into it. This is a lifelong process. Learning about our new cultural patterns at home, in school, and at work affects our worldview and our new interpretation of the world.

Example

- A young immigrant who has lived most of his life in the United States calls himself an American and identifies with the American popular culture, yet his home life still includes beliefs and traditions from his native country.

Alternatively, **acculturation** is the learning of a supplementary culture. This is when we deliberately learn about a second culture, often because we are visiting or living in the new culture. In this case we adapt to a second culture without abandoning our native cultural identity.

Example

- A woman from the United States who lives and works abroad for a number of years continues to self-identify with her home country, even though she is fluent in the language of the new country and enjoys its culture and traditions.

Our cultural background influences our expectations at an unconscious level. We are frequently unaware that our judgments are being formed not, as we think, on the basis of objective facts but rather on the basis of attribution. To be cognizant of the elements of culture requires an awareness not only of our own culture but also the culture of others.

What the teacher can do

Teachers can help students see that beliefs, values, norms, and attitudes are part of every culture and that different cultures often value the same things, even though it is not always evident. By helping to make the invisible elements more accessible, teachers can help students understand why others view the world in a different way as well as encourage students to think about their own values. For example, if Makoto and Paul, mentioned at the beginning of this section, had realized the underlying cultural values from which the other was operating, they would have had a better chance of understanding each other.

Teachers can use Activity 1.4 to challenge students to think about their own cultural values and to compare them with others. The activity encourages students to make decisions about what matters most to them. The activity is also helpful to teachers in that they can learn more about their students' thoughts and beliefs.

Activity 1.4	*Cultural values clarification*
Level	Intermediate – Advanced
Handout	Page 192
Tip	Show how cultures may value the same thing differently.

Steps:

1. Make copies of the handout for Activity 1.4. Pass them out to the class.
2. Model how to use the chart. Draw a horizontal line on the board and number it 1 to 5 from left to right. To the left of number 1 write "It is important to have a job that you love." To the right of number 5 write "It is important to have a job that pays a good salary." Ask students to think about these statements and decide which they think is most important. Ask them to choose the number on the continuum that best represents their opinions.
3. Point out that there are seven separate items to think about. Explain the vocabulary if needed.

(continued on next page)

4. Give the class 5 minutes to complete the chart. Tell them to circle the answer that best represents their opinions, just as you did in the example.
5. Form pairs. Have students compare and discuss their answers. If students are from various cultural backgrounds, mix the pairs.
6. Draw the chart from the handout on the board. For each item, take a poll of how many students circled each number. Keep track of the totals on the board.
7. To finish the activity, have the class study the results of the poll. If any item has an unusually low or high total, ask students to talk about why they chose that answer.

Teaching notes:

• If students are all from the same culture, see if there is any variation in the answers. If not, point that out and mention that if the class included various other cultures, answers could be different. If you are familiar with other cultures, you may want to offer ideas on how students from those cultures might have responded.

 Help students understand how culture works.

In addition to beliefs, values, norms, and attitudes, culture is made up of a number of other key dimensions, such as identity, the hierarchy of society, and gender roles. Ann, one of the authors, does not usually have her position as a female university professor challenged, but there have been times when students from other cultures have needed to adapt and adjust their cultural views. Ekliel, from Afghanistan, was in Ann's advanced ESL writing class. Often he did not pay attention to the lesson, displayed arrogance when asked to participate in class, and answered Ann's questions in a disrespectful tone. At times when Ann was explaining something, Ekliel would question her explanation. It seemed to be his way of showing his unwillingness to accept having a female as his professor, a position traditionally held by males in Afghanistan. Ann decided to speak to Ekliel privately and talked about her academic achievements and the accepted role of women as professors in U.S. society. She also talked about her role as his teacher and her expectations of him as a student. Tensions were noticeably lessened after their conversation.

What the research says

Hofstede et al. (2002, p. 40) categorize five dimensions of a culture: identity, hierarchy, social gender role, truth value, and virtue. These researchers suggest that culture may be defined as the way a group of people teaches these perspectives and how they resolve any issues around them.

DIMENSION	CONTINUUM
Identity	Collectivism ⟵⟶ Individualism
Hierarchy	Large power distance ⟵⟶ Small power distance
Social gender role	Feminine ⟵⟶ Masculine
Truth value	Strong uncertainty avoidance ⟵⟶ Weak uncertainty avoidance
Virtue	Long term orientation ⟵⟶ Short term orientation

The first dimension of culture—**identity**—can be described on a range from **collectivism** at one end to **individualism** at the other. According to Ting-Toomey (1999, p. 67), individualism stresses individual identity, focuses on individual rights, and emphasizes individual needs. Individualistic cultures encourage the *I* **identity** and individual goals. On the other end of the spectrum, collectivism stresses the *we* **identity** and focuses on group rights and group-oriented needs. Collectivistic cultures encourage dependence as a way to promote harmony and cooperation within the group.

The second dimension—**hierarchy**—can be described on a range from large **power distance** at one end to small **power distance** at the other. Power distance describes the degree of acceptance of the unequal distribution of power by the less powerful members of a culture (Hofstede and Bond, 1984). Ting-Toomey observes that in cultures with a small power distance, people are inclined to value an equal distribution of power, equal rights, and the idea that rewards or punishments should be granted based on how a task is executed (1999, p. 71). In cultures with a large power distance, on the other hand, people accept an unequal distribution of power. They seem to accept a chain of command regarding one's rights, unbalanced role relations, and the idea that rewards and punishments should be determined by factors such as age, rank, status, title, and seniority. Cultures with a small power distance tend to seek equality, whereas cultures with a large power distance have allowed inequalities of power and wealth to grow within their societies.

The third dimension of culture—**social gender role**—includes the question of roles for females and males. In traditional gender roles, men are expected to be forceful, tough, and materialistic, whereas women are expected to be humble, sensitive, and worried about the quality of daily life. When we look at this dimension, we are looking at the degree to which a society reinforces the traditional male and female roles regarding achievement, control, and power.

The fourth dimension—**truth value**—ranges from strong **uncertainty avoidance** at one end to weak **uncertainty avoidance** at the other. Uncertainty avoidance measures the degree to which members of a culture feel threatened by situations that are uncertain or unknown to them. It also describes their attempts to steer clear of such situations. For instance, a person from a strongly **collectivistic society** might feel threatened by being asked to act as the single representative of that culture. If uncertainty avoidance is strong, the individual feels a powerful threat and makes every effort to stay away from being put on the spot. Weak uncertainty avoidance cultures promote risk taking, whereas strong uncertainty avoidance cultures favor rules and laws, which make it very clear how people are expected to behave and thus help members avoid risks.

The fifth and final dimension of culture—**virtue**—ranges from **long-term orientation** to **short-term orientation**. This dimension refers to the time perspective and the attitude of perseverance of a society. Ting-Toomey (1999, p. 74) notes that cultures valuing long-term orientation stress social order, respect hierarchy, believe in collective face-saving, practice long-term planning, are centered on thrift, and focus on long-term outcomes. On the other end, cultures valuing short-term orientation emphasize personal survival, respect personal dignity, believe in individual face-saving, practice short-term planning, are centered on spending, and focus on short-term outcomes.

What the teacher can do

Teachers can encourage students to discover cultural dimensions by sharing concepts of culture along a continuum. Before doing this, be sure that students understand the idea of a continuum and how it works. One good illustration is that of color. Choose items in the classroom that are varying shades of blue and line them up from darkest to lightest. Alternatively, use the example of height. Line up students from shortest to tallest and place their names on a list.

Teachers can also help students gain an awareness of these various cultural dimensions by using concrete examples, as some of these ideas may be difficult to grasp in the abstract. An example is the idea of an individual versus a group.

Teachers can use Activity 1.5 to introduce students to the concept of the **critical incident**. A critical incident offers students a brief story or vignette in which some type of cultural miscommunication takes place. Students read and discuss the incident to try to understand why the miscommunication took place and how it could have been prevented. Critical incidents are used in activities throughout this book and provide a useful tool to help students share their opinions, values, and beliefs.

Activity 1.5	*Culture in action*
Level	Intermediate – Advanced
Handouts	Pages 193 – 194
Tip	Help students understand how culture works.

Steps:

1. Make copies of the two handouts for Activity 1.5.
2. Present and explain the concept of critical incidents to the class. Tell students that a critical incident is a cross-cultural problematic situation. The incidents are concerned with various dimensions of culture. Inform students that there are no right or wrong answers but that there are solutions.
3. Ask students to work in groups of 3-4. Pass out the handouts for Activity 1.5. Assign each group one critical incident. Have students read the critical incidents and questions and discuss what they think caused the conflict.
4. If a group finishes early, assign another critical incident.
5. As a class, discuss each critical incident, the solutions from each group, and the area of cultural conflict manifested. Page 189 outlines possible interpretations that you can share with the class if no one has suggested them.

Teaching notes:

- Each critical incident presents an area of conflict designed to stimulate discussion and to make students aware of and sensitive to cultural differences.
- *Alternative:* If necessary, simplify the vocabulary used in the critical incidents.

6 Build awareness about stress caused by cultural adjustment.

When students spend time in another culture, their adjustment to the new culture can cause feelings of stress. Becoming aware of possible intercultural stumbling blocks and overcoming them can help students become comfortable in a new culture.

Chia-Chang, a student from Taiwan, was used to eating a diet consisting mostly of noodles and vegetables. When he arrived to study in the United States, he found he didn't like the largely fast-food diet of American college students. Chia-Chang felt he could not eat most of the food and found himself hungry most days. This increased his stress level and began to affect his ability to concentrate in class and when studying. Finally, a fellow student mentioned a nearby neighborhood that had a number of Chinese restaurants and grocery stores. The ability to anchor himself in the familiar by buying and eating food he was accustomed to helped Chia-Chang reduce his stress so that he was able to function at a more productive level.

What the research says

Whether or not we are conscious of it, we are directly influenced by our cultural upbringing. We often presume that the needs, desires, and assumptions of others are the same as ours when in reality they are not. This can create problems when communicating with individuals from other cultures. To help avoid frustration and reduce misunderstanding, Barna (1988, p. 322) highlights potential stumbling blocks or obstacles that can hinder effective intercultural communication. We first need to acknowledge the existence of these stumbling blocks and then learn to avoid them. To do this may require a change in our mindset and the way that we view the world.

Common Stumbling Blocks

Assumption of similarity

When people from different cultures first meet and each person wears similar clothes, speaks the same language, and uses comparable rituals, we feel a sense of confidence rather than a sense of anxiety because no differences seem apparent. Only by assuming that subtle differences do in fact exist and that new rules for behavior are needed can our interpretation be adjusted so that we can really understand these differences.

Language difference

Components of language include vocabulary, grammar, idioms, slang, dialects, and many other features. The sociocultural aspects of language also include **cultural competence**, or knowing what to say, how to say it, when and where to say it, and why it is being said. We sometimes are under the impression that we understand what is being said when in fact we do not. Consequently, we can misinterpret the words of others. (Discussed in Chapter 2.)

Misinterpreting nonverbal communication

Gestures, postures, and other body movements, which are easily observable, are often misunderstood. Time and spatial relationships, which are more subtle and more difficult to grasp, are even more prone to misinterpretation. (Discussed in Chapter 3.)

Preconceptions and stereotypes

Barna (1988) defines stereotypes as "overgeneralized beliefs that provide conceptual bases from which to 'make sense' out of what goes on around us" (p. 326). We are not objective where others are concerned, which can make stereotypes difficult to overcome and correct, even when we have definite evidence that they are wrong. Stereotypes continue to exist because they are firmly rooted as either myths or truths in our culture and because they tend to rationalize prejudices. (Discussed in Chapter 4.)

Immediate evaluation

Rather than attempting to understand the thoughts and feelings conveyed from the worldview of others, many of us all too quickly move to approve or disapprove of the actions and assertions of other people. This tendency to evaluate is further intensified when emotions are involved. Our own particular culture or way of life naturally always seems to us to be the right one. This outlook hinders open-mindedness and, as a result, the attitudes and behavior of others are only considered from our own point of view rather than from the other's point of view.

High anxiety or stress or 'internal noise'

Anxiety is a basic part of the other stumbling blocks because of the uncertainties and risk factors involved. Being positive prepares us to meet these challenges energetically. However, once stress increases our body loses its energy and a defense mechanism appears whether we want it to or not.

What the teacher can do

Teachers can help students avoid these stumbling blocks by first making them aware of them. However, this is not enough. We need to help students go beyond simply knowing that people have different customs, goals, and mindsets and help them begin to develop empathy toward people who are different from them regardless of how foreign others may appear. Recognizing and understanding these so-called obstacles is the first step toward navigating through them, just like a ship trying to go around an iceberg without crashing into it.

Spending time in a new culture can be stressful. A number of symptoms can occur that indicate problems in adjustment, often referred to as **culture shock,** which is explained in more detail in Chapter 5. Teachers can use Activity 1.6 to help students recognize symptoms of culture shock and learn steps they can take to help themselves relax and feel less stress in their new surroundings. (See next page.)

Activity 1.6	***Stress busters***
Level	Intermediate – Advanced
Handout	None
Tip	Build awareness about stress caused by cultural adjustment.

Steps:

1. Write the following on the board: feeling tired, eating more or less, tight muscles (especially in shoulders and jaw), difficulty concentrating, difficulty sleeping, irritability, headaches, worrying, and unhappiness.
2. Introduce the topic of culture shock by explaining that someone experiencing a new culture and feeling stress about it can have some or many of the symptoms on the board. If necessary, define stress: mental and physical responses to events that upset us in some way.
3. Ask students to think about other causes and symptoms of stress. Write their ideas on the board.
4. Ask students about any ideas they have or strategies they use for dealing with stress. Write their ideas on the board.
5. If students haven't mentioned the following, add them to the list on the board:
   a. deep breathing
   b. progressive muscle relaxation
   c. meditation (mindfulness, guided imagery, repetitive prayer)
   d. exercise (yoga, tai-chi, walking)
   e. massage therapy (by others, by self)
6. Share information with your students about how to explore these and other techniques at your institution's health center, by doing research online, or by checking their local library or community center.
7. Have students think about a personal plan that could help them reduce stress.

Teaching notes:

- Some students may be reluctant to discuss this topic. Be sensitive to student needs. Speaking about stress and feelings publicly may not be considered appropriate in some cultures.
- *Alternative:* Invite a professional to visit your class to talk about stress and techniques for dealing with stress. Your institution may offer such services or support through the health center or learning resource center.

Conclusion

In this chapter we explored the concept of culture. We looked at ways of defining culture and describing culture and its characteristics. We examined varied cultural concepts including big *C* culture and little *c* culture, elements of culture, cultural perspectives, and dimensions of culture. Finally, we reviewed the stumbling blocks or obstacles to avoid when engaging in intercultural communication.

The activities in this chapter have encouraged students to examine their own definition of culture, to become more aware of the hidden aspects of culture, to grasp some of the underlying values and assumptions behind culture, and to try out techniques to reduce stress and tension brought on by difficulties in cultural adjustment. Teachers who can understand and convey these ideas to their students can help them apply what they have learned and practiced in the language classroom to their lives outside of school.

Check your understanding

After reading this chapter and using the activities with your class, check your comfort level with the following:

- ❏ I can articulate my own definition of culture.
- ❏ I have raised culture to a conscious level for my students.
- ❏ I have pointed out the hidden aspects of culture to my students.
- ❏ I understand that cultures can value the same thing differently.
- ❏ I feel that my students understand and can talk about how culture works.
- ❏ I have learned about the stress caused by cultural adjustment and know techniques to help my students reduce that stress.

CHAPTER 2

CULTURE AND LANGUAGE

Consider these questions:
- How do you think language and culture are related?
- Do you change how you use your language in different contexts or situations? For example, compare how you speak to your classmates with how you speak to your teachers, friends, your parents, and other members of the community.
- How does written language differ from spoken language?

As a young American teaching English in China, Joe would walk to the cafeteria each day at lunch time. He was teaching at a medical school and would almost always run into the same elderly doctor coming from the other direction. Although his Chinese was very limited, he was finally able to understand her standard greeting, "Have you eaten yet?" "No, no," he would say, pointing to his empty rice bowl and chopsticks. Joe thought it seemed obvious that he hadn't eaten yet. Besides, he was just going into the cafeteria. He thought, "She sees my empty bowl. And she asks me this same question each day. She doesn't seem to pay attention to details." After a few weeks, someone finally explained to Joe that in China a standard greeting is "Have you eaten yet?" In many languages, phrases such as this one are not meant literally. Food is such a key part of Chinese culture that its purpose and meaning is to express polite concern for someone's well-being. Joe had understood the literal meaning of the Chinese language, but he did not grasp the cultural intent behind the words.

For many years linguists and anthropologists have studied the relationship between language and culture and have found the two to be closely connected. This connection raises a number of questions. Is our view of the world dependent on what language we speak, or does language depend on culture? How closely are language and culture related? Is it possible for us to understand a culture fully without knowing the language?

There are serious implications here for teachers. If language and culture are indeed closely intertwined, then the teaching of culture and the teaching of language must go hand in hand. How then can teachers help students become more successful learners of both language and culture? How can teachers equip themselves to help students improve their language and cultural skills?

TIPS FOR CULTURE AND LANGUAGE

The eight tips in this chapter offer specific suggestions about how teachers can encourage language-learners to explore the connection between language, culture, and thought. With each tip, we provide a summary of the research related to the tip and offer practical ideas for what teachers can do in the classroom. Some of the activities include photocopiable handouts. These are located in Appendix A on pages 195–200.

TIPS

1. Understand the relationship between culture, language, and thought.
2. Identify different speech communities.
3. Recognize the influence of gender on language.
4. Explore the differences between spoken and written language.
5. Understand the meaning of language in context.
6. Identify speech acts in daily communication.
7. Understand the concept of face.
8. Recognize communication styles and registers.

In this chapter we discuss the connections between culture, language, and thought. We look at how language affects our thought processes, how culture and language are bound together, and how language is used in different contexts. We consider the differences between written and spoken language and between men's and women's use of language. When teachers understand the relationship between language and culture, they are better able to help their students build an awareness and understanding of this connection. Students then have a better sense of how language and culture are interconnected and how these connections affect them both in and out of the classroom.

Understand the relationship between culture, language, and thought.

When you live in a culture, the language of that culture is everywhere. You are surrounded by it and immersed in it. You hear it on the street, in the music, and in the movies. You hear and see it in the supermarket and on the subway and bus. You breathe it in the scent of the markets, the restaurants, and the coffee shops. Language-learners who live in a new culture begin to absorb the new language by listening to it, practicing it, and using it in real situations. When learners see how language and culture are fused together and reflect each other, they become more aware of their environment and can understand how it affects their second-language development.

Ann, one of the authors, teaches an advanced ESL speaking and listening class. Her student Ming, who is from China, decided not to live off campus. She chose to live on campus with American roommates. In this way, Ming knew she would have to use English in her daily life. "Living with Americans has helped me to learn English related to fashion, sports, and relationships, since those were the topics that we talked about. I feel not only has my English ability really improved," Ming said, "but I also feel that I understand American culture a lot better."

What the research says

A special relationship exists between culture, language, and thought—an almost inseparable bond. Claire Kramsch (1998, p. 3) highlights three ways in which language and culture are bound together: First, "language expresses cultural reality" in that the words a person uses for a common experience are shared by others and reflect the beliefs, attitudes, and worldview of the speaker. Second, "language embodies cultural reality" in that the choice of the spoken, written, or visual form generates meanings that are understood by a person's cultural group. Third, "language symbolizes cultural reality" in that language reflects a person's social identity. The ways that we perceive, believe, evaluate, and act are a reflection of our culture.

Moran (2001) claims that language not only symbolizes the products, practices, perspectives, communities, and people of a culture but that language itself is also a product of that culture. For Moran, "the words of the language, its expressions, structures, sounds, and scripts reflect the culture, just as the cultural products and practices reflect the language. Language, therefore, is a window to the culture" (p. 35). Moran regards language and culture as two sides of the same coin, each side mirroring the other.

To what degree then is culture shaped by language? The idea that language affects the thought processes of its users is known as the **principle of linguistic relativity** or the **Sapir-Whorf hypothesis**. Speakers of different languages perceive and express the world around them differently because of the ways in which language influences a person's thinking and behavior. Because languages differ in grammatical structures, in linguistic categories, and in other ways, Sapir and Whorf, the originators of the principle, concluded that the speakers of different languages have different ways of viewing the world. Language serves as a filter of its speakers' perceptions and influences the way that a cultural group categorizes experience. As Samovar and Porter (2004, p. 143) put it, the Sapir-Whorf hypothesis argues that "language is not simply a means of reporting experience but, more important, it is a way of defining experience."

The strong version of the Sapir-Whorf hypothesis holds that language *determines* thought. It suggests that we are prisoners of our language and that the way we think is determined by language. Damen (1987, p. 125) describes the strong version as one in which "languages structure perception and experience, and literally *create* and *define* the realities people perceive." On the other hand, the weak version of the Sapir-Whorf hypothesis holds that language *influences* but does

reality, life, experience, the world, values, perspective, what is important, roles, relationships

not *determine* thought. It suggests that a relationship exists between language and culture. This weaker version is more readily accepted today (DeCapua and Wintergerst 2004, p. 23).

What the teacher can do

Teachers can help students see the relationship between language, culture, and thought by making the connection explicit. To do this, teachers need to have a clear sense of their own view of the relationship between language and culture. One way to clarify points for students is by sharing personal experiences. Ann, one of the authors, has often found that translation into English does not adequately reflect the meaning of a word in her first language. A case in point is when she tells her colleagues about the German word "Gemuetlichkeit." In translation this word simply means "cozy atmosphere." However, this translation does not capture the true essence of the word for German speakers, which means the warmth generated in making people feel at home, extremely comfortable, and very much at ease.

Teachers can use Activity 2.1 to help students begin to understand the relationship between language, culture, and thought. The activity gives students the opportunity to share their ideas about their own language with their classmates and at the same time get a better sense of the new language they are learning. Students are asked to consider the concept of relationship and family and to describe how these work in their own languages and cultures.

Activity 2.1	***Describing relationships***
Level	Beginner – Intermediate
Handout	None
Tip	Understand the relationship between culture, language, and thought.

Steps:

1. Tell students they are going to talk about family and family members. Ask students to give you English words that identify family relationships. Write them on the board.
2. Draw a family tree on the board and use the list of vocabulary words on the board to identify the relationships on the tree.
3. Point out the word for each relationship on the tree. Ask students to say the word for each relationship in their language.
4. This next step gets students to think about how languages might work differently. Write the following on the board: my older sister, my younger brother, my oldest aunt on my mother's side, my younger cousin. Ask students to think about these relationships and ask the class how to say them in their language. You may want to have students write the words on the board. Then point out that in English there isn't just one word; you need a few words to describe the relationship. Compare this with the other languages: do they need more than one word?
5. Talk about how the different ways we use words lead to different ways of thinking about the world. For example, are family relationships closer if people know clearly how they are related? Ask students how this may influence their own views of family and relationships. Ask volunteers to share their ideas.

(continued on next page)

6. Have students draw a family tree using the English words to identify the family members they include. Then have students write the relationship words in their own languages.

Teaching notes:
- Some common language differences found in ways to describe families are
  - English has only one word for *sister* and for *brother*. Many languages use different terms that also describe birth order, for example, *older sister* or *younger sister*, using single vocabulary words.
  - In English, the words *aunt, uncle,* and *cousin* do not indicate which side of the family the person is related to. In some languages the word for a family member includes this information.
  - In some languages, one honorary title is used for a whole group. For example, in the Philippines, all older relatives are called *aunt* or *uncle*. If people are quite a bit older, they are called *grandma* or *grandpa*.

2 Identify different speech communities.

Each of us belongs to different social groups and units. These groups may be formed by family ties, by our work and occupation, or by common interests such as hobbies, music, or sports. Each group forms its own speech community. In a speech group or community, we develop a certain way of speaking that is common to the group. We may use common expressions or vocabulary terms that make it clear that we are members of the group. For example, at a conference, a group of teachers of English to speakers of other languages might use terms such as *L2*, *fossilization*, *phoneme*, or *silent period*. These terms are not familiar to those who are not part of this speech community. Other examples of speech groups or communities could be mathematics teachers, politicians, or a sports team.

Our membership in speech communities determines not only the language we use but also the parameters within which we use it. That is, a speech community uses language based on established rules and sets limits or boundaries for its use. Distinguishing between these communities can help learners realize that there are different speech communities not only in the classroom but also outside of the classroom. It is important for learners to be aware of this distinction so that they can use appropriate language for the different situations they encounter.

What the research says

Each culture uses its own language to communicate among its members. The language is learned as a child grows up and becomes socialized into the culture. Aspects of a language reflect the ideas and values of that culture and its subgroups. To describe the interconnected nature of language and culture, Agar (1994) proposed the term *languaculture*. Each language consists of certain elements that are universal to all languages and other elements that are particular only to that specific language. All languages have rules that govern their sound and grammar systems and semantic and pragmatic rules that regulate the language that speech communities use.

Hymes (1974a) identifies these speech communities as groups of people who use similar rules as guideposts for how they use language and how they understand others' use of language. He describes categories for analyzing and describing speaking patterns in given speech communities and provides a framework for the development of sociolinguistic rules. He uses the term speech event to refer to a specific context involving speech, such as a classroom lecture, a private conversation, or a talk given in a church. A speech event usually consists of one or more **speech acts** that are not identified by the grammar used but by how they are interpreted (Hymes 1974b, p. 52). Speech acts are culturally defined: A native speaker can distinguish between a complaint or a compliment, a refusal or an apology.

As language users we belong to different social groups—families, professions, clubs, and organizations—whose view of the world is framed through their interaction with other members of the same group. This worldview or *Weltanschauung* is apparent in the language that we use and in the linguistic code that governs it. In other words, what is said, what is discussed, how it is said, and what interaction style is used all help to distinguish members of different groups. For example, teachers, politicians, doctors, lawyers, and scientists are professional groups who form their own speech communities as a result of their specialized vocabulary. For example, "Unlike my opponent who lives in a fantasy world, I view the issues from a realistic perspective" illustrates the language used by politicians.

 ## Voices from the Classroom

> *Shortly after arriving to teach in Japan, I went on a sightseeing trip with a group of colleagues. I didn't speak much Japanese, but I had learned enough to know that it is a customary sign of respect to add the expression* san *after a person's name. Thus everyone in our sightseeing group was called by their name followed by* san. *One person was Yuko-san, one was Masaki-san, and so on.*
>
> *I was puzzled, however, when the trip organizer, while giving briefings, referred to someone as "Mina-san." I didn't remember anyone named Mina in the group, and I was pretty sure that I knew the names of everyone. Each time the organizer said "Mina-san," I would look around and try to see whom he was talking to. Only later did I find out that the expression* san *is also attached at the end of the word* all *when addressing a group of people collectively. So* mina *was actually the Japanese word for* all, *and the organizer used it whenever he talked to all of us.*
>
> *—Najma Janjua*
> *Kagawa Prefectural College of Health Sciences*
> *Kagawa, Japan*

What the teacher can do

Teachers can help students recognize speech communities by building awareness of the distinct vocabulary words found in different speech communities. Students can then see how vocabulary and speech acts distinguish insiders from outsiders in a group. Teachers can explain the concept of **in-groups**—when an individual is included and is viewed as a member and **out-groups**—when an individual is excluded and viewed as a non-member. This concept makes sense for students of most ages. An example can often be created centering around the school or institution where classes are held. Schools sometimes have their own terms of reference for different spaces within the school or for groups or activities. For example, students at Middlebury College in Vermont use the term "Febs" to describe first-year students who begin their studies in February rather than in September as most other students do.

Teachers can use Activity 2.2 in which students attend a group or organizational meeting to get a better sense of the kind of language that a particular speech community uses. This activity serves several purposes. First, it gets students out of the classroom and into the "real world" of language use. Second, it helps students understand and distinguish between the types of language used by different speech communities. Third, it provides students with the opportunity to try out their language in a real-world setting.

Activity 2.2	*The language of meetings*
Level	Intermediate – Advanced
Handout	Page 195
Tip	Identify different speech communities.

Steps:

1. Make copies of the handout for Activity 2.2.
2. Tell students that they are going to work on a project that includes attending the meeting of a group or organization on campus or in the community.
3. On the board, write a list of possible meetings students could attend, such as a student meeting or Board of Education meeting at a school, a town or civic committee meeting, etc. School and community calendars are a good source of information. Include dates, times, and locations.
4. Ask students to choose the meeting they will attend. Form pairs or small groups based on the type of meetings students have chosen.

5. Pass out the handout for Activity 2.2. Go over the directions. Tell students that it's important to write down the words and phrases they hear. Suggest that each student take notes and then compare them with a classmate's.
6. Tell students how you would like them to report their findings to the class: an oral presentation, a written report, a poster board of information, etc.
7. During student presentations, you may wish to highlight certain words or expressions and go over them with the class.
8. To finish the activity, ask: "What can you conclude about speech communities from this activity? How does language vary from one group to another?"

Teaching notes:

- Prepare a list of appropriate school or local meetings. If possible, contact the organizers of the meetings to let them know that some of your students may attend and their purpose.
- Let students know if you have or have not contacted meeting organizers about their attendance.
- If you are teaching in a country where English is not commonly used, students can still observe a meeting and analyze the language used in that speech community.
- *Alternative:* Record meetings of local public government bodies, such as school boards or city councils, shown on TV. These meetings are usually part of the public record and are not subject to copyright. You may also be able to obtain minutes or transcripts of these public meetings.

3   Recognize the influence of gender on language.

Different types of speech occur within different speech communities, but there are also differences in the way that men and women communicate. On the surface, men and women use the same vocabulary words and sentence structure. However, men are more likely to view interactions in a hierarchical way, where one person is superior to the other. Women are more likely to want to be connected and feel a sense of closeness through empathy and therefore see interactions from a non-hierarchical viewpoint. Understanding these differences can help learners acknowledge that men and women use language differently and help them to interpret interactions with the other gender appropriately.

What the research says

Researchers are interested in differences in language used by men and women—especially when they are speaking. How does their use of language differ? Tannen (1990, p. 77) suggests that, "For most women, the language of conversation is primarily a language of rapport: a way of establishing connections and negotiating relationships . . . . For most men, talk is primarily a means to preserve independence and negotiate and maintain status in a hierarchical social order." Conversational rituals are particularly evident in the workplace where the ways in which men and women communicate often influence who gets heard, who gets promoted, and what gets done.

Wood (1994, p. 142) identified seven characteristics of women's talk. Particularly when they are talking with each other, women tend to give and receive equal **turns in conversation**; they show support and sympathy for each other; they use questions to probe for greater understanding of feelings; they work hard to keep the conversation going; they are responsive to the comments of others; they speak in concrete and personal terms; and they are sometimes tentative or apologetic. On the other hand, men do not usually acknowledge feelings but focus more on gathering data or solving problems. They tend to express superiority and maintain

control, dominating the conversation. They are not very responsive, may assert themselves, and may speak in abstract terms removed from personal experience.

Maltz and Borker (1982, p. 213) suggest that men and women have their own "cultural" differences. They hypothesize that when giving minimal responses in conversations, nods and *mm-hums* by women are saying something like "I'm listening to you; please continue," but that for men there is implied the stronger meaning of "I agree with you" or at least "I follow your argument so far." Maltz and Borker list five additional areas in which men and women tend to hold differing conversational assumptions that can lead to communication problems between genders.

WOMEN'S CONVERSATIONAL ASSUMPTIONS	CONVERSATIONAL SITUATION	MEN'S CONVERSATIONAL ASSUMPTIONS
Seen as part of conversational maintenance	Asking questions	Seen as requests for information
Used to make an explicit acknowledgement of what has already been said	Linking an utterance to the preceding utterance	What has been said is not necessarily acknowledged and is sometimes explicitly ignored
Viewed as personally directed, negative, and disruptive	Displays of verbal aggressiveness	Viewed as one conventional organizing structure for conversational flow
The topic is developed progressively and shifts gradually; topics can change quickly	Topic flow and topic shift	The topic is narrowly defined and then adhered to until finished; then the topic can change
Viewed as opportunities to share experiences and offer reassurances	Problem sharing and advice giving	Heard as an explicit request for solutions; advice or a lecture is given

As Gray (1992, pp. 21-22) puts it, if a woman comes home at the end of the day and complains about a problem that she had during the day, the immediate and impulsive response of the man is to try to solve her problem. In fact, the woman may simply want a sympathetic ear to listen to her. Although this is not true in English, there are some languages such as Japanese in which male and female users are required to use different forms. Men use one set of verbs, and women use another. In other languages such as Thai, the speaker is required to use a different form depending on whether he or she is addressing a man or a woman.

Gender differences also exist in the use of language learning strategies. Oxford (2001, p. 1) found that females use language learning strategies significantly more than males, yet in certain cultures males use particular types of language learning strategies more than females. Oxford (2001, p. 4) also reported gender differences in social and linguistic development, noting that "according to hundreds of studies (Maccoby and Jacklin, 1974) females show greater interest than males in social activities, prefer 'gentle' interaction to aggressive interaction, and are more cooperative and less competitive than males."

What the teacher can do

Teachers can help students recognize the influence of gender on language by first helping them understand some of the differences between the conversational styles of men and women. Making them aware of differing gender communication styles is a start. Making these differences explicit is the best way to get students on the road to comprehending the differences in gender communication.

Teachers can use Activity 2.3 to help students explore and discuss these differences in the classroom and prepare them for the outside world.

Activity 2.3	***He said, She said***
Level	High beginner – Advanced
Handout	None
Tip	Recognize the influence of gender on language.

Steps:

1. Form small groups of same-gender students.
2. Write the following on the board:

    Women talk more than men.
    Women talk more for the purpose of maintaining relationships.
    Men talk more to get things done.
    I feel comfortable talking to members of the opposite sex.

3. Ask the groups to talk about the statements and share their opinions.
4. Write the following on the board:

    I think that when women communicate they are too _____.
    I think that when men communicate they are too _____.

5. Ask the class to share how they would complete the sentences.

Teaching notes:

- It is important to be culturally sensitive when dealing with this topic. Some students may not want to share their opinions in front of the entire class.

- Deborah Tannen's books *You Just Don't Understand: Women and Men in Conversation* and *Talking from 9 to 5—Women and Men in the Workplace: Language, Sex and Power* provide useful stories for class discussions.
- *Alternative:* If time permits, share the findings of Wood (1994) and Maltz and Borker (1982) with the class. Ask students if these characteristics of male and female communication hold true in their experience.
- *Alternative:* Extend this activity to include a writing assignment.

 ## Explore the differences between spoken and written language.

Often students do not realize that spoken language and written language have distinct differences. Spoken English is relatively informal, repetitive, and interactive. Speakers may take long pauses and talk over or interrupt each other. On the other hand, written language is relatively formal. Writing is usually more concise and less repetitive. Exploring the differences between spoken and written English can help students use language more appropriately in various contexts.

What the research says

Kramsch (1998, pp. 38-40) summarizes seven characteristics of conversational speech in English that differentiate it from expository writing.

CONVERSATIONAL SPEECH	EXPOSITORY WRITING
Transient, not permanent	Permanent, can be retrieved
Additive; items from prior turn-taking talk are attached; participants build on the utterances of others	Hierarchically ordered and generally linear in nature
Aggregative; uses formulaic expressions to maintain dealings between speakers	Avoids formulaic expressions but promotes analysis
Superfluous or wordy; vocabulary and ideas are repeated	Avoids redundancy; too much repetition is not considered appropriate
Grammatically loose	Grammatically tightly structured
Focus is on people; attempts to involve the listener	Focus is on the topic
Dependent on context	Reduced and away from context

Brown (2007, pp. 326–327) notes additional features of the spoken language that distinguish it from writing and that can be challenging to students learning English.

FEATURES OF SPOKEN LANGUAGE

CLUSTERING
Fluent speakers group words together rather than uttering each word

REDUCED FORMS
Speakers use contractions, elisions, and reduced vowels

PERFORMANCE VARIABLES
The speaker is permitted to pause and hesitate, using filler words and expressions such as *uh, you know, like*

COLLOQUIAL LANGUAGE
Informal terms are permitted and common

RATE OF DELIVERY
The speaker controls the rate of delivery for the listener; a reader can read at his or her own pace

STRESS, RHYTHM, AND INTONATION
Rhythmic and intonation patterns can be important in conveying meaning in spoken language

Other researchers have found connections between writing and meaning. In 1966, applied linguist Robert B. Kaplan suggested that patterns of writing found in academic essays varied depending on language and cultural background. According to Kaplan, who studied the essays of international students' writing in English, American and British students wrote essays in linear fashion, whereas speakers of Arabic and Hebrew were likely to repeat points to reinforce them. Asian students made circular arguments in which the main point was revealed only at the end. Essay writers of Romance languages such as French, Spanish, and Italian were likely to make points, only to veer off in another direction before returning to the topic at hand, as were writers in Russian but following a somewhat different pattern.

In the same way that there is a strong and a weak version of the Sapir-Whorf hypothesis, there have been various interpretations of Kaplan's findings. In fact, Kaplan himself and others (Leki, 1991) have retreated somewhat from the strong version of his article; nevertheless, any composition teacher who has worked with students from a variety of languages and cultural backgrounds can attest to the ways in which cultural thought patterns vary and persist in written text.

Many ESL/EFL teachers have discovered that students in their writing classes cannot distinguish between what is appropriate in written English and what is appropriate in spoken English. The challenge of understanding these distinctions has been made more difficult by the speech-like abbreviations used by students sending text messages. In many instances students may have a good command of the spoken language or what Cummins (1979) terms basic interpersonal communication skills (BICS) used in daily interpersonal exchanges. However, they may attempt to use this type of language in academic writing where it is not appropriate, demonstrating a lack of cognitive academic language proficiency (CALP).

What the teacher can do

Teachers can help students explore the differences between spoken and written language by making the differences explicit. Teachers can elicit some of the differences from students themselves, making use of examples from text messages or from students' writing. It can also be helpful to examine different genres of speaking and writing. Kaplan's descriptions of rhetorical styles can be beneficial for intermediate and advanced students.

By making the differences between spoken and written English explicit, teachers can help students understand these differences and improve their writing. Activity 2.4 is designed to make some of the differences between spoken and written English clearer to students.

Activity 2.4	*Writing vs. speaking*
Level	Intermediate – Advanced
Handout	Page 196
Tip	Explore the differences between spoken and written language.

Steps:

1. Make copies of the handout for Activity 2.4.
2. Find a talk or news program appropriate for your students and for which transcripts are readily available. A good source can be found by visiting www.cnn.com and searching for "transcripts."
3. Find a written news article on the same topic.

(continued on next page)

4. Ask students to read the written article.
5. In class, watch the selected program and have students read along with the transcript.
6. Ask the class to compare the language used in each. Point out the differences between oral and written English characterized by Kramsch (1998) and Brown (2007a). Outline the key features on the board.
7. Pass out copies of the handout for Activity 2.4. Go over the directions.
8. Form pairs or small groups. Ask students to compare the texts and summarize their answers as a group.
9. To conclude the activity, ask: "Do you find spoken language or written language more difficult to learn? Did this exercise help you understand the differences between spoken and written English?"

Teaching notes:

- The primary purpose of this activity is to help students see the differences between spoken and written English. If time permits, repeat the activity with another topic.

 Understand the meaning of language in context.

Communication does not and cannot take place in a vacuum. Fluent speakers of a language vary their speech depending on the context. They know how to use formal language in formal situations and when to switch to informal language if necessary. Vocabulary choice, expressions, and degrees of directness are used differently in different contexts. These variances can sometimes cause difficulties in communication. **Pragmatics**—the branch of linguistics that studies language in context and especially the conveying and interpreting of meaning—is most relevant to Joe's situation in the following incident.

When Joe was teaching English in China, he was once visited in his apartment by a group of Chinese students, most in their thirties. Joe wasn't feeling well, and as the evening wore on, he began to make what were typical hints in English to suggest that it was time for the students to leave. He yawned and said, "Gee, it's getting pretty late" and "We sure have a lot to do tomorrow" and "It's been great to have you visit." However, the students did not interpret these suggestions as gentle requests to leave. It was only when he said very directly, "It's time for you to go now" that the students realized that they were being asked to leave.

What the research says

According to David Crystal (1985, p. 240), pragmatics is "the study of language from the point of view of users, especially of the choices they make, the constraints they encounter in using language in social interaction, and the effects their use of language has on other participants in the act of communication." LoCastro

(2003, p. 15) defines pragmatics as "the study of speaker and hearer meaning created in their joint actions that include both linguistic and nonlinguistic signals in the context of socioculturally organized activities." In other words, pragmatics examines how a speaker uses language in social situations and what the listener understands. For example, when a teacher says to a student, "You're late," the student needs to recognize that this is not simply a statement of fact but a complaint with the implied meaning that the student should not be late again. Understanding the meaning of language in context will help learners be aware of polite behavior and the sometimes hidden meaning of language.

Pragmatics involves analysis of the speakers' meaning in context. It focuses on the linguistic text and on social elements such as age, social status, and social distance of the speakers. Pragmatics seeks answers to the following questions, which are used by researchers to analyze texts:

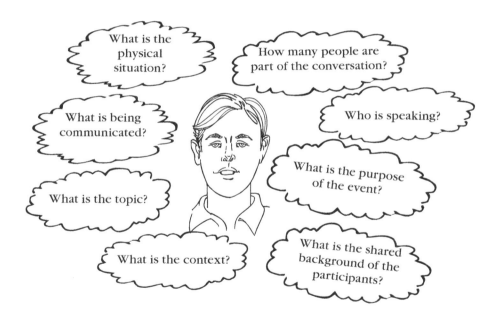

The key to pragmatics is to understand the intention of the speaker beyond the actual meaning of the words spoken. Pragmatic usage differs across languages (Kasper and Blum-Kulka, 1993, Thomas, 1983, 1984). A speaker's intended meaning is conveyed through language that is either correctly interpreted or misinterpreted in different cultural contexts because each speaker and listener brings along his or her own cultural norms of interpretation, underlying worldview, and cultural thought patterns. When speakers do not use or do not understand situationally appropriate language, pragmatic failure occurs. Contributing to this failure may be regional, ethnic, gender, and class differences within a community or across cultural boundaries.

The study of pragmatics requires looking at assumptions, communicative goals, and especially speech acts to understand how language is used in different interactions and situations. Context plays an especially important part in spoken language because it helps us identify communicative intent, or the actual intended meaning of the words themselves.

Let's consider the statement, "It's hot in here." At the sentence level, if this sentence is taken literally, the statement is understood as a fact about the temperature in the room. At another level it can be understood as an indirect request or as a directive with the meaning, "Please turn up the air conditioner" or "Please open the window." The listener can accurately understand the intended meaning of the statement only when the context in which the statement is uttered is understood. Statements like "It's hot in here" do not present a problem for speakers who share the same knowledge about that language, the same rules of speaking, and the same understanding of the context in which the statement is made. DeCapua and Wintergerst (2004, p. 243) note that this is so because the speakers "understand intuitively the complex relationship between the function or intended function of an utterance, the form or structure by which it is expressed, and the situational variables affecting the intended meaning." In short, if the frame of reference is the same for speakers, then misunderstandings will be avoided.

 ## Voices from the Classroom

I remember back when I was a young student who had just arrived from Turkey. I walked around trying to communicate with my dictionary and grammar books my first year in the United States. I didn't know that understanding a language involves not only knowledge of the language itself but also knowledge of characteristics of the culture until the death of my next-door neighbor's mother.

I didn't know what to say to my friend. I knew that sorry *was the right word, but was it enough? I asked one of my Turkish friends who had been in the United States for ten years. She told me that I could buy a greeting card to express condolences. I went to the store and I saw a card that said, "Get well soon." I thought that this would be perfect for the situation because my friend wasn't feeling well.*

Of course, it wasn't the right card for the situation, but at least I made my neighbor laugh and I learned something that day. I learned that language wasn't the only target for me; I needed to learn about the new culture too.

—Meral Muyesser
Burlington County College, New Jersey

What the teacher can do

Teachers can help students to understand the meaning of language in context by creating an awareness of the role of pragmatics in language use. This awareness is crucial if students are to function effectively in their new language. One way to do this is to take an expression that is thoughtful, polite, and courteous and then gradually make it stronger and more intense. You could begin with "Would you mind closing the door, please?" and gradually work your way up to "Shut the damn door!" Then discuss with the students under what circumstances each of these expressions might be uttered and the appropriateness of each utterance.

Teachers can use Activity 2.5 to reintroduce students to the concept of the critical incident to examine issues related to the use of language in context. A critical incident offers students a brief story or vignette in which some type of cultural miscommunication takes place. Critical incidents are used in activities throughout this book. Activity 2.5 focuses on giving students practice regarding the appropriateness of language in different situations.

Activity 2.5	*Language in context*
Level	Intermediate – Advanced
Handouts	Pages 197 – 198
Tip	Understand the meaning of language in context.

Steps:

1. Make copies of the two handouts for Activity 2.5.
2. Review with students that a critical incident is a cross-cultural problematic situation. The incidents are concerned with various dimensions of culture. Inform students that there are no right or wrong answers but that there are solutions.
3. Ask students to work in groups of three or four. Pass out copies of the handouts for Activity 2.5. Assign each group one critical incident. Have students read the critical incidents and questions and discuss what they think caused the conflict.
4. If a group finishes early, assign them another critical incident.
5. As a class, discuss each critical incident, the solutions from each group, and the area of cultural conflict manifested. Pages 189-190 outline possible interpretations to share with the class if none of the groups suggest them.

Teaching notes:

- Each critical incident presents an area of conflict designed to stimulate discussion about the situation described and make students aware of and sensitive to cultural differences.
- *Alternative:* If necessary, simplify the vocabulary used to describe the critical incidents.

6 Identify speech acts in daily communication.

We use language for many different purposes. An understanding of those purposes is necessary to use language effectively. The term **speech act** refers to the utterances made by a speaker, the intent of those words, and the effect of those words on the listener.

For example, in a classroom, when the teacher says, "I can't hear myself think," it is an indication to her students that they are talking too much or too loudly and that they should stop and be quiet. A native speaker of English would understand what is being conveyed. However, an English language learner might not be aware of the meaning and intent of the utterance and may continue talking. It is important for learners to discern the meaning behind the words to be sure that they understand what is being communicated.

What the research says

Speech act is a term that stems from the work of the language philosopher John Austin (1962). Any utterance by a speaker can be a speech act, and each speech act contains three components: the words spoken, the intention behind the spoken words, and the effect of the spoken words on the listener.

In order to understand a speech act, the listener must have the necessary linguistic, sociocultural, and pragmatic knowledge. Each culture's speech acts reflect its norms, values, and beliefs. When a student in the United States is working on an assignment in class and asks another student for help, the teacher might ask the students, "Is there a problem?" The intent of these words is to find out whether a student needs the teacher's help. The effect of these words prompts the student to stop asking his classmate and go directly to the teacher for help. This act reflects the norms, values, and beliefs in the United States that suggest that students do their work independently in class, not talk when working on an assignment, and do what the teacher asks.

Searle (1969) developed a taxonomy of speech acts that he grouped according to common functional characteristics. The following are some examples of Searle's taxonomy of different types of speech acts.

SPEECH ACT	DESCRIPTION	EXAMPLES
Directives	Attempts to get the listener to do something or not do something	Asking, questioning, inquiring
Representatives	Commits the speaker to the truth of a statement	Asserting, concluding
Commissives	Makes a commitment to doing something	Promising, threatening, offering
Expressives	Conveys a psychological state	Thanking, apologizing, welcoming, congratulating
Declaratives and performatives	Affects the surrounding environment	Declaring, firing from employment, ordering someone to do something

Searle's classification of speech acts provides an important contribution to cross-cultural pragmatics. As students gain pragmatic knowledge of the language of study, they are better able to avoid miscommunication and potential misunderstandings.

What the teacher can do

Teachers can help students identify speech acts in daily communication and develop pragmatic and sociolinguistic awareness by using activities that Judd (1999, p. 154) classifies into three broad categories: cognitive awareness activities, receptive skill development, and productive use activities.

Cognitive awareness activities help learners become consciously aware of the differences between native and target language speech acts. These types of activities emphasize both the linguistic aspects of the speech act, especially the grammar, and the sociolinguistic features of the speech act. These sociolinguistic features include the situations, the participants, the status of those involved, and so on. Commonly used techniques in cognitive awareness activities are presenting and discussing research findings on speech acts and obtaining information through observations, questionnaires, or interviews.

Receptive skill development activities, according to Judd, help students identify and comprehend speech acts. These activities demonstrate the functions of speech acts and give students practice in comprehending these language features as they occur in natural speech. Audio or video recordings with or without closed captioning are often used. Both teacher-generated materials and natural data can be used. Special attention is given to the linguistic forms used and to the sociolinguistic variables of the speech event: the environment, age, gender, participants' status, and formality levels.

Productive-use activities utilize specific speech acts for student practice. Judd mentions the use of cloze-type exercises, in which selected words from the speech acts are deleted, and simulation or role plays, which produce pragmatic features, to capture student interest and help them learn. In short, it is important for teachers to give students opportunities to practice speech acts in the second language so that students can understand the pragmatic meanings when they encounter these outside of the classroom.

The teacher can use Activity 2.6 to give students practice in identifying and using speech acts. This activity is what Judd would classify as a cognitive awareness activity. By helping students learn about speech acts, we prepare them to be aware of the language they use during interactions. By making students aware of the purpose for which language is used, or its so-called language function, teachers focus students' attention on the practical aspects of language use.

Activity 2.6	***Language functions***
Level	Intermediate – Advanced
Handout	Page 199
Tip	Identify speech acts in daily communication.

Steps:
1. Make copies of the handout for Activity 2.6. Review the directions and examples. Explain the concept of language functions.
2. Give students 5-10 minutes to complete the chart.
3. Ask the class for ways in which these functions in English differ from their first language.
4. Form pairs or small groups. Have students compare their answers.
5. Copy the chart on the board. Ask volunteers for examples of their speech acts. Write them in the chart.
6. After reviewing the answers, ask students what they learned about speech acts and language functions.

Teaching notes:

- You may wish to correct student responses if they contain grammatical or other errors.
- Encourage students to share corresponding speech acts from their own cultural and linguistic background.
- *Alternative:* If you are teaching in a country where English is spoken, assign your students to gather examples from overheard conversations or from radio or television programs.

 Understand the concept of face.

The concept of **face** is a universal phenomenon and an important component of individual identity. Face refers to the public image of a person and plays a role when communicating with others. In certain cultures, **facework,** or the communication behaviors a person uses to maintain a positive image of the speaker and listener, plays a dominant role.

Kumi, a student from Japan, was studying English in the United States. When her teacher asked whether she was clear about using the present-perfect tense, Kumi nodded affirmatively. When the teacher asked her for a sentence to illustrate the present perfect, Kumi was unable to produce one. She hadn't actually understood the verb tense. Saving face is an important concept in Japanese culture. In order to save face, Kumi pretended to know the answer.

What the research says

The notion of face is particularly evident in Asian cultures, where it is the key to fitting into a social group and upholding social harmony. Facework refers to specific social strategies used to protect the positive image of the communicators. Ting-Toomey (1999, p. 38) contends that as resourceful communicators, individuals "often use creative facework behaviors to protect their vulnerable emotions such as pride and shame, or honor and dishonor" and that facework differs across cultures. Facework includes the communicative behaviors that speakers use to save their own face or that of their listener's, to maintain their image, and to gain the respect and approval of others.

LoCastro (2003, p. 111) holds that the Chinese concept of face is twofold: Acquired face is "earned through social behavior in life" as a result of moral conduct or birth, and ascribed face is "what every individual is entitled to receive as a human being." Tensions can arise when different expectations exist about how face is shown and to whom it is shown. In order to have successful social interactions, a person's actions need to show respect for the face of conversational partners.

The perception of face may be colored by patterns of cultural communication. For example, people from the United States are known for speaking directly. They like to get right to the point and not "beat around the bush." They don't necessarily feel a need to establish relationships before entering into personal conversations or business transactions. When they ask a question, they expect to receive a direct answer. Imagine the potential difficulties when a person from a culture that values directness is communicating with someone whose culture is more indirect and who thinks that harmony and agreement are more important than directness. If individuals from Mexico or Japan were asked a question that they couldn't answer affirmatively, they might be concerned about the loss of face for the questioner or for themselves. In such a case, they might say, "yes" to save face, even though, from the point of view of the American, the "real" or "true" answer would be "no."

The human desire for public self-image, or face, is universal. Brown and Levinson (1987) use the term **linguistic politeness** to describe the use of language to carry out social actions in which face is mutually respected. Issues of face become particularly apparent when the words of a speaker threaten the public image of the listener. When a face-threatening act occurs, the speaker can adopt a politeness strategy such as an apology to soften this threat. The speaker also needs to be aware that the power relationship between the addresser and the addressee, the social distance between them, and the degree of imposition are culturally defined (Brown and Eisterhold 2004, p. 60).

What the teacher can do

Teachers can help students build awareness of the concept of face by using a contrastive approach to show varieties of responses to different situations as well as conversational gambits and responses that could be face-threatening.

Teachers can use Activity 2.7 to present the concept of face and to identify potential cultural differences connected with this concept. In this way students become aware of this concept in their own and other cultures.

Activity 2.7	*Maintaining face*
Level	Intermediate – Advanced
Handout	Page 200
Tip	Understand the concept of face.

Steps:

1. Make copies of the handout for Activity 2.7. Pass out the copies.
2. Explain the vocabulary if needed. Ask students to fill out the chart by checking the answer that best represents their cultural background.
3. Form pairs or small groups and ask students to share their answers. If possible, try to vary cultures and first languages within groups.
4. If possible, project the chart on the board or on a screen. Ask students to share their answers and mark them on the chart. You may want to use abbreviations.
5. To conclude the activity, ask students to give a summary of what this activity has taught them about the concept of face and cultural background.

Teaching notes:

- This activity works best with students from a variety of cultures. If students are all from the same culture, you may want to point out that the answers would be different if other cultures were involved and offer some examples.
- There are no right or wrong answers to these questions. However, point out that answers will vary from culture to culture.

8 **Recognize communication styles and registers.**

Spoken and written language styles may shift depending on the social or conversational setting. **Communication styles** incorporate an individual's word choice, discourse patterns, and nonverbal cues. While native speakers may vary their use of communication styles in different situations, these styles also differ cross-culturally. For example, when the teacher asks him a question, Xiao Jia from China simply avoids eye contact and answers the question, whereas Carolina from Brazil looks straight at the teacher and answers the question.

Register refers to how one uses language in a particular situation and depends on the degree of formality of a situation and the relationship between the speakers. For example, one of Ann's colleagues, Gaetano, who is from Italy, uses formal academic language when giving a speech to an audience filled with his peers. When talking with his friends, however, he uses informal language or conversational language filled with slang and idiomatic expressions. Understanding the concepts of communication style and register can help students understand what language is appropriate to use when, where, with whom, and about what topic.

What the research says

Communication style is affected by subject matter, audience, occasion, shared experience, and purpose of the communication. Brown (2007, p. 235) defines communication styles as "not social or regional dialects, but sets of conventions for selecting words, phrases, discourse, and nonverbal language in specified contexts." Variables such as setting, status, gender, and age can make important differences in how speakers determine which language to use to convey their messages. These decisions may differ cross-culturally depending on how we perceive and use language.

A communicatively competent person does not speak the same way all of the time (Wolfson, 1989). Competent speakers shift style to indicate social distance. They do not speak the same way to close friends as they do to strangers. In addition to the relationship between the speakers, the patterns or style of speech used are also influenced by the background of the speaker and by the particular speech event.

Brown (2007a, p. 237) views register as related to stylistic variation and not as a synonym for communication style, because "registers are commonly identified by certain phonological variants, vocabulary, idioms, and other expressions that are associated with different occupational or socioeconomic groups. Register sometimes enables people to identify with a particular group to maintain solidarity." However, choosing the appropriate level of formality can often be a challenge cross-culturally. For example, in Germany, a letter sent to a female professor holding a doctorate would be addressed to (translation) Mrs. Professor Doctor Ann Wintergerst. This level of formality is above that considered acceptable in the United States, where use of more than a single prefix at a time would be considered incorrect.

McCarthy (1991, p. 32) defines register as "the linguistic features of the text that reflect the social context in which it is produced." He also notes that register is closely tied to choice of vocabulary words so that lexical choices are often significantly affected by the situation and the context of the conversation.

What the teacher can do

Teachers can help students appreciate communication styles and registers by demonstrating a wide variety of these in the classroom and by their choice of teaching materials. Whereas students at the beginning levels of language learning are simply concerned with conveying basic meaning, students at intermediate levels can begin to learn to express themselves using a style and register appropriate to the context.

Teachers can use Activity 2.8 to give students an opportunity to practice varying levels of formality. This will help them appreciate the nuances of language.

Activity 2.8	***Shut the door***
Level	Intermediate – Advanced
Handout	None
Tip	Recognize communication styles and registers.

Steps:

1. Write the following on the board: Shut the door. Shut the door, please. Would you please shut the door? Would you be so kind as to shut the door? Gee, it's a little chilly in here. Shut the damn door!
2. Ask students to identify which sentence they think is the most and least polite. Review their answers.
3. Discuss which sentences would be appropriate to use with different people.
4. Write the following on the board: What time is it? Hand me those scissors. Bring me a glass of water.
5. Form pairs or small groups. Ask each group to choose one of the sentences and write a list of possible ways to express the meaning ranging from very polite to rude.
6. Ask groups for their ideas and write them on the board. Discuss the sentences and the students' ideas.

Teaching notes:

- *Alternative:* A similar task can be done using intensifiers such as "What in the world do you think you're doing?" and gradually inserting language that makes the expression progressively ruder (e.g., "What the hell do you think you're doing?").
- Caution students not to use rude expressions. They may be useful for comprehension purposes, but they can get students into trouble if they use them without fully comprehending their impact on the listener.

Conclusion

In this chapter we explored the connection between language, thought, and culture. We examined the use of language in speech communities and its use in the context of the communication. We discussed the role of speech acts and we took into account the role of communication styles and register. We considered the difference between written and spoken language and the ways in which men and women use language differently. We also looked at the concept of face in communication. Understanding these concepts helps teachers in the classroom to equip learners with useful tools to use in real communication situations.

Check your understanding

After reading this chapter and using the activities with your class, check your comfort level with the following:

❏ I know how to help students see the relationship between culture, language, and thought.
❏ I can distinguish between speech communities.
❏ I can help my students recognize the influence of gender on language.
❏ I understand the differences between spoken and written language.
❏ I understand the meaning of language in context.
❏ I can help my students identify speech acts in daily communication.
❏ My students understand the concept of face.
❏ I can help students appreciate communication styles and registers.

CHAPTER 3

CULTURE AND NONVERBAL COMMUNICATION

Consider these questions:
- What are some examples of gestures with special meanings?
- Do you know of any gestures used in your culture that have different meanings in other cultures?
- What are some ways to communicate nonverbally without using gestures?

In Chapter 2 we explored the relationship between language and culture. In this chapter we move beyond spoken and written language to consider nonverbal communication. When most people think of nonverbal communication they think of gestures. You might be familiar with stories of misinterpretations of certain gestures. For example, in some cultures, the

53

American "okay" signal, made by holding up the hand while forming a circle with the thumb and the forefinger, is offensive. In others, holding up two fingers can be an insult.

However, nonverbal communication also includes the way in which people interact in time and in space. It encompasses facial expressions and sounds that are not words, such as intonation patterns. Nonverbal communication also includes **proxemics,** the distance at which two speakers relate; **kinesics,** or movement; and **haptics,** which refers to touch. As teachers, we need to work with our students to build their awareness of nonverbal communication and to use it appropriately in the target language and culture.

TIPS FOR TEACHING ABOUT NONVERBAL COMMUNICATION

The seven tips in this chapter give explicit advice to teachers about how they can encourage language-learners to explore their knowledge of nonverbal communication. With each tip, we provide a summary of the research related to the tip and offer practical ideas for what teachers can do in the classroom. Some of the activities include photocopiable handouts. These are located in Appendix A on pages 201–206.

 **TIPS**

1. Identify basic concepts of nonverbal communication.
2. Emphasize the connection between verbal and nonverbal communication.
3. Understand the functions of nonverbal communication.
4. Help students understand the concept of physical space.
5. Introduce various concepts of time.
6. Emphasize differences between high- and low-context communication.
7. Explore kinesics, movement, and gestures in nonverbal communication.

In this chapter we examine research findings on nonverbal communication. We explore the ways that teachers can help students grasp key concepts. We also look at ways of engaging students in the study of gestures and other nonverbal cues found in everyday life. The classroom activities promote the active engagement of students in cultural learning, making use of their abilities to recognize and convey meaning without speech. After completing the activities, students will have an increased awareness of the varied communication styles used by their classmates and people from other cultures.

1 Identify basic concepts of nonverbal communication.

Nonverbal communication functions for us at a primal level and is therefore extremely important in the communication of feelings and emotions. As far as we know from anthropologists and other researchers, before spoken language, humans' primary means of communication consisted of grunts, gestures, and other nonverbal cues. The primacy of nonverbal communication can be seen from the earliest stages; infants communicate via movements before mastering language, for example. Nonverbal communication and the interpretation of nonverbal communication differ from culture to culture, and understanding its different forms and functions is an important part of learning to communicate across cultures.

Ann, one of the authors, teaches an advanced ESL writing class. One day Marcos, a student from Greece, asked Ann if he could be excused from the next class in order to meet his mother at the airport. She was flying in for a visit. Ann nodded the head up and down indicating that it was okay with her. Ann was surprised to see Marcos in class the next day. She discovered that nodding the head up and down means *no* in some parts of Greece. Because of this nonverbal miscommunication, Marcos thought Ann had not given him permission to be absent and so his mother had to take a taxi from the airport.

What the research says

"If language is the key to the core of a culture, nonverbal communication is indeed the *heart* of each culture. Nonverbal communication is omnipresent throughout a culture—it is everywhere," according to Stella Ting-Toomey (1999, p. 120). Other researchers agree. The anthropologist Ray Birdwhistell (1974) found that more than 65 percent of a conversation is communicated through nonverbal cues. Porter and Samovar (1988) make the point that nonverbal communication and culture are closely linked. They contend that most nonverbal communication is culturally based; thus, a particular gesture or action symbolizes, only the meaning a particular culture has attached to it.

Members of a culture recognize those realities that have meaning or importance for them. For example, Vietnamese is a tonal language in which upward and downward intonation patterns carry distinct meanings. People from other cultures may find the speech of Vietnamese people to have a "sing-song" quality. If the language of the listener doesn't include tones, the nonverbal sounds from a Vietnamese speaker may be challenging to distinguish at first.

The members of a culture interpret nonverbal experiences through their own personal frame of reference, as well as through their own cultural frame of reference. Failure to recognize observable nonverbal signs and symbols or interpret them correctly can lead to a breakdown in communication (Samovar and Porter 1988, p. 28). In order to fully enter into a new culture and communicate accurately, we need to identify the rules, be aware of the underlying cultural values, and understand the connection between the functions and interpretations of nonverbal behavior (Ting-Toomey, 1999).

An effort to understand and use correct nonverbal communication in a new culture can have significant benefits. O'Sullivan (1994, p. 63) described his experiences attempting to learn the language and culture of Iran. Although he was unable to speak the language fluently, he did use many nonverbal communication strategies to help him function in his new culture. For example, by putting his hand on his heart and inclining his head to the side, he was able to approximate the correct nonverbal communication used for greeting another man. Although his verbal greeting may have had errors, his nonverbal greeting was clearly understood.

The values, norms, and beliefs of a group are reflected in their patterns of verbal and nonverbal behavior. Nonverbal behavior often carries a heavy affective load, but

the meaning of an emotional gesture varies from one culture to another. For example, the Japanese smile when they are angry, feel sad, or fail, whereas Americans smile to signal joy, happiness, and contentment. When the meanings attached to the non-verbal cue—in this case the smile—are not understood in the same way by the speaker and the listener, there is the possibility that one of the communicators may feel disrespected.

Nonverbal behavior accounts for the majority of the communication that occurs within any given group (Ting-Toomey, 1999). Because members communicate and perceive meaning so well within their own groups, they attain a level of comfort. They communicate with minimum effort and frustration because the behavior patterns of their group members are so predictable that little effort is required for them to function effectively (Bennett, 1998).

What the teacher can do

Teachers can help students understand the basic concepts of nonverbal communication by developing their awareness of these concepts and how they are used across cultures. In-class demonstrations of a variety of nonverbal behaviors can be useful. At the most basic level, teachers can have students from different cultures indicate some common gestures with different meanings such as *come here, stop,* and *me.*

A student who can interpret a variety of nonverbal cues is more likely to have successful cross-cultural interactions. Activity 3.1 is designed to build student awareness of different nonverbal communication signals by using critical incidents. In each of these critical incidents, nonverbal communication causes some type of cultural miscommunication.

Activity 3.1	*Nonverbal communication dimensions*
Level	Intermediate – Advanced
Handouts	Pages 201 – 202
Tip	Identify basic concepts of nonverbal communication.

Steps:

1. Make copies of the two handouts for Activity 3.1.
2. Present and explain the concept of critical incidents to the class. Tell students that a critical incident is a cross-cultural problematic situation. The incidents are concerned with various dimensions of culture. Inform students that there are no right or wrong answers but that there are solutions.
3. Ask students to work in groups of 3-4. Pass out the handouts for Activity 3.1. Assign each group one critical incident. Have students read the critical incidents and questions and discuss what they think caused the conflict.
4. If a group finishes early, assign another critical incident.
5. As a class, discuss each critical incident, the solutions from each group, and the area of cultural conflict manifested. Page 190 outlines possible interpretations to share with the class if none of the groups suggest them.

Teaching notes:

- Each critical incident presents an area of conflict designed to stimulate discussion about the situation described and to make students aware of and sensitive to cultural differences.
- *Alternative:* If necessary, simplify the vocabulary used to describe the critical incidents.

 ## Emphasize the connection between verbal and nonverbal communication.

In the United States there is a saying: "Actions speak louder than words." This suggests that doing something is better than talking about doing something. So too, nonverbal behavior appears to have a greater impact than mere verbal behavior. For example, when U.S. President Richard Nixon gave his State of the Union address on American television in 1969, the public was distrustful because the audience perceived his posture as stoic and his eyes as unfriendly.

As teachers, we sometimes give mixed messages. Nodding the head may mean we are telling students that their answers are correct or that we agree with their comments. However, in other circumstances, we may nod our head simply because we are too busy at the moment to deal with the question or comment and need to keep things moving in the classroom.

What the research says

The term nonverbal communication, or what Hall (1959) calls "the silent language," refers to all types of nonverbal interaction, including **paralanguage**—the use of body language—and the use of the voice to make sounds that are not words. This includes features such as pitch, stress, volume, and rate of delivery. Paralanguage even takes into consideration the contextual elements found in human interaction (Damen, 1987). These elements include body movement, the use of time and space, and whatever other nonlinguistic elements help to get the message across. These behaviors are learned and vary cross-culturally.

Paralinguistic cues are also used to manage conversations. These cues include silence, pauses, and **backchannel behavior** such as "uh huh" and "yeah," spoken by the listeners to indicate that they are paying attention to what is being said. But there are many subtleties in the use of these cues. For example, a drop in pitch when saying "Excuse me" in English can indicate anger, frustration, anxiety, or impatience, whereas speaking the same words with a drawn out or slight rising tone shows friendliness or a relaxed attitude.

Nonverbal communication can carry a powerful emotional meaning. Nonverbal messages can supplement, underscore, replace, or even disagree with the meaning of the messages conveyed with words. These nonverbal messages can be intentional or unintentional. For instance, some experts can tell when a person is lying by observing his or her nonverbal behavior.

People provide context and clarify the meaning of verbal messages through the use of facial expressions. However, miscommunication can occur when a nonverbal signal means different things to people in other cultures, such as the common hand gesture in which the thumb and middle finger are brought together in a circle. In the United States this sign means "okay," in Brazil it is an insult, and in Japan it is a symbol for money. Birdwhistell (1970) contends that no body movement has the same social meaning in all societies. So nonverbal communication is affected by cultural, situational, and individual variations.

 Voices from the Classroom

As an American, I was teaching English in Burundi, located in central Africa. It was before class, and I was upstairs, outside the Dean's office, waiting to ask him a question. I looked down into the courtyard and saw that several of my students had arrived. So I waved to them and said, "Hi." Moments later they were all upstairs, crowding the narrow corridor. When I asked why they had come upstairs, they replied, "You told us to come." Then I realized that my wave had been misinterpreted. In the United States my gesture meant "Hi," but in Burundi the same gesture meant "Come here."

— *Sue Rosenfield*
Boston University

Cross-cultural differences can lead to ambiguities in interpretation, especially when there are multiple nonverbal cues during a single interaction. In addition, nonverbal communication patterns can be layered with other factors such as personality, gender, socioeconomic status, and a particular communicative context, all making these patterns even more difficult to understand and interpret correctly.

Damen (1987) cautions that nonverbal *behavior* does not necessarily involve nonverbal *communication*. Simple nonverbal behavior such as nodding only becomes nonverbal communication when a cultural message of agreement or disagreement is sent and received. In short, if there is no shared message, nonverbal communication has not taken place, only nonverbal behavior. Once these behaviors are given meaning and evaluated by the listener, they become part of the nonverbal communication system or code of a particular cultural group. After spending only a few days in Japan, for instance, a visitor is often struck by the desire to bow and repeat, "Thank you very much" whenever anyone performs the slightest task.

According to Ekman and Oster (1979), culture is the dominant factor that shapes the rules for how diverse emotions in nonverbal behavior are to be conveyed or concealed as well as under what circumstances. Ekman (1982) argues that social or cultural rules affect the display of emotions, and he reaffirms the need to be aware of these rules and understand them.

What the teacher can do

Teachers can point out the importance of nonverbal messages during the delivery of verbal messages. It is possible that what a person says with words can be in disagreement with what he or she demonstrates through gestures and actions. Students need to learn how to decipher nonverbal codes and interpret them appropriately. To help students gain this knowledge, the teacher might consider playing the part of a speaker whose nonverbal communication gives a different message from his or her spoken words. For example, a superior at work or a parent might ask a worker or teenager if he or she would be willing to perform a particular task. The person might respond "Yeah," which means "yes," but if the facial gesture or body language indicates displeasure about being asked to do something then the nonverbal gesture delivers a message that is contrary to the spoken words.

Teachers can also model appropriate nonverbal communication in the target language. For example, Japanese students may put their index finger on their nose as a way of self-identification. The teacher can demonstrate how one self-identifies in the United States, by pointing and placing one finger to the chest.

Teachers can use Activity 3.2 to help students recognize the differences in meaning that sounds and intonation patterns can convey in the United States. (See next page.)

Activity 3.2	*Hmmmmm?*
Level	Intermediate – Advanced
Handout	None
Tip	Emphasize the connection between verbal and nonverbal communication.

Steps:

1. Write the following items on the board. Tell students you are going to say each one and they need to interpret what each sound is communicating.
2. Have students number a piece of paper from 1 to 5. Say each item and have students write their answers. You may wish to overemphasize the intonation patterns slightly so that each one is clear.

1. Hmmm   4. Umm- humm

2. Hmmm   5. Hmmm

3. Umm-humm

Meanings: 1. I didn't hear you. 2. That's interesting. 3. Indicates yes or agreement. 4. Indicates no or disagreement. 5. Indicates pleasure or satisfaction.

3. Go over the answers. Say each item again and have students repeat.

Teaching notes:

- *Alternative:* Form pairs or small groups. Have students take turns producing nonverbal sounds and guessing the meanings.
- *Alternative:* Write the meanings of several intonation patterns on index cards. Have students take turns choosing a card and saying "Hmmm" or "Umm-hmmm" to match the meaning on the card.

3 Understand the functions of nonverbal communication.

Nonverbal communication does not occur in a vacuum. It does not exist independently of meaning. When we use a smile, a shrug, or a "Hmmm?" response, we do so in order to convey meaning or emotions and often to achieve a particular purpose. For example, in the United States if a teacher would like to get her students involved in a classroom activity, she would add a smile of encouragement as she gives her verbal instructions. Her goal is to signal to students that she is encouraging them to take risks and not to be overly concerned about failure. This achieves more positive results in terms of student involvement than when she does not smile. Cross-culturally a teacher's smile might present a problem for those students for whom a smile holds different cultural interpretations. For instance, as stated earlier, in Japan a smile can signal anger, sadness, or failure.

What the research says

Nonverbal communication can vary not only in use but also in function. DeCapua and Wintergerst (2004, p. 149) cite Ekman and Friesen (1969) and Patterson (1990) who identify the most important functions of nonverbal behavior as follows: expression of emotions, reinforcement of verbal messages, substitution for verbal communication, contradiction of verbal messages, management of communicative situations, and conveyance of messages in ritualized forms.

Ting-Toomey (1999, p. 116) identifies five functions of nonverbal communication.

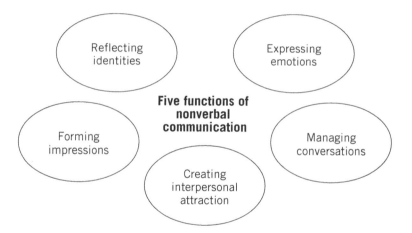

The first function of nonverbal communication is to reflect our identity. Ting-Toomey (1999, p. 115) likens nonverbal cues to "name badges" that we use to alert others about our group memberships. Unspoken signals such as our choice of clothes or jewelry, our **vocalics**—voice qualifiers such as accent, pitch, volume, articulation, resolution, and tempo—and our vocalizations—sounds or noise such as laughing and crying, moaning and groaning, yawning, and hesitation or silence—send the world a message about who we are. The person receiving these messages forms attitudes and impressions based on them.

The second function of nonverbal behavior is the expression of emotions and attitudes. Emotions and attitudes can be communicated to the listener through **kinesics,** which are facial expressions and gestures, and vocalics, or voice qualifiers. These cues and their meanings vary from culture to culture. The messages sent and received depend on what cues the speaker and listener have been exposed to and how their culture has conditioned them to respond to those cues. In the United States, speakers may demonstrate facial expressions that indicate the emotions of anger, distrust, fear, happiness, sadness, and surprise. In Japan speakers are less likely to express emotions through facial expressions. It is easy to see how miscommunication can happen if speakers are not familiar with the way that facial expressions are interpreted in another culture.

The third function of nonverbal communication, according to Ting-Toomey, is conversation management. Kinesics and **oculesics**—eye movement—play important roles in conversation management. In the United States, signals to indicate conversational turn-taking are given by changing body posture, displaying ending gestures, and halting eye contact. These nonverbal cues are not necessarily used in conversations in Asian, African, or Latino cultures.

A study of conversational management during business negotiations revealed that Brazilians tend to interrupt twice as much as Americans or Japanese. The French also interrupt, but only when the conversation has reached a certain level of informality. In Asia it is a signal of respect to avoid sustained direct eye contact with the elderly or with any high-status individual. The opposite, however, is true in the United States, where failure to make eye contact when speaking to another person is considered impolite.

The fourth and the fifth functions of nonverbal behavior are forming impressions and creating interpersonal attraction, otherwise known as trying to make a good impression (Ting-Toomey 1999, p. 126). We are culturally conditioned to examine the posture and facial expressions of others to learn more about them. Many people form first impressions when meeting individuals before anyone has even had a chance to say anything. We look, for instance, at politicians to see if we feel that their body language lends credibility to their statements. Facial expressions and posture are frequently cited in books about international business communication as areas requiring special attention when communicating with those from another culture. We also "read" the nonverbal communications of others to decide whether we like them and would like to spend more time with them.

What the teacher can do

Teachers can help students understand the functions of nonverbal communication by demonstrating the use of tone, facial expressions, gestures, eye contact, touch, and space. Teachers can check whether the students in the class grasp how these nonverbal patterns reflect different cultural backgrounds, practices, and perspectives and the effect that they may have on a conversation by asking them to do role plays.

Improving conversational management will help students succeed in academic and social communication tasks. Teachers can use Activity 3.3 to give students an opportunity to practice different types of nonverbal communication used in conversational management.

Activity 3.3	*Stop or go?*
Level	High beginner – Advanced
Handout	None
Tip	Understand the functions of nonverbal communication.

Steps:

1. Introduce the topic: conversational management. Explain that people give different nonverbal cues when they are interested or uninterested in a conversational subject. They use nonverbal cues to show interest in continuing a conversation or when they want to end a conversation.
2. Write the following nonverbal cues on the board. Go over any vocabulary students don't know.
   a. Gazing intently at the speaker to indicate interest.
   b. Looking over the speaker's shoulder as if there is something more interesting that you would like to go and do.
   c. Responding with enthusiastic nonverbal sounds (e.g., "Um-hmm!").
   d. Responding with unenthusiastic, monotone nonverbal sounds.
   e. Tapping a hand, finger, or foot to indicate boredom.
   f. Avoiding eye contact with the speaker.
3. Choose a volunteer. Without identifying which one, role-play one of the cues. Ask the class to identify which cue you are role-playing and the meaning.
4. Form pairs. Choose a dialogue from your textbook. One student is the primary speaker and the other is the respondent. Have them practice the nonverbal behaviors listed above one by one. Then ask students to switch roles.
5. To finish the activity, ask the class to describe what happened during their role plays. Was it clear to them when the listener was interested and when he or she was not? Could they tell when the listener wanted to end the conversation?

Teaching notes:

- *Caution:* An intense gaze may be disconcerting. Be sure that students, especially males, understand that an overly intense gaze directed at a female may be unwelcome or perceived as intrusive or rude.
- If your class is high beginner or low intermediate, choose a simple dialogue or prepare a dialogue based on language you have already presented and practiced.

Help students understand the concept of physical space.

In 1959 anthropologist Edward T. Hall wrote *The Silent Language* and explained how patterns of **spatial behavior** can vary from culture to culture. Spatial behaviors are part of the communication process and, like other forms of nonverbal communication, can carry a greater weight in conveying meaning than the spoken word.

In an intermediate ESL writing class that Ann taught, two students illustrated the potential for misunderstanding. Anders from Norway and Arash from Iran were asked to work together on a writing activity. Anders felt very uncomfortable because Arash was sitting so close to him that he could barely move during the activity. Anders finally asked Arash to move his chair farther away. Arash considered the proximity to be acceptable because his culture permits a much closer use of space during interpersonal interactions, whereas Anders' culture had a different point of view.

What the research says

The term **proxemics** refers to the use of physical space, such as distance between people and physical positioning of people in relation to one another (Ting-Toomey, 1999). Proxemics encompasses relative distance and physical orientation. Because people in different cultures use space differently, they may sometimes unknowingly violate the personal space of others. This use of space is a function of each individual culture.

The illustrations on page 65 show a model developed by Hall (1966) to describe the use of personal space in the United States. Think about other cultures with which you are familiar. How are they the same or different regarding the use of space during interactions?

The zone of personal and social distance in the Middle East is much smaller than that in the United States. Because individuals usually adjust the space between them until they find their own level of comfort, one can imagine what Davis (1990) describes as a comic dance between a person from the Middle East and a North American. In this "dance," the person from the Middle East keeps attempting to get closer and closer, while the North American seeks a more comfortable distance by continuing to withdraw and move further away.

If the space between two people is reduced to nothing, then they are touching. Touch—also known as **haptics**—refers to behaviors with hands, lips, and arms. This behavior can vary in duration, intensity, and frequency. The perception, function, and meaning of touch can vary across cultures because different cultures have different standards, expectations, and rules regarding touching.

Intimate

touching to 1.5 feet

Personal
(the so-called
American
personal space
"bubble")

1.5 to 4 feet or about an arm's length

Social distance
for general public
contact

4 to 12 feet

Public (signals
some type of formal
relationship)

12 to 25 feet

Examples of touch include shaking hands, taking a patient's pulse, hugging, kissing, kicking, romantic touch, poking, or grabbing. In the United States, adult friends of small children will sometimes pat them on their heads. In Thailand, however, the head is considered sacred, and to touch another's head with the flat of the hand is rude. In the United States, touching or patting children you don't know is inappropriate. But in China or the Philippines, strangers may feel entitled to stroke or touch the children of others.

What the teacher can do

Teachers can build their own awareness of the functions of proxemics and haptics in nonverbal communication. They can then help students grasp the concept of space by having them demonstrate how distance and touching are viewed in their respective cultures and then comparing these views with those of other classmates.

Teachers can share any information about appropriate proxemic behavior in the target culture. For example, identifying and demonstrating appropriate behavior such as greetings or leave-takings or the amount of pressure and the length of time for a handshake are practical and useful information for students. Activity 3.4 helps students compare proxemic behaviors and spatial distances across cultural groups.

Activity 3.4	*Give me my space!*
Level	High beginner – Advanced
Handout	None
Tip	Help students understand the concept of physical space.

Steps:

1. Ask a student volunteer to join you at the front of the class.
2. Start a conversation with the student and stand a distance of 4 feet away. As you are talking, move closer to the student, until you are approximately 2 feet away. Finish the conversation from about 1 foot away.
3. Ask the class to say what they observed about the student's behavior during the exercise.
4. Ask the student how he or she felt during the exercise.
5. Explain the concept of space and proxemics as discussed above. Talk about proxemics in U.S. culture using the information in the diagram on page 65. You may want to draw the diagram on the board.
6. Form pairs. Ask each pair to have a short conversation at 4 feet, 2 feet, and 1 foot apart.
7. To finish the activity, ask pairs to talk about their experiences. How comfortable did students feel at each distance?

Teaching notes:

- You may want to let the student volunteer know in advance what is going to happen during Step 1.
- As you teach Step 5, it is important that students from cultures that allow a closer speaking distance understand how uncomfortable this can be for students from cultures where such proximity is not appropriate.
- *Alternative:* Conduct a similar exercise focusing on eye contact. Have students talk while maintaining strong eye contact and then talk while avoiding eye contact.

Introduce various concepts of time.

Some of us always arrive at an event at the exact time it is scheduled to begin, whereas others never get there until well after the appointed hour. Concepts of punctuality, however, are a matter of cultural perspective. What is considered *on time* for one culture is not necessarily the same in another culture.

For example, we tend to generalize that Germans usually arrive at the agreed upon time and that Latin Americans usually arrive after the agreed upon time. Though such generalizations are a reflection of the culture as a whole, there are, of course, exceptions based on individual personalities. In Ann's advanced ESL speaking/listening class, Christophe from Germany was usually late for Ann's class, whereas Maria from the Dominican Republic was usually on time.

What the research says

Time is viewed differently by Eastern and Western cultures, and even within these cultures, ideas about time differ from one country to another. For example, Americans often say that "time is money," which suggests that they are fast-paced, action-oriented, and linear time-oriented. Many Eastern cultures view time not as linear or capable of being managed but as cyclic, flexible, or adaptable (Lewis, 2000). People in Western cultures, especially those from the United States, think of time as something fixed in nature, something around them from which they cannot escape, and something that is ever-present in their environment, like oxygen. They think of time as a road that extends into the future along which they progress and that this road has distinct parts. This perception of time is linear and is quite different from ideas about time held by Latin Americans. For example, Mexicans value the *mañana* tendency in terms of what Lewis calls cyclical time, in which time is viewed as coming around again and again.

Hall (1983) considers **chronemics**—the use of time—from three different perspectives. The first is monochromic time or M-time. This is the view of time typically used by North Americans and Northern Europeans who do one thing at a time. Hall's second perspective is polychromic time or P-time. This is the view found in many other parts of the world where people do multiple things at the same time. A third perspective is that of synchrony—coordinating actions in time through mutual understanding. Latin Americans, who are members of polychromic (P-time) cultures, consider time to be more flexible, in contrast to those who are members of monochromic (M-time) cultures, such as the Swiss, who consider time to be rigid and fixed.

How important is time? Is time something to be spent, wasted, or given? Is it central to one's day and life? Or is it more or less in the background, taking a back seat to interpersonal relations? Levine (1997) recounts his experiences as a Westerner teaching in Brazil. He found that, as a teacher, it was quite unnecessary

and unexpected for him to either begin or end class at the appointed hour, nor was punctuality expected by most other university students and teachers in making or keeping appointments. Levine and Wolff (1985) conducted a psychological study to find the relative accuracy of bank clocks and compared it to the speed at which people walked and the time it took to buy a stamp in the post office. Japan and the United States were found to have the most accurate clocks and to move the fastest. In Italy and Indonesia, the pace of walking was slower, the clocks were less accurate, and it took longer to buy a stamp. Clearly, different concepts of time prevailed in these different countries and cultures.

What the teacher can do

Teachers can introduce students to varying concepts of time. They can use explicit examples in the classroom of ways that time works in different cultures. They can lead discussions about time, punctuality, and cultural differences. It is important that the teacher make sure students understand what is considered appropriate regarding time in the target culture.

Teachers can use Activity 3.5 to show students how time is viewed in different cultures. It gives students a chance to share how they view time, how it is viewed by their own culture, and how this might affect them in the new culture.

Activity 3.5	*Take your time*
Level	High beginner – Advanced
Handout	Page 203
Tip	Introduce various concepts of time.

Steps:

1. Make copies of the handout for Activity 3.5. Pass them out to the class.
2. Explain the vocabulary if needed. Ask students to complete the chart.
3. Ask the class to share what they found out about how different cultures view time. What similarities or differences did they find?
4. To finish the activity, ask: "What do these behaviors tell you about the perception of time in these cultures? What can you learn from the differences?"

Teaching notes:

- Students may grasp these concepts better if you illustrate them with examples of cultures that have very different ideas about punctuality, such as Canada vs. Saudi Arabia.
- Ask students for their own examples and experiences of dealing with time in different cultural contexts.
- General answers about the United States are as follows: For parties or events in a home, it would be uncomfortable for the hosts if guests arrived early. It is appropriate to arrive on time or 5 to 10 minutes after the appointed time. For business meetings or classes, it would be appropriate to arrive 5 to 10 minutes early. Arriving after the appointed time would be considered impolite. If you are meeting friends at a café or restaurant, arriving 5-10 minutes early or at the appointed time is appropriate. If you are running late, you should call your friends to let them know. In the United States, students should be on time or early to class.

6   Emphasize differences between high- and low-context communication.

Some cultures communicate more explicitly. Messages are spelled out directly in speech or writing. But in other cultures, many messages are communicated indirectly. Learning about a new culture means paying special attention to how messages are communicated compared to what you are familiar with.

Ann, one of the authors, is an English professor at St. John's University. She finds that sometimes people seem offended by her directness. She was brought up in Germany and then lived much of her adult life in New York City—both known as places where direct communication is the norm. She doesn't *beat around the bush* but likes to *tell it like it is*. For those who are not accustomed to direct communication, this can be uncomfortable.

Ann's behavior contrasts with that of Ragiv, the manager of a large corporation in India, where Joe was acting as a language consultant with a team of other specialists. The manager, who had been educated in the West, asked for a meeting and spoke in rather oblique terms about how some kinds of behavior went over better than others in India. Eventually it became clear that the Indian members of the team did not appreciate some of the kinds of humor the Westerners were using, although at no time did Ragiv come out and state this directly.

What the research says

To understand the differences between high- and low-context communication, we should bear in mind that "members of individualistic cultures predominately use low-context communication and tend to communicate in a direct fashion, and members of collectivistic cultures predominately use high-context messages when in-group harmony is important and tend to communicate in an indirect fashion" (Gudykunst and Kim 2003, p. 69). Cultures such as the Japanese are labeled **high-context** cultures, a term coined by the anthropologist Edward Hall. According to Hall (1998, p. 61), "a high-context communication or message is one in which most of the information is already in the person, while very little is in the coded, explicit, transmitted part of the message." In other words, the message that is being conveyed is implied or internalized in the person. Cultures such as that of the United States are regarded as **low-context** cultures, because the bulk of the information is in the explicit code or language (Bennett, 1998).

In low-context messages, the situation or context plays a minor role in communication; the messages are explicit and direct, and they are conveyed largely through spoken language. In a low-context culture, if a woman felt too warm she might say directly, "It's warm in here. Would you please open a window?" High-context messages, on the other hand, are implicit and indirect; they are conveyed largely through the context or the social situation in question. In the same situation in a high-context culture, the woman might fan herself due to the heat, but she would do so in silence and probably not say anything directly about opening a window.

Lustig and Koester (2003, p. 112) note that Hall's high- and low-context cultures include three further characteristics: the use of covert or overt messages, the importance of in-groups and out-groups, and the orientation to time. Covert or implicit messages are found in high-context cultures, whereas overt or explicit messages are found in low-context ones. As far as in-groups and out-groups are concerned, it is easily discerned who belongs to the group and who does not in high-context cultures, where the concern of the group is above that of the individual. This is less evident in low-context cultures, where there is much greater flexibility with in-groups and out-groups. As for time orientation, high-context cultures are more open and flexible in this regard, whereas in low-context cultures time is highly organized. Differences in the way time is regarded in Mexico as opposed to Switzerland illustrate the characteristic use of time in high- and low-context cultures.

What the teacher can do

Moving from a high-context to a low-context culture or vice-versa can be challenging for students. Teachers can illustrate the differences between high- and low-context cultures by giving examples of the behaviors of the different cultural types. Teachers can share their own experiences and examples with their students. The students themselves can also be valuable resources for each other.

Teachers can use Activity 3.6 to help students understand the difference between high- and low-context cultures. In this activity students play the role of someone communicating in a high- or low-context culture.

Activity 3.6	*Can't you take a hint?*
Level	High beginner – Advanced
Handouts	Pages 204 – 205
Tip	Emphasize differences between high- and low-context communication.

Steps:

1. Make copies of the two handouts for Activity 3.6.
2. Tell students that they are going to play a game. The object of the game is to get the other person to do or say something. However, they won't know what it is that the person wants them to do or say.
3. Form pairs of student A and student B. Pass out the handouts for Activity 3.6. Give Handout 3.6A only to student A and Handout 3.6B only to student B. Tell students to read only the information on their own handout and not to look at their partner's handout.
4. Following the directions on the handout, Student A should go first. When Student A is finished, it is Student B's turn.
5. After the students have finished, ask them how successful they were in getting their partner to do or say what they wanted. How did they feel during the game?
6. Explain the concept of high- and low-context communication as outlined above. In high-context communication, it is the context of the situation itself that conveys most of the meaning, rather than the words. In low-context cultures, such as that of the United States, communication is usually fairly verbally explicit, although it can occasionally be indirect.

(continued on next page)

7. To finish the activity, ask the class to talk about difficulties they could have or have had when communicating with someone from a culture with a different communication style.

Teaching notes:
- This activity is most interesting in a class with students from both high-context and low-context cultures.
- Note that the directions on the two handouts are slightly different. Student A is told to speak directly (low context.) Student B is told to speak indirectly (high context.)

 ### Explore kinesics, movement, and gestures in nonverbal communication.

The ways in which we move our bodies also send messages to our listeners, and, not surprisingly, the interpretation of these messages can vary from one culture to another. Even within the United States, we talk about "reading" the body language of another person. Indeed, it is not difficult to tell when someone from our own culture is ill at ease or uncomfortable.

Sometimes, however, the body can signal a message that seems to be quite different from the one being conveyed verbally. Nonverbal experts like Birdwhistell (1970) say that body language is more reliable than verbal language when attempting to identify which of the two conflicting meanings conveys the true feelings of the speaker.

What the research says

Birdwhistell (1970) pioneered the study of body movement, which he named kinesics, and identified meaningful units of body movement, called kinemes. Kinemes include facial expressions and many other movements such as those involving the eyes, head, shoulder, torso, and hands. Posture and pantomime are also part of the study of kinesics. Affective considerations such as respect, humiliation, and disgrace can be conveyed kinesically (Taylor, 1974).

Certain familiar gestures carry different messages across cultures. For example, East Asians find touching students on the head, hugging them, passing something over their head, and pointing with the foot to be offensive. For Arabs, touching members of the opposite sex, hugging them, showing the sole of the foot, handing a person something with the left hand, turning your back during a conversation, and winking are offensive. For Latin Americans, the American "okay" sign is a rude and inappropriate gesture.

Anthropologists believe that body language became more explicit with the help of speech, and, as speech became more developed, gestures became less needed (Lewis 2000, p. 134). However, today, humans still use body language to convey meaning. Italians, South Americans, most Latin Americans, Africans, and Middle Easterners are known to be demonstrative in their use of gestures. In contrast, Japanese, Chinese, Finns, and Scandinavians use only minimal body language in their communication. Members of the Finnish and Japanese cultures are socialized to use fewer gestures and facial expressions and to avoid what is seen as an unseemly demonstration of emotions.

We also send messages to our listeners by the way we use eye contact. Eye contact, or **oculesics**, refers to eye behaviors including gaze, blinking, winking, glancing, and squinting. Again, cultures differ in regard to their preferences about eye contact. The Japanese, for example, avoid direct eye contact in many situations, whereas Americans usually insist on it.

Lewis (2000, p. 135) describes cultures that are people-oriented and talkative as multiactive. He notes that the body language of multi-active people, such as the French, those from the Mediterranean, Arabs, Africans, and Latinos, includes features that differ from those of the quiet-group people. The following table (adapted from Lewis 2000, p. 136–139) presents a comparison of how body language differs between those he categorizes as multi-active people and those he categorizes as quiet-group people.

PART OF THE BODY	ACTION AND MEANING OF MULTI-ACTIVE PEOPLE	ACTION AND MEANING OF QUIET-GROUP PEOPLE
Eyes	Speakers keep close eye contact as they convey their message. This is so in Spain, Greece, and Arab countries where the power distance is greater and where staring implies dominance and reinforcing one's position and message.	In Finland and Japan, such intense eye contact is considered staring and is rude. The Japanese avoid eye contact 90% of the time.
Nose and ears	Twitching, snorting, or sniffing with the nose can signal being alert, disapproving, or disdaining something. This is so for the French and Hispanics. Tugging the earlobes alludes to tasty food for the Portuguese but may have sexual overtones for Italians.	Quiet-group people tend not to use the nose very much. Blowing one's nose in public is considered rude in Japan.

(continued on next page)

PART OF THE BODY	ACTION AND MEANING OF MULTI-ACTIVE PEOPLE	ACTION AND MEANING OF QUIET-GROUP PEOPLE
Mouth	Latin Americans may purse the lips or kiss their fingertips to express praise. Saudi Arabians may blow at their fingertips to request silence.	These gestures are not used in Asian countries or in Nordic cultures.
Shoulders	These are very mobile in multiactive people. Latin Americans keep their shoulders back and down when they are calm but push them up when they feel anxious.	People from northern cultures keep their shoulders still.
Arms and hands	Italians, the Spanish, and South Americans gesture with their arms while speaking. Latin Americans and Arabs use their hands most expressively.	Excessive gestures may be viewed as insincere, overdramatic, and unreliable by people in Northern Europe. Northern Europeans do not use their hands as much when they speak.
Legs	The legs are kept together in formal situations and crossed in more informal situations. Lewis describes the walking style of Latin Americans as bouncy, the style of Germans as marching, and the style of Americans as swaggering.	Lewis describes the walking style of the British and Nordic people as neutral.
Feet	The feet are "the most honest part of the body" but often the most forgotten part. Stamping the feet shows anger in Italy and Latin American countries.	In the United States, repeatedly tapping a foot on the floor indicates boredom. Showing the sole of the foot when seated is considered rude in many Arab countries.

What the teacher can do

Teachers can help students explore kinesics, movement, and gestures by demonstrating appropriate and inappropriate behavior in the classroom. This can also be done by engaging students in role plays, showing films, or displaying pictures that feature different kinds of nonverbal behavior. Teachers must also be sure that when they communicate with their students verbally that they do so with an awareness of the importance that the nonverbal dimension plays in their own interactions.

Teachers can use Activity 3.7 to help students understand how gestures can communicate different messages and meanings in different situations and cultures.

Activity 3.7	*How do you say ...?*
Level	High beginner – Advanced
Handout	None
Tip	Explore kinesics, movement, and gestures in nonverbal communication.

Steps:

1. Have your class stand in a circle. You may need to move desks and tables out of the way so there is room to move.
2. Introduce the activity. Tell students they should not talk but only act out the information they hear. Discussion will take place at the end of the activity.
3. Tell students that you will state an action and they need to demonstrate this action in their country or culture nonverbally. Remind students they are not going to talk, just act.
4. Ask: "How would you _____?"

agree with a speaker	show you don't care
answer 'yes'	point to yourself
disagree with a speaker	ask someone to come here
answer 'no'	indicate people should be quiet
show you aren't sure of an answer	indicate someone is crazy
show you don't know something	

5. Ask the class what differences they noted in the actions. Repeat any actions necessary or that had a variety of responses.
6. To finish the activity, demonstrate the nonverbal behavior that would be considered appropriate in the target culture.

Teaching notes:

- If you have a monocultural group, compare your students' gestures with those of the target culture.
- *Alternative:* Ask your students to use the same list of behaviors to interview people outside the class. Ask them to take notes and report to the class.

Conclusion

In this chapter we have studied the basic concepts and key functions of nonverbal communication. We have made connections between verbal and nonverbal communication. We have looked at how the use of personal space and the use of time vary across cultures. We have also considered high-context and low-context communication and how cultures communicate with greater or lesser amounts of verbal directness. We examined, too, the potential misunderstandings that can arise from differences in gestures, posture, and other body movements.

Check your understanding

After reading this chapter and using the activities with your class, check your comfort level with the following:

- ❏ I have introduced the basic concepts of nonverbal communication.
- ❏ My students can differentiate between verbal and nonverbal communication.
- ❏ I have explained the concept of cross-cultural space to my students.
- ❏ I have given my students a clear understanding of varying concepts of time.
- ❏ My students understand high- and low-context communication.
- ❏ I know the roles of kinesics, movement, and gestures in nonverbal communication.

CHAPTER 4

CULTURE AND IDENTITY

Consider these questions:

- What makes you the person you are? What do you feel makes up your personal identity?
- What parts of your identity come from your culture? In other words, how has your culture influenced who you are?
- When you think of your own identity, do you think of yourself as more of an individual or more as part of a larger group? What different groups are you a part of?

Our identities are shaped by our family life and upbringing, by gender, by the social groups to which we belong, and by the cultural and ethnic groups of which we are a part. Students in our English-language classrooms have their own identities. Including activities about culture and identity can help students gain new insights into their identities by reflecting on their lives, the environment they grew up in, and their beliefs. Helping students learn more about their identities can be a rewarding aspect of teaching, although teachers are cautioned that these types of personal conversations may occasionally cause some students to feel uncomfortable.

Living in a new culture can be threatening to our personal identity. When Joe, one of the authors, taught English in China, he found that some aspects of his own identity were lost to him. In the United States, he was considered to be well-educated and knowledgeable about the world, and this was an important part of his identity. In China, because his initial command of Chinese was minimal, his knowledge and education were not evident except to those who could speak English. At times, Joe, despite his master's degree, felt his status reduced almost to that of a child.

TIPS FOR EXPLORING CULTURE AND IDENTITY

The six tips in this chapter will help teachers give specific advice about how to explore culture and identity. With each tip, we provide a summary of the research and offer practical suggestions for what teachers can do in the classroom. Some of the activities include photocopiable handouts. These are located in Appendix A on pages 206–210.

 **TIPS**

1. Explore personal identity.
2. Explore gender identity and roles.
3. Build awareness of social identity and roles.
4. Recognize differences among cultural identities.
5. Identify cultures as either individualistic or collectivistic.
6. Show how ethnic identity influences social identity.

This chapter examines the place of identity within culture. It explores concepts of identity and considers group memberships. It looks at our many different identities and our varied roles in social life. The activities promote an awareness of cross-cultural differences, offer ways to look at one's own identity and roles, and suggest what to watch out for when working with culture and identity.

① Explore personal identity.

Our sense of self or identity comes from a variety of different sources. Ting-Toomey (1999, p. 28) categorizes identities or self-image areas into **primary identities** and **secondary identities**. Primary identities have an impact on our lives on an ongoing basis, whereas secondary or situational identities are changeable from situation to situation. Primary identities include personal identity, gender identity, cultural identity, and ethnic identity. How these identities are formed and communicated is largely interconnected with our culture.

Personal identity exists in each human being, whether or not we choose to examine it. Many of us go through life never taking the time to look closely at this aspect of our lives and the impact it has on us and others. However, our sense of personal identity is absolutely central to who we are as individuals. It also strongly influences the ways in which we interact with others.

Andry, from Madagascar, was an art student. His teachers and fellow students respected him as a talented young man with great gifts of perspective and color. His art work depicted the people around whom he was raised—his parents, grandmother, friends, and fellow villagers back home. Every pencil sketch he put on paper included a picture of a baby drawn in red, which became his trademark. Andry said that he included the red baby as a reminder of his origins and as a symbol of how he sees the world—from the perspective of a newborn.

What the research says

Our life story, experiences, background, and personality traits all affect the development of our personal identity. The family in which we are raised also plays a key role in defining who we are. Personal identity sets us apart in relation to other individuals. Our personal identity becomes clear when we consider our self-concepts or the characteristics that define us and make us unique from others in our in-groups. The role models around us influence the formation of our distinct or unique self, too.

Personal identity is defined by Ting-Toomey (1999, p. 35) as "the sentiments and information an individual has regarding her or his personal self-images. These personal self-images are linked to her or his unique personalities, drives, goals, and values." Our personal identity, or our uniqueness, makes us different from others who are in our cultural and social groups, and it is this personal identity that has a direct impact on our self-concept, or the mental image we have of ourselves.

Personal identity includes many factors. One is our age. We tend to speculate about someone's age and then categorize the individual as either young or old, but differences in age play out in different ways depending on the culture. In the United States, younger people frequently steer away from contact with the old. However, "in collectivistic cultures, for example, old people have high status, and, therefore, young people tend to show respect to them. Age, however, does not tend to provide status in individualistic cultures" (Gudykunst and Kim 2003, p. 116).

Another factor that influences personal identity is **social class**. Each of us belongs to a social class and identifies with one. Whether this identification is positive or negative depends on our satisfaction with our place on the social scale. Although social class structures differ from one society to another, the factors that determine social class identity are similar across cultures. These factors include income, occupation, education, family background, lifestyle, possessions, manner of speaking, and attitudes and beliefs.

Although it may have lost significance to some in modern Western cultures, religion is another key aspect of personal identity for many people around the world. For many, religion helps define both their sense of self as well as their worldview. Religious beliefs can help give individuals a sense of their own place in the universe as well as ideas about how that universe is organized. Interaction with "sacred wisdom" (Samovar and Porter 2004, p. 89) through scripture or holy books gives guidance in the living of daily life and gives rise to moral and ethical beliefs and behaviors. English language teachers, particularly those in the United States where it is commonly thought that religion has no place in the classroom, may nevertheless find that it has a significant impact on the behavior and the sense of identity of some students.

 ## Voices from the Classroom

I was working as a tutor in the writing center at a state university in New Mexico. Maria, originally from Puerto Rico, was in her early fifties. Although her writing skills were adequate, she never seemed to be able to get the "A" grades that she wanted. When I learned more about her and her academic and cultural background, I discovered that she was a very religious woman. Her writing was heavily influenced by her religious background and by the oral culture in which she had been raised. For instance, she began her academic essays by acknowledging God. She then concluded her essays by thanking God and her teachers. Although this might have been suitable for a presentation in her native Puerto Rico, it was not appropriate for university-level academic writing in the United States.

After reading one of her essays, I demonstrated various writing patterns and styles to her. I showed her how writing differs from culture to culture, discipline to discipline, and person to person. I convinced her that academic writing needed to be different from religious writing. Eventually she organized her papers as I suggested. After a few weeks, she came into the Writing Center and thanked me and told me that she had received an "A" on one of her papers. Maria became a successful writer in her classes by learning to write appropriately for the situation.

—*Marohang Limbu*
University of Texas at El Paso

Our personal identity is linked to our cultural and social identities, and these linkages become particularly evident when we live abroad. For instance, when our cultural identity is threatened, we may interpret it as an affront to our sense of self. People who may not be particularly patriotic in their native culture can find themselves standing up for their country when it is disparaged by others.

Difficulties in language learning can also lead to threats to personal identity. Even students whose language skills are generally good but whose pronunciation creates miscommunication may suffer crises of personal identity. In some classrooms a student whose accent causes miscommunication may be embarrassed in front of the entire class. Not only is the student's cultural identity threatened, but so is his or her personal self-esteem.

What the teacher can do
Teachers can help students explore personal identity by first ensuring that they themselves have a good sense and feel for their own identity through self-reflection, journaling, and talking with others. By their willingness to explore their own issues of identity, teachers can provide good models for students to investigate their personal identities.

Personal identity can be a challenging area for classroom discussion. Students of many ages may feel awkward talking about themselves and about aspects of their lives that make up their personalities. It may be best to avoid activities that require students to share intimate knowledge, although some writing tasks may lend themselves to this sort of disclosure. Exercises and activities that encourage and permit students to explore their own personal identity include questionnaires, discussions, journaling and other writing assignments, and reading and discussion of essays, stories, or biographical writings of others.

Teachers can use Activity 4.1 to engage students in an exploration of self. By exploring their own personal identities through art, students may come to a better understanding of themselves and their classmates. Note that this activity accommodates the learning style of more visual learners. (See next page.)

Activity 4.1	***Who am I?***
Level	High beginner – Advanced
Handout	None
Tip	Explore personal identity.

Steps:

1. The goal of this activity is for students to create a collage to represent their personal identities. A simple form of collage involves selecting, cutting, and pasting photographs, printed text, handwritten texts or drawings, and/or digital images and text onto paper.
2. Prepare a model of the type of collage that you would like to see your students produce. Show students your collage to introduce the activity.
3. Two weeks before the start of the project, ask the class to bring in magazines and newspapers with photographs. Encourage students to bring all types of magazines so that there are a variety of photographs and text to choose from.
4. Decide if you want to devote class time to this activity or ask students to do their collages as homework. Instruct students accordingly.
5. Tell students the project is to make a collage that represents their personal identity. They should include information they feel represents who they are, their interests, their views, etc. Point out that they can use photos, bits of text, their own drawings or writings—anything that helps portray how they see themselves.
6. Have students bring their completed collages to class. Display them around the classroom. Ask students to walk around the room and enjoy the collages. Give the class an opportunity to ask any questions about their classmates' collages.

Teaching notes:

- If the collages are made during class, supply poster board, glue, scissors, paper, and any other supplies needed.
- Make sure students use copies of personal photographs, not originals. Advise students to lay out their collage first and then glue or tape.
- A collage is a great opportunity for experimentation. Encourage your students to try different things and not be overly concerned with "getting it right." Grading this activity is not recommended.

 Explore gender identity and roles.

Men and women engage in varied roles in different cultures. Societies usually have specific roles that they expect men and women to fulfill. Thus the term **gender identity** comprises both a person's own individual gender identification and society's conceptualization of gender roles. An example of this can be seen in reactions to women in power in the United States. Although the United States claims to be a country in which women and men have equal rights, a quick look at the national legislature reveals that most senators and representatives in the U.S. Congress are men. Despite the supposed equality, the numbers tell a different story. There are also different expectations of behavior of women in power. People expect men to give their opinions forcefully. However, when a woman engages in the same behavior, she may be described as aggressive or harsh.

What the research says

Gender roles are a fundamental part of identity. Pleck (1977, p. 182) defines gender roles as "the psychological traits and the social responsibilities that individuals have and feel are appropriate for them because they are male or female." Gender role expectations can be learned and unlearned. These roles lead men and women to relate to others in markedly different ways (Tannen, 1990), and this affects not only gender identities but also social identities.

There are significant differences in gender roles across cultures. Hofstede (1980) claims that clear differences in gender roles can be seen in cultures that are highly masculine. In highly masculine cultures, men are expected to be strong, aggressive, and focused on success, whereas women are expected to be reserved, gentle, and concerned about the quality of life for others. In other words, in a highly

masculine culture, the distinction between masculine and feminine roles is clearly emphasized. In a highly feminine culture, on the other hand, gender roles are not so obviously distinguished; the roles of both men and women tend to overlap.

When in cross-cultural situations, we should not assume that the commonly accepted masculine and feminine roles of our own culture will be identical in another culture. And it may well be that these different expectations of the roles of men and women are well established and change is not desired. Differences in gender identity may lead individuals to different expectations about their lives and careers. There may be some careers that are socially acceptable for men and others for women. There are also often different expectations of men and women in most family roles; for example, fathers and mothers may have different roles in child care.

Gender identity and gender roles are also factors in expressions of sexuality. What may pass as acceptable behavior for men, for instance, is often unacceptable for women in many cultures. Another fundamental part of gender identity is sexual orientation. Over the past half century, same-sex relationships have become increasingly socially acceptable in some Western cultures and even legally sanctioned, whereas the same behavior is illegal and completely unacceptable in other parts of the world.

As noted in previous chapters, gender also makes a difference in language use, nonverbal communication, and sociolinguistic patterns. Women may be less direct in speech, may use a different form of eye contact, and may be less likely to interrupt than men. Because language and its use are a fundamental part of identity, these differences in communication make up a key part of gender identity.

What the teacher can do

Teachers can help students explore gender identity and gender roles by having them discuss their views based on their own cultures. Building this kind of awareness will encourage students to go beyond their visible identities and reveal cultural and societal variations in male and female roles.

Teachers can use Activity 4.2 to help students explore gender identity and roles and the ways that they are perceived and understood. The activity has students look at men and women in the media. For example, the depiction of men and women in the news provides material for discussion of how a culture views the accomplishments and achievements of men versus women. Although television and movies may not present entirely realistic portraits of the way people are, they often mirror common cultural attitudes.

Activity 4.2	*Who is he or she?*
Level	High beginner – Advanced
Handout	None
Tip	Explore gender identity and roles.

Steps:
1. The goal of this activity is for students to create a poster that represents their view of gender identity and roles.
2. Ask the class to brainstorm qualities and characteristics that they associate with women and then generate a similar list for men. Write the ideas on the board.
3. For homework, have students find visual images that represent the qualities and characteristics listed on the board. These images can come from their own photographs, from magazines or online sources, etc. Assign students a due date for bringing their images to class.

4. Form small groups. Ask each group to make two posters: one that represents women and one that represents men.
5. To finish the activity, display the posters around the room. Discuss the various presentations of images. Do students feel that these depictions of masculine and feminine qualities and characteristics are accurate and realistic? Are they creations of the media?

Teaching notes:

- *Alternative:* Ask students to write a paragraph. (Adjust the length of the assignment as appropriate for your students.) Ask students to answer these questions: What are the main qualities and characteristics of men? of women? How are they the same? How are they different?

 Build awareness of social identity and roles.

In the United States there is a saying: "Show me who your friends are and I'll tell you who you are." This means that the people with whom we surround ourselves, the groups to which we belong, and the roles that we have in life all affect our **social identity**. In addition to our individual sense of self—our personal identity—and our gender identity, we each have a social identity. Social identity is built on the things we have in common with others in our cultural group as well as how others see us.

The **social roles**, or socially expected behavior patterns, that we hold and the ways in which we execute them affect our social identity. At times we are judged solely on our roles and then either accepted or rejected by others as a result.

When Ann, one of the authors, assigned students to work in pairs in her intermediate ESL writing class, Sana from Pakistan was left without a partner. She felt left out and couldn't understand why she wasn't paired with another student. Sana thought that it was probably due to her weak writing skills. When Sana asked Ann why she didn't get a partner, Ann told her that students were paired randomly, and, with an odd number of students, the teacher becomes someone's partner. Ann explained this procedure to the class, which made Sana feel better because her classmates were now aware that it wasn't a question of her writing ability or that she was Pakastani. She also realized that she had lucked out by getting paired with her teacher.

What the research says

Social identity becomes apparent when we consider the self-concepts that we share with other members of our in-groups. In-groups are a group of people for whom we show concern, with whom we cooperate without seeking rewards, and without whom we find ourselves in distress (Triandis 1988, p. 75). In other words, our social identity is not only linked to the roles we play in life such as student, teacher, parent, or sibling or to our physical features such as ethnicity, gender, or age but also to the memberships we hold, such as when we belong to a club, an organization, or a political party. Our membership in select societies links us to our in-groups with whom we share many commonalities.

 Voices from the Classroom

A number of years ago I was teaching in a country where the government did not permit public disagreement with its policies. The students were watching a video segment I was showing of a television news program. In it a man was testifying before the U.S. Congress about the high cost of living for the middle class. He became very excited and emotional while speaking.

Afterwards my students were very quiet. I asked what was wrong. One student asked, "What happened to that man? Did they kill him?" I told him no, he hadn't been killed. They mulled over this a while and finally another student said, "But they put him in prison, right?" I said no; the man testified and then went home. But I began to wonder if I had inadvertently implied something about their country and its political climate, where no citizen would be allowed to embarrass or criticize the government on television. I realized also that during my stay, I had been making value judgments based on the norms of my own culture.

— *Sue Rosenfield*
Boston University

During the process of **socialization**, children view themselves initially as members of their families. Once they have developed an awareness of various social groups, they start to form social identities. Tajfel (1978, p. 63) defines social identity as those parts of a person's self-concept that arise from the knowledge of his or her membership in a social group, including the value and emotional importance connected to that membership. As children grow older, their group memberships expand based on their interests. They may become in-group members of the softball league, the chess club, the Mexican folk dancing group, or the Democratic Party, for example. Membership in these in-groups and out-groups is a key part of our identity or self-concept (Lustig and Koester 2003, p. 141).

When we belong to a particular cultural group, we add to our social identity by learning about our traditions, language, religion, genealogy, and social structures. By internalizing our culture's beliefs, values, norms, and worldviews, we connect with that culture and identify with it during the formation of our self-concept. Whether the groups are related to work, religion, age, common interests, or other things, we identify with them and they mold our social identity.

Social structure, an inherent component of culture, includes not only formal rules and behaviors but also **social roles**. The roles that we play are one contributing factor to our social identities. Social roles are the cultural expectations of how people in a social position are to behave (DeCapua and Wintergerst 2004, p. 194), and they vary within and across cultures. For example, we may hold the role of teacher, parent, doctor, judge, consumer, and so forth. Each of these roles is defined by its own characteristics and behaviors.

Each culture has its own expectations that define the parameters in which the members function. Some social roles are given to us simply by virtue of who we are, such as the roles defined by gender, age, or the social status of the family into which we are born. Other roles depend on our own actions, such as the roles we gain by educational achievement, hard work, or marriage. Certain cultures expect a degree of personal attention in role relationships. For example, doing business in Greece requires a certain level of friendship or friendly attitude, although not at the expense of conducting a successful business transaction. A strong distinction is not made between these two role identities. In the United States, business people exhibit more rigidity, coldness, and concern about legal issues in business dealings, and friendship is left for more social settings.

By the same token, differences exist in the level of formality considered desirable in a relationship. For example, in some classrooms in the United States, teachers and professors encourage students to call them by their first names, a practice that would be considered disrespectful in other cultures. Another aspect of social identity is the degree of hierarchy in role relationships. For example, Asian cultures are highly influenced by Confucianism, which clearly delineates the attitudes and roles of members of the society. As a result, these countries have hierarchical role relationships. Many African cultures, too, have comparable role expectations. To avoid cultural misunderstandings, it is crucial to know and understand the role expectations of other cultures.

Another aspect of social role identity that relates to social structure is the idea of status or the relative position of importance. When people speak to each other, they do so from their own perspective, from their status within the social structure, and from the status they attribute to the person addressed. The words used in verbal communication reflect the status or position of the speaker and that of the addressee. In some languages, certain forms of address make these roles explicit. For example, the formal *vous* and the informal *tu* in French, the formal *Sie* and the informal *du* in German, and the formal *usted* and the informal *tu* in Spanish can signal not only power and status among speakers but also position or social class and distance or closeness. Sometimes the use of these terms is a personal matter, however our choice of pronouns, forms of address, or names can also indicate our ability to communicate fluently in a culturally appropriate manner.

What the teacher can do

Social identity is a complex topic because of the multiple groups to which each of us belongs. Teachers can help students grasp these ideas by calling attention to the multiple groups to which students and other individuals belong. Furthermore, teachers can also point out the function of roles as part of social identity by involving students actively in classroom activities that examine these roles.

Teachers can use Activity 4.3 to help students analyze and recognize social identity. Using role play allows students to get a sense of the concept and helps to further their understanding of the function of roles as part of social identity. Role plays also create a memorable language learning experience.

Activity 4.3	*Who are you?*
Level	High beginner – Advanced
Handout	Page 206 – 207
Tip	Build awareness of social identity and roles.

Steps:

1. Make copies of the two handouts for Activity 4.3. Pass them out to the class.
2. Explain the concept of a role play. Students choose a character and role-play how the person would act in the situation. Remind students that they are taking on the character's social identity and social role. Have them think about any differences in social status of the characters, etc. To provide a model, demonstrate one of the role plays with a student in front of the class.
3. Form pairs and assign role plays. Ask students to imagine what the character is like based on his or her social identity and role. Students might invent the name and age of the character, where he or she is from, and what he or she looks like.
4. Give the class time to practice. Walk around and provide feedback and help as needed.
5. Have students act out their role plays in front of the class.
6. To finish the activity, ask the class to discuss the following questions:
   - How did you feel about taking on the role of another person? What was easy about the role? What was difficult?
   - What ideas or thoughts do you have about culture and identity after role-playing your character(s)?

Teaching notes:

- If you want the dialogues to be more impromptu, limit the amount of time students have to practice.
- *Alternative:* To provide a more structured interaction, form pairs, assign role plays, and have students write the dialogue before acting it out in front of the class. Remind students that the role play should focus on different identity roles.
- *Alternative:* To give students a sense of both identities, ask them to switch roles and repeat the role play.

Recognize differences among cultural identities.

Cultural identity, which is determined by our cultural background—and all that goes with it—is tied to social identity and personal identity. The strength attributed to cultural identity depends on our worldview, our memberships, and our multiple identities. This makes sense in light of the many identities we hold and the varied identities that exist cross-culturally. When people are studying or living in a new country, they are generally more inclined to say that they are Chinese, French, Russian, or Vietnamese, for example, because they are eager to reveal their cultural identity. When the perception is positive, people permit their cultural identity to assume a prominent place. When the perception is negative, they tend to avoid its mention when interacting with others.

Ankita, from India, was proud of her cultural identity because her country is receiving increased recognition for its skilled workforce, including computer technologists, doctors, and pharmacists. Her parents were both doctors. When Rolando from Colombia found that many people associated his country with illegal drugs and political upheaval, he was less open with others about his origins and often just said he was from Latin America.

What the research says

Our sense of self is closely tied to our **cultural identity**. Gudykunst and Kim (2003) highlight two dimensions of cultural identity that affect our contact with people from other cultures: the strength of our identification and the content of our identities. Some people identify more strongly with their own culture than others. However, the strength of the identification can vary depending on the circumstances. For example, people tend to have a stronger sense of cultural identification while they are abroad. When they are at home, their cultural identification is not called into question or questioned openly; they just live it daily. Similarly, the content of their cultural identity, or those things connected with being a member of a culture, is often more positive or apparent after having lived abroad.

A key element that affects our cultural identity is whether we have membership in an individualistic culture or in a collectivistic culture and the respective values that each type of culture holds. For example, the culture of the United States is described as an individualistic culture, and the culture of Japan is a collectivistic culture. Gudykunst and Nishida (1999) found that citizens of the United States who have a strong identification with their culture tend to value freedom, pleasure, social recognition, and independence more so than their fellow Americans who have a weak identification with their culture. So too, Japanese, who have a strong identification with their culture tend to value self-sacrifice, harmony, and traditions more so than their fellow Japanese who have a weak identification with their culture.

Cultural identity in the past was easier to define because common cultural practices and face-to-face interactions were associated with particular groups. In today's open societies, however, the boundaries of particular social groups as well as the linguistic and cultural identities of the members are much more difficult to define. The idea that one language equals one culture is no longer true. People nowadays exhibit multiple identities that are changeable over time. When their cultural identity is threatened, they  attach great importance to maintaining their language. Kramsch (1998, p. 77) asserts that "although there is no one-to-one relationship between anyone's language and his or her cultural identity, language is *the* most sensitive indicator of the relationship between an individual and a given social group."

 Voices from the Classroom

I was teaching an oral presentation class for non-native English-speaking undergraduates in the United States. One of my students, Jae, was a twenty-four-year-old Korean. In class, Jae had trouble adapting to the presentation style commonly used in the United States. Even after working extensively on the organization of his talks, he could not manage to organize his ideas in a way that would be clear to a U.S. audience. For example, he would give the details about a certain point before providing a general overview.

After a while, I realized the nature of the problem. Jay had first come to the United States when he was fourteen to attend high school and college. After living in the United States for six years, he returned to Korea for two years of military service. Back in Korea, he felt he had lost touch with his own culture and had to work hard to develop a Korean communication style. When he returned to the United States to finish college, he was afraid of losing his newly redeveloped Korean identity. Because of this fear, a seemingly simple adjustment such as learning and using a typical pattern of organizing ideas in English became a challenging cultural barrier.

— Cara Costello
Carnegie Mellon University

Another construct of cultural identity is **social distance**. H.D. Brown (1999, p. 39) defines social distance as "the cognitive and affective proximity of two cultures which come into contact within an individual," where the term *distance* indicates ways in which the two cultures are different. For example, Canadians are culturally similar to western Europeans, whereas both are dissimilar to Chinese. So the social distance between Canadians and western Europeans is closer than that between Canadians and Chinese. Schumann (1976, p. 136) hypothesizes that when the social distance between two cultures is great, the learner will have more difficulty learning the second language. On the other hand, when the social distance between two cultures is small, the learner will have less difficulty learning the second language.

Because the measurement of actual social distance presents a challenge, Acton (1979) devised a way to gauge *perceived* social distance. He believes that it is not the actual distance between cultures that is relevant but the *perceptions* of the learners through their own filtered worldviews that form their reality. In other words, how a learner perceives his or her own culture as it relates to the target language culture can be of great importance in the classroom and in life.

What the teacher can do

Helping students build an awareness of social distance gives learning about culture a place of greater importance in the second-language classroom. Teachers can help students differentiate between various cultural identities by making them aware of their own cultural practices and those of their classmates. When students encounter a situation that has the potential of leading to a misunderstanding, they may be able to rescue themselves if they are aware of what might cause the pitfall.

An effective way for teachers to help students understand and learn about their own culture as well as the culture of others is to offer a variety of reflection activities. These can include self-reflection about how to avoid cultural mishaps; discussions with their classmates, friends, or family members; readings about the historical development of a culture; and examination of current cultural practices as portrayed in films, books, and other cultural artifacts. Activity 4.4 uses critical incidents to encourage students to reflect on cultural identity. (See next page.)

Activity 4.4	*Culture and me*
Level	High beginner – Advanced
Handouts	Pages 208 – 209
Tip	Recognize differences among cultural identities.

Steps:

1. Make copies of the two handouts for Activity 4.4.
2. Review with students that a critical incident is a cross-cultural problematic situation. The incidents are concerned with various dimensions of culture. Inform the students that there are no right or wrong answers but that there are solutions.
3. Ask students to work in groups of three or four. Pass out the handouts for Activity 4.4. Assign each group one critical incident. Have students read the critical incidents and questions and discuss what they think caused the conflict.
4. If a group finishes early, assign another critical incident.
5. As a class, discuss each critical incident, the solutions from each group, and the area of cultural conflict manifested. Go to pages 190-191 for possible interpretations to share with the class if none of the groups suggest them.

Teaching notes:

- Each critical incident presents an area of conflict designed to stimulate discussion about the situation described and to make students aware of and sensitive to cultural differences.
- *Alternative:* If necessary, simplify the vocabulary used to describe the critical incidents.

5 Identify cultures as either individualistic or collectivistic.

A key element of cultural identity relates to the nature of the culture in which we find our identity. Does the culture value **individualism**, in which primary importance is placed on the individual, or **collectivism**, in which the well-being of the group takes priority? Individualism and collectivism have many implications for students and teachers, even to the extent of influencing the ways that individuals learn.

What the research says

Our relationships with the larger social group to which we belong are essential because we must live and work together for our culture to survive. However, we need to find a balance between showing concern for ourselves and showing concern for others (Lustig and Koester, 2003). This relationship between the individual and the group is at the heart of identity, according to Hofstede et al. (2002, p. 35). The following diagram represents their individualism–collectivism index.

Highly Individualistic Cultures ⟷		Highly Collectivistic Cultures
Individuals take care of themselves and their immediate family first. The autonomy of the individual and the self are most important.	**Characteristics**	Individuals work for the good of the group and suppress their identity for the benefit of the group. The needs of the group come before the needs of the individual.
United States, Australia, Great Britain, Canada, Hungary, the Netherlands, New Zealand, and Italy	**Example Cultures**	Guatemala, Ecuador, Panama, Venezuela, Colombia, Pakistán, Indonesia, and Costa Rica

A culture's position on the individualistic-collectivistic continuum is also linked to its position on Hofstede's power distance index (PDI), which measures a society's perception and level of human equality and inequality. (Hofstede, et al., 2002)

Low Power Distance Cultures ⟷		High Power Distance Cultures
Tend to be individualistic and minimize social or class inequalities	**Characteristics**	Tend to be collectivistic and believe that hierarchy and different levels of equality are acceptable and appropriate
Austria, Israel, Denmark, Switzerland, Great Britain, Germany, Australia, and the United States	**Example Cultures**	Malaysia, Russia, Mexico, Bangladesh, China, Arab countries, West African countries, and Singapore

Lustig and Koester (2003, p. 119) note that "The consequences of the degree of power distance that a culture prefers are evident in family customs, the relationships between students and teachers, organizational practices, and in other areas of social life." For that matter, even language is affected by social hierarchy as described earlier in our accounts of the formal and informal forms of "you" in German, French, and Spanish.

Individualism and collectivism have an effect on the way that students learn. Researchers have found that different cultural groups fall into distinct **learning style** preferences, what Ehrman and Oxford (1990, p. 311) define as "preferred or habitual patterns of mental functioning and dealing with new information." Reid's (1987) investigation into the perceptual learning style preferences of native and nonnative speakers found that English speakers rated individual learning as the highest, whereas ESL students did not. She noted that "It is probable that culture—in particular, previous educational experience—enters into student learning style preferences for group and individual learning" (p. 98). In their study Wintergerst et al. (2002) found that American students studying a foreign language also preferred individual work in contrast to their ESL counterparts, who preferred group work. In another learning styles study Wintergerst et al. (2003) found that Russian ESL/EFL students and Asian (Chinese, Korean, and Japanese) ESL students preferred group work over individual work, a linkage with their cultural identity of collectivism. Nelson (1995, p. 14) notes that Chinese learning is characterized by cooperation, a natural consequence of the Confucian philosophical tradition and the value of collectivism in that culture. This is in sharp contrast with the U.S. preference of individualism and competition.

What the teacher can do

Teachers can help students identify cultures as either individualistic or collectivistic by having them think about their own culture and identify their cultural characteristics. Teachers can bring in readings, such as short stories or articles, that are illustrative of individualism and collectivism. Advanced students can be referred to page 125 of Lustig and Koesters', book *Intercultural Competence: Interpersonal Communication across Cultures*, which gives country ratings on the individualism-collectivism dimension adapted from Hofstede. Students can also go to page 53 of Hofstede's, *Cultures and Organizations: Software of the Mind*.

Teachers can use Activity 4.5 to help build awareness of what marks a culture as individualistic or collectivistic and then to identify cultures based on those characteristics.

Activity 4.5	*Alone or with others?*
Level	Intermediate – Advanced
Handout	None
Tip	Identify cultures as either individualistic or collectivistic.

Steps:

1. Present the concept of individualistic and collectivistic cultures. Draw the top part of the table on page 93 on the board. Point out the characteristics of each culture on the continuum.
2. Write the students' home countries on the board. Ask students if they think their own culture is more individualistic or more collectivistic.

3. Ask students to think of examples of phrases, expressions, situations, or proverbs that illustrate either the collectivistic or individualistic nature of their culture. Write examples on the board; for example, "The nail that stands up will be hammered down." "The squeaky wheel gets the grease." "All for one and one for all."

4. To finish the activity, have volunteers share their ideas with the class.

Teaching notes:

- If students seem unaware of how their culture behaves with regard to individualism and collectivism, ask some gently leading questions.

- If all of your students are from the same cultural background, contrast their background with that of an English-speaking country like Australia, New Zealand, the United Kingdom, Canada, or the United States.

- *Alternative:* As a homework project, have students think about or find well-known stories about a heroic figure in their home country. Ask students to say whether these people were heroes because of an individual or a group accomplishment.

 ## Show how ethnic identity influences social identity.

Does your **ethnic identity** influence your way of life, how you live, how you think, and how you behave? If your answer is yes, then you have demonstrated the influence of your ethnicity—your racial, national, tribal, religious, linguistic, or cultural origin or background.

Ann, one of the authors, finds that most often the African students in her English classes identify with their ethnic connection more strongly than students from other parts of the world. When asked to talk about his social identity, Donkor from Togo spoke more about the influences of his cultural group, his parents and religion, and his language than about what he saw as his role in society.

What the research says

Our ethnic identities define who we are and influence all facets of our lives from language to customs to rituals to values and beyond. Our reactions and responses to other people are connected with our assumptions about their ethnicity. Many of us automatically compartmentalize people and consciously or unconsciously place ethnic labels on them. We categorize people by ethnicity on the basis of cultural, social, psychological, physical, or other characteristics. Turner (1987) cautions that once we classify ourselves as members of a particular ethnic group, we categorize others as non-members and therefore as members of different ethnic groups than our own.

In the past, the United States viewed ethnicity from an assimilationist point of view. This point of view suggests that when a person moves to a different country, he or she should give up his or her former culture and take on the characteristics of a new culture. This view was popular before World War II when immigrants to the United States were predominantly of European ancestry. Sociologists used to speak of the country as a vast *melting pot*. Today a more pluralistic view of ethnicity predominates. Our ethnic identity may or may not be displayed when we are interacting with another person, depending on whether or not it is in our self-interest to do so. For instance, there are a large number of Spanish speakers in the United States. In some interactions, the use of Spanish might be seen as an asset, whereas in other interactions it may be viewed as a disadvantage. Today, rather than expecting new immigrants to melt into American society, people in the United States hope to take advantage of the new people's unique strengths and think of society as more of a salad bowl or mosaic, in which many individual parts make up the whole.

Ethnicity is defined not only by skin color and national origin but also by language. Language is an essential aspect of ethnic group membership; it connects members emotionally and creates solidarity among members. Just as they vary in the strength of their cultural identities, some people identify more strongly with their ethnic groups, whereas others identify more weakly (Gudykunst and Kim, 2003). Gaines et al. (1997) found that African Americans, Asian Americans, and Latino Americans tend to have stronger ethnic identities than European Americans. Also, like the content of cultural identities, the content of ethnic identities may be highly individualistic or highly collectivistic, depending on national heritage and the strength of identity.

What the teacher can do

One way teachers can help students identify ethnic identities is by having them watch and analyze films or television programs. Films are an excellent classroom tool because they provide students with the opportunity to look at situations objectively and to experience the lives of others through a visual medium.

Films show different cultures as well as provide content for developing language skills. Teachers can use Activity 4.6 to help students examine the lives of fictional characters; this activity is less threatening than examining their own lives in the public setting of the classroom.

Activity 4.6	*Ethnic identities in film*
Level	Intermediate – Advanced
Handout	Page 210
Tip	Show how ethnic identity influences social identity.

Steps:

1. Make copies of the handout for Activity 4.6. Pass them out to the class.
2. Choose a film that highlights ethnic roles within a culture. Some suggestions are *My Big Fat Greek Wedding* (2002), *Guess Who's Coming to Dinner* (1967), *Bend it Like Beckham* (2003), *Pleasantville* (1998), and *Witness* (1985). See more suggestions on page 126.
3. Discuss the questions with the class before watching the movie.
4. During the movie, stop as often as necessary to explain any key plot or language points that may be difficult for students to understand.
5. Form pairs. Have students answer the questions on the handout.
6. To finish the activity, discuss the answers with the class.

Teaching notes:

- The purpose of this activity is to focus on differences in ethnic identity. Try to keep the focus of the discussion on ethnic identity rather than on cultural differences in general.
- *Alternative:* Using the closed-caption feature during the film will provide language support for lower-level learners.

Conclusion

In this chapter on culture and identity we examined personal identity, gender identity, social identity, cultural identity, and ethnic identity. We investigated the place of roles as part of social identity. We also identified and categorized individualistic and collectivistic cultures and their link to Hofstede's power distance index.

Identity is a key element in the way that we see ourselves as individuals and the way that we interact with others, both within our own first culture and when we come into contact with those from other cultures. We presented a number of ways to help students come to grips with issues of identity, including watching films, role play, examining critical incidents, making a collage, and using visual prompts and graphic organizers for classifying.

Check your understanding

After reading this chapter and using the activities with your class, check your comfort level with the following:

- ❑ I am confident that my students know how to explore their own personal identities.
- ❑ I help my students understand the concepts of gender identity and roles.
- ❑ I know how to help my students recognize social identity and the function of roles as part of that identity.
- ❑ I assist my students in learning how to recognize differences among cultural identities.
- ❑ I am confident that my students can identify cultures as either individualistic or collectivistic.
- ❑ I help my students understand ethnic identity, how it applies to them, and how it influences social identity.

CHAPTER 5

CULTURE SHOCK AND CROSS-CULTURAL ADJUSTMENT

Consider these questions:
- Have you ever experienced "culture shock"? What was it like? How did you know that you were experiencing it?
- What adjustments have you had to make when encountering a new culture?
- What stereotypes do you think people from other countries have about your culture? Why do you think people have these ideas? Is there any truth in them?

Even with the many differences among cultures that we still have already explored, we still find that cross-cultural experiences can lead to surprising results. In earlier chapters, we included discussions of challenges in communication with both spoken language and nonverbal communication. We also highlighted the importance of cultural identity. In this chapter, we focus on the difficulties of adjusting or adapting to a new culture and on the challenges of intercultural conflicts. The tips in this chapter help teachers guide language-learners to understand causes of cultural distress and in turn help them be better prepared to deal with these situations.

TIPS FOR CULTURE SHOCK AND CROSS-CULTURAL ADJUSTMENT

The five tips in this chapter offer specific advice about how to help students explore issues stemming from cultural conflict and from problems with adjusting to a new culture. With each tip, we provide a summary of the related research and offer practical ideas for what teachers can do in the classroom. Some of the activities include photocopiable handouts. These are located in Appendix A on pages 211–214.

TIPS

1. Recognize the causes and stages of culture shock.
2. Identify the symptoms of culture shock.
3. Counter the effects of culture shock.
4. Examine your own cultural style.
5. Reduce cultural conflict.

This chapter discusses culture shock and cross-cultural adjustment. It revisits potential barriers to cultural understanding, explains the concept of culture shock, and offers suggestions to minimize its effects. It reemphasizes the importance of knowing one's own cultural style as well as being familiar with the new culture to help reduce cultural conflict. The activities promote an awareness of cross-cultural differences, provide sample critical incidents for analysis, and give insights to help students achieve successful outcomes in the face of cultural conflict.

 Recognize the causes and stages of culture shock.

Although people from different cultures often share some basic cultural concepts, there are other concepts that can be seen as irrational or even contradictory to one's own way of doing things. Having a working knowledge of the basic concepts of other cultures can help our students interact successfully with a new culture as well as diminish the level of culture shock they experience upon entering their new environment.

Joe, one of the authors, graduated from college and then traveled to work overseas. He was three months into his first year of teaching English in Hangzhou, China, when he experienced the difficult phase of culture shock. The excitement of the honeymoon stage had worn off. Living in China no longer seemed so fascinating; instead, the trials of daily life became irritating. He had less desire to go out and experience the new culture and spent a few weeks largely cooped up in his apartment, reading novels in English and talking with other Americans. Even though he was aware that he was experiencing culture shock, it took a little while to shake it off.

What the research says

Entering a new culture is a developmental process involving several steps (Adler, 1977; M. Bennett, 1986, 1993; Weaver, 1993). In one view, adaptation to a new culture is a process in which a person's worldview is expanded to include behaviors and values appropriate to the host culture (Bennett 1998, p. 25) so that the behaviors and values of the new culture are added to the existing behaviors and values of the original culture. Bennett's view contrasts with the idea that adapting to a new culture is a process of **assimilation**. Assimilation is when the new culture and its beliefs and values replace those of the original culture, either fully or partially and either by choice or by necessity.

Adapting to a new culture while not giving up our existing cultural identity is called **acculturation**. Acculturation is not an easy process. When we change from one culture to another, our worldview and our self-identity are disrupted as are our ways of thinking, acting, feeling, and communicating. The anthropologist Kalvero Oberg (1960) notes four stages of acculturation. The first stage, the **honeymoon stage**, is filled with excitement and euphoria about everything that is new. In the second stage, the aggressive stage, better known as **culture shock**, we feel the distress of experiencing many cultural differences and search for fellow citizens of our native land to help us through our unhappiness. The third stage, the **adjustment stage**, leads the way to a gradual adaptation where some problems are resolved while others linger on. Slowly but surely we accept the cultural differences around us. The fourth and final stage is called the **recovery stage,** in which we accept the new culture and develop a bicultural identity.

Distinct stages of development are apparent as a person proceeds through acculturation, and it is the second stage that usually causes particular difficulty. Oberg (1960) coined the term **culture shock** and depicted it as an occupational disease of people who have been transplanted abroad. Researchers have described the causes and symptoms of culture shock in a number of ways:

the discomfort experienced while abroad; being disoriented in different and unfamiliar cultural contexts due to loss and change (J. Bennett 1998, p. 216)

a recurring collision between one's culture and a contrasting culture, including a feeling of helplessness and sometimes even entrapment (Barnlund 1998, p. 47)

Culture Shock

a removal or distortion of many of the familiar cues one encounters at home and the substitution for them with other cues which are strange (Hall 1959, p. 199)

the feeling of being like a fish out of water due to the loss of familiar signs and symbols of social interaction in daily life (Weaver 1994, p. 165)

Culture shock has three basic causes: the loss of familiar cues, the breakdown of interpersonal communication, and an identity crisis exaggerated by cultural differences (Weaver, 1994). Beginning as infants, we are surrounded by familiar social cues that help us make sense of our world. The loss of these cues results in the removal of comfortable and predictable signposts. The breakdown of communication results in frustration, anxiety, and alienation from others. An identity crisis develops when we are no longer able to think and solve problems effectively in the way our own culture has programmed us to do.

Ann, one of the authors, remembers her own experience of culture shock as an American traveling abroad:

When I first visited Italy, I had taken a semester of beginning Italian before my departure to have some basic Italian survival skills. I felt quite confident with my limited Italian ability. Little did I know that upon arriving in Rome, I'd be completely lost. What I thought would be a pleasant visit turned into a nightmare! I was unable to communicate with anyone. I couldn't even get on a bus. It was embarrassing! I was on my own in a country with a language in which I could not even communicate. After the first week and multiple attempts to shop for groceries, find restaurants, and visit tourist sites, I finally relaxed and convinced myself that if I did get lost, someone would help me get back to my apartment. After I changed my attitude, I was able to deal with my daily chores and enjoy the next part of my Italian adventure.

There are different terms used to describe the many stages of culture shock. Peter Adler (1977) was one of the first authors to describe this experience in terms of what is now the classic five-stage model of culture shock:

Stage 1	Contact	We first meet cultural differences.
Stage 2	Disintegration	We experience confusion and lose self-esteem.
Stage 3	Integration	We experience anger. We rebuff the new culture and reaffirm the old culture.
Stage 4	Autonomy	We begin to feel self-assured and the new cultural situations are not problematic.
Stage 5	Independence	We treat both the old and the new culture with respect.

Whether researchers identify four, five, or six stages of culture shock, the end result is the same. Culture shock takes place in distinct emotional stages (Shaules, 2007). Some researchers use graphic visualizations to depict the stages of culture shock. In one version, a U-curve pattern is used to signal elation, an initial high, or the honeymoon period, which dips to a downturn or low to signal a sharp decline due to adjustment difficulties. This is then followed by an upswing to signal adjustment. In another version, a W curve is used. This is similar to the U curve but includes an additional readjustment stage upon return to the native culture.

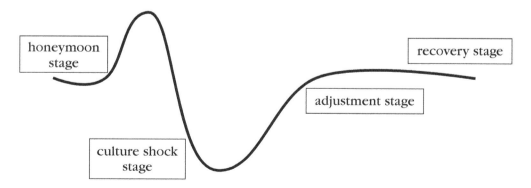

Although the stages of culture shock are fairly well established, they are experienced differently by each individual. Some people experience the effects more strongly and deeply. The length of time of each phase can also vary. It is possible, however, to predict which individuals will cope better with the symptoms of culture shock. The Intercultural Adjustment Potential Scale, developed by Matsumoto et al. (2001) measures the extent to which individuals possess the psychological coping strategies that aid with cultural adjustment. The scale measures the extent to which individuals are able to regulate their emotions, use critical thinking skills, and be open and flexible when encountering new experiences. Those who score higher on this scale are more likely to experience positive intercultural encounters.

What is important for teachers and students to remember, and as Brown (1999) suggests, is that the experience of culture shock is the norm for anyone learning a second language in a new culture.

What the teacher can do

Teachers can help students recognize the causes of culture shock by teaching them that both cultural conflict and culture shock are normal parts of the acculturation process. Students experiencing discomfort are going through the same thing that many others have gone through before them. Students whose first language is not English may arrive in class with different cultural backgrounds, from many parts of the world, and with vastly different life experiences. They can be unprepared for the changes they encounter in their new environment and the ways in which things are done that are different from their own culture. Teachers can help students who are experiencing culture shock by making the underlying causes explicit.

Many people who travel abroad and find themselves in new cultures are not aware of the reasons for their discomfort. Teachers can help students understand that invisible social cues and unstated assumptions about reality have a real impact on their own experiences of life in the new culture. Teachers can further help their students over these hurdles by encouraging them to reflect on the situations that have led them to experience culture shock. By doing so, students are in a better position to adapt more readily to their new cultural environment.

Teachers can help students identify the stages of culture shock by clearly outlining and explaining these stages. They can help students understand these stages by sharing with them their own experiences in encountering a new culture. They can ask about what experiences students have had and help students understand where they are in the process of cultural adjustment.

Teachers can use Activity 5.1 to help students identify the stages of culture shock and to understand that different reactions and different cultural experiences, both positive and negative, are completely normal.

Activity 5.1	***Stages of culture shock***
Level	High beginner – Advanced
Handout	None
Tip	Recognize the causes and stages of culture shock.

Steps:

1. Discuss the basic concepts of cultural adjustment with your class. You may wish to refer to the sections in this chapter on identifying the causes and recognizing the symptoms of culture shock. It may also be helpful to give an example of your own experience with culture shock.
2. Draw the diagram from page 103 on the board. Talk about the diagram and how it represents culture shock. Make sure students understand the terms.
3. Explain that with time people move through the stages of cultural adjustment. Tell students that everyone experiences culture shock but that the duration and intensity vary from one person to another.
4. Ask the class to think about their experiences in a new culture. Have them write down a few notes about their ideas. If the class size is small, ask students to describe their own experiences of cultural adjustment. If the class size is larger, have students work in pairs or small groups first.
5. An important goal of this activity is to reassure students that culture shock is normal.

Teaching notes:

- You can point out that the pace of the stages can vary based on the amount of time someone is in the new culture. For example, the cycle of adjustment may be accelerated or may not be completed during a short-term visit.
- Familiarize yourself with any student services offered at your school or institution that could offer support. Share this information with your class.
- You may want to point out that some people experience "reverse culture shock" when returning to their culture and country.

Identify the symptoms of culture shock.

One of the challenges of dealing with culture shock is its invisibility. When we experience the symptoms of culture shock in another country, we may not recognize them. They are also not immediately recognizable to others. No one comes up to us and says, "Oh, you're going through culture shock." Rather, a number of seemingly unrelated symptoms can inform us about what we are experiencing. These symptoms may appear initially to be simple depression or withdrawal, but whether these symptoms are mild or extreme, they affect our ability to cope with new cultural experiences.

Prem, from Sri Lanka, was a student in Ann's intermediate English as a second language writing class. He was considered a good student in his home country but was aware that his English skills were weak. In Ann's class, whenever he was called on, he became extremely nervous. Although the class was small, he did not seem comfortable working with other students. Prem was unable to cope with the material, the students, or the teacher. At one point he even stopped doing homework. The shock of entering a new culture was so jarring to him that it clearly affected how he was dealing with his studies. Because he was unable to adjust to the new culture, he ended up failing the course.

What the research says

When we experience culture shock, we may find that the values and behaviors rewarded at home are not rewarded the same way or at all in the new culture. The new culture makes new demands on us, but if we are not ready for them we may become overwhelmed and unable to cope.

How individuals react and how intense their reactions are depend not only on the nature and length of a stressful cultural encounter but also on the psychological make-up of the individual (Weaver, 1994). Some individuals cope better and can adjust faster than others. When the culture is completely different from ours, however, we are inclined to experience a more severe case of culture shock. Kohls (1996, p. 92) divides the symptoms of culture shock into three categories: overall symptoms, withdrawal symptoms, and aggressive symptoms. Kohl's overall symptoms include "anxiety, homesickness, boredom, depression, and fatigue." His withdrawal symptoms include "physical and/or psychological withdrawal, need for excessive amounts of sleep, and avoiding contact with host nationals." His aggressive symptoms include "exaggerated cleanliness, irritability, stereotyping, and verbal aggressiveness."

What the teacher can do

Teachers can help students recognize the symptoms of culture shock by having them participate in class activities that highlight their individual experiences. Hearing that other students have experienced or are experiencing the same issues and how they are dealing with them can be very reassuring to students. Teachers may want to share an experience of how they successfully dealt with culture shock. This self-disclosure on the part of the teacher may help students be more comfortable in deciding to share their own experiences.

Teachers can use Activity 5.2 to give students an opportunity to develop a deeper understanding of the symptoms of culture shock. Students are often not aware that some of the emotions and difficulties they are having are indeed culture shock. Identifying some symptoms or causes of culture shock help them think about their own experiences and at the same time realize that their classmates might be in the same boat. (See next page.)

Activity 5.2	***Culture shock symptoms***
Level	High beginner – Advanced
Handout	None
Tip	Identify the symptoms of culture shock.

Steps:

1. Write "culture shock" on the board. Ask the class what they think it means.
2. Write the following culture shock symptoms on the board: depression, withdrawal, boredom, irritability, annoyance, hostility, fatigue, trouble studying, homesickness, crying easily, drinking, sleeping a lot, trouble sleeping, nervousness, eating a lot, and spending a lot of time alone.
3. Introduce and teach the words by listing definitions, asking students to find the definitions, or describing a situation for each. Make sure students understand the words before moving on.
4. Write each symptom on a piece of paper.
5. Form small groups and hand out the pieces of paper.
6. Tell students they are going to role-play or mime the culture shock symptoms. They are not allowed to speak during the role play and may use only facial expressions or body movements. The class will guess the symptoms.
7. Circulate among the groups and offer help if students don't understand the vocabulary.
8. Erase the board. Have each group role-play their symptoms in front of the class. As the class guesses, write the correct symptom on the board.
9. To finish this activity, discuss the culture shock symptoms on the board. Explain that having any of these symptoms is very common when living in a new culture. Ask students if they have experienced any of these symptoms.

Teaching notes:

- You can mime one of the symptoms to model the role plays. Some of the symptoms will work with two students participating in the role play. You may need to encourage shy students to "ham it up" a little.

3 Counter the effects of culture shock.

Everyone who encounters a new culture by living in it will experience some form of culture shock. Although the timing and the severity of the experience will vary from person to person, we can predict what some of the symptoms are likely to be. Because we can anticipate the effects of culture shock, we can also take proactive steps to counter these symptoms.

Hideki, from Japan, was accustomed to bowing whenever he encountered an elder or a superior. As a student in the U.K., he would stop, bow, and address his professors saying "Good morning, Professor" or "Good afternoon, Doctor." The formal mode of address was acceptable at a university, but finally someone told Hideki that although bowing was a sign of respect in Japan, it was not seen as an appropriate method of greeting in Britain. Hideki was grateful that someone alerted him to this because he did not want to draw attention to himself in his new cultural surroundings and hoped to fit in.

What the research says

To help cope with cross-cultural adjustment stress, Weaver (1994, pp. 177–182) offers the following broad strategies:

- understand the process of adjustment, so that stress is anticipated and the severity of our reactions can be minimized
- develop coping strategies that facilitate adjustment to another culture swiftly and efficiently
- learn something about the new culture before leaving home and have realistic expectations of the new culture
- develop skills that will facilitate cross-cultural understanding, communication, and adaptation through cross-cultural training or orientation

Using a cognitive approach, Milton Bennett (1993) proposes six stages in the process of achieving overall intercultural sensitivity:

STAGE	REACTION
Denial	We deny the existence of cultural differences and live in isolation.
Defense	We recognize differences and form strategies to counter them.
Minimization	We still recognize differences but don't consider them important.
Acceptance	We recognize cultural behavior not as different but as existing in a particular cultural context.
Adaptation	We develop skills to deal with the differences.
Integration	We are able to move into different cultural viewpoints.

Storti and Bennhold-Saaman (1997, p. 210) suggest a reflective approach to coping with culture shock. They encourage individuals working and living in international settings to take an active role in their own physical, mental, and emotional health by making lists and then either reflecting on or acting on the items. Understanding the possibilities for action can be encouraging. Storti and

Bennhold-Saaman suggest thinking about the following actions as ways of creating a positive experience in a new culture:

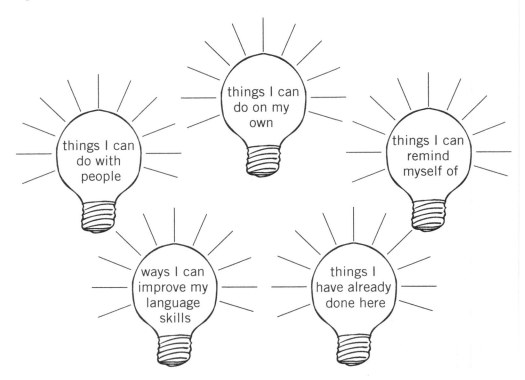

Another way of coping with the effects of culture shock is by getting to know your host country. Kohls (1996, p. 61) suggests taking time to do some of the following:

- Read a short history of the country.
- Learn the basic factual information about the country, such as natural resources, political structure, family organization, religion, art, and so on.
- Develop a "human profile" of a typical average host national.
- Learn some of the specific cultural "dos and don'ts" for foreigners. What are the expected behaviors, manners, and unspoken rules?
- Learn about present-day problems and current national affairs.
- Seek out a sympathetic person from your own culture to find out what problems you are likely to encounter.
- Be sure to know how to meet basic logistical needs such as shopping, banking, and medical needs.
- Explore the landscape. Find the principal sights, monuments, and historic areas.
- Identify the nation's heroes and heroines.

If we are not in tune with our own cultural values and beliefs, then those of the new culture are less understandable to us. Awareness, however, is just one part of cultural understanding. Being nonjudgmental about what we see and how we interpret it is another. Janet Bennett (1998, p. 221) reminds us that nonevaluation is essential when attempting to develop **cultural empathy,** a term defined by Milton Bennett as using our imagination to intellectually and emotionally participate in an unfamiliar experience. To gain cultural empathy, we must be willing to give the new culture equal status to our own.

What the teacher can do

Teachers can help counter the effects of culture shock by encouraging students to try some of the ideas and suggestions outlined above. Teachers can create reading or listening assignments that help students become familiar with the new culture and its people. If you are teaching in an English-speaking environment, organize contact assignments so that students go out into the community.

Teachers may have students who are experiencing real difficulties dealing with the effects of culture shock. Teachers can use Activity 5.3 to encourage students to share ideas and coping strategies for cultural adjustment. For this activity, it is important that students are somewhat familiar with each other and that they feel comfortable relating their personal life experiences to others.

Activity 5.3	*Coping with culture shock*
Level	High beginner – Advanced
Handout	None
Tip	Counter the effects of culture shock.

Steps:

1. Use the information from pages 101-106 to present the concept of culture shock and its causes, stages, and symptoms with the class. Draw the illustrations of culture shock from page 110 on the board.
2. Ask the class to brainstorm two or three possible ways of dealing with the stress of culture shock. Write student ideas on the board. (For examples, see page 110.)
3. Form small groups. Ask each group to brainstorm two or three other ideas for dealing with culture shock.
4. To finish the activity, ask the groups to share their ideas. Add the information to the board so that students have a list.

(continued on next page)

Teaching notes:

- If possible, complete Activity 5.2 before doing this activity.
- *Alternative:* If you are working with lower-level students, you may wish to develop a list of ideas for coping with culture shock to give them, rather than requiring them to generate a list on their own. Then have students rank the strategies from most helpful to least helpful.

 Examine your own cultural style.

Individuals carry with them their own cultural experiences, beliefs, and worldviews. These can make it difficult to adapt to a new cultural environment because the members of the new culture may hold a very different set of experiences, beliefs, and worldviews.

For example, what might be considered a small and insignificant "white lie" in one culture might be seen as a serious display of untruthfulness in another culture. An international student in the United States might tell his teacher that he lost his homework, when in reality he did not complete it. If the teacher discovers the student in this lie, the consequences could include a lower grade in the course. For the international student, culture shock has occurred.

What the research says

What we decide to say and how we decide to say it depends on who we are as individuals and as cultural beings. We possess both a **cultural style** and a **communication style**. Our cultural style is revealed when we behave in a manner that is acceptable in our home culture. What we say to someone and how we say it reveals our communication style. When considering communication styles, Peterson (2004, p. 156) outlines a number of areas that vary from culture to culture.

CULTURAL VARIATIONS IN COMMUNICATION STYLES	
Direct/indirect	The method of giving feedback How conflict style is handled Levels of openness revealed in discussion The concept of face
Level of formality	Using title and last name versus using first name power issues
Vocal indicators	Aspects of the voice: inflection, volume, speed, accent, and pitch
Conversation flow	Examples: interrupting, turn-taking, and ending conversations

Nonverbal communication	Examples: gestures, posture, silence, and nodding
Eye contact	How direct/indirect eye contact is construed: as a test, as truthful, as respect
Physical distance	How close or far away we position ourselves; how much we say using gestures and our bodies

Peterson (2004, pp. 161–165) notes that knowing our own cultural style means knowing the strengths and weaknesses that are connected with it. He offers eleven traits or competencies that are crucial to dealing successfully with people from other countries and cultures:

Cultural self-awareness: the establishment of firsthand experiences with other cultures, best achieved through travel abroad.

Cultural awareness of others: knowledge about the differences among people, countries, and cultures that leads to behavioral changes that make people more effective when dealing with others.

Cultural sensitivity: respect and acceptance of other cultures combined with the skills to demonstrate that acceptance.

Cross-cultural communication skills: verbal and nonverbal behaviors that are helpful to function effectively across cultures.

Tolerance for ambiguity: the ability to accept and deal with uncertainty without becoming upset.

Flexibility: the ability to adjust to other ways of doing things based on the new culture's practices.

Open-mindedness: the realization that there is more than one way of doing things and that others do things differently based on their cultural context.

Humility: a quality that gradually emerges if individuals can realize that they are not always the sole focus in every cultural situation encountered.

Empathy: the ability to put one's self in the shoes of another to gain a different perspective.

Outgoing personality: being an extrovert rather than an introvert can have a positive influence on the success of a cultural encounter. Not all extroverted personalities are well suited to new encounters, but most are.

Self-reliance: the ability to depend on one's self and to act independently.

What the teacher can do

Teachers can help students examine their own cultural styles by building empathy, self-awareness, and a tolerance for ambiguity. This gives students a solid foundation when they are trying to understand the cultural style of someone from another culture and helps them navigate the cultural conflicts they may feel within themselves. Teachers can also present an example of their own experiences and their own cultural style.

Teachers can use Activity 5.4 to offer students an opportunity to examine their own particular cultural style and compare it with the styles of other students in the class.

Activity 5.4	*My cultural styles*
Level	Advanced
Handouts	Pages 211 – 212
Tip	Examine your own cultural style.

Steps:

1. List the cultural competencies from Peterson (2004) on the board: cultural self-awareness, flexibility, cultural awareness of others, humility, cultural sensitivity, cross-cultural communication skills, empathy, tolerance for ambiguity, open-mindedness, outgoing personality, and self-reliance.
2. Ask the class to say what they think the concepts mean. Explain any words they don't know.
3. Make copies of the two handouts for Activity 5.4. Pass them out to the class.
4. Ask students to read the descriptions of Peterson's cultural competencies on Handout 5.4A. Answer any questions students may have.
5. Ask students to fill in the chart on Handout 5.4B. Make sure students understand how the rating system works.
6. To finish this activity, ask volunteers to share some of their answers with the class.

Teaching notes:

- *Alternative:* If you want to do this activity with lower-level students, choose four or five competencies and simplify the language.
- You can also hand out Handout 5.4A for students to read as homework. Do Handout 5.4B and have the related discussion in class.

5 Reduce cultural conflict.

When we find ourselves in the company of other individuals who look like us, dress like us, and act like us, we assume that they see what we see, hear what we say, and understand what we mean and what we intend. However, if we insist on working under these assumptions, we may find ourselves experiencing misunderstandings and conflict. How then can we best minimize these cultural misunderstandings? When we are dealing with a different culture, we are working from a different mindset, controlled by different norms, and we have different goals (Lewis, 2000). We must acknowledge that we do not all have the same experiences, come from the same background, or have the same values. Thus, we need to be cautious that our perceptions do not overinfluence how we think and how we behave toward others.

What the research says

Negative intercultural experiences may lead people to make global judgments about a cultural group. These negative judgments may be reactions of culture shock or the result of learned **prejudice**. Sometimes a particular minority group is continuously disparaged, such as illegal immigrants in the United States. Other groups can become prejudiced against the minority group because of **ethnocentrism,** which is the feeling that one's own group is better than another's.

Shaules (2007, p. 66) uses the term "sojourner" to describe someone venturing into another culture. He notes that

> Among sojourners, prejudice functions primarily out of conscious awareness and often results from judging behavior based on criteria that the sojourner assumes is neutral and absolute, but which is actually based in hidden cultural assumptions. Shedding light on this phenomenon—and using neutral terminology to do so—can help sojourners become aware of this process and may help them suspend judgment.

Being able to see a situation as sensible when rooted in the viewpoint of another's culture represents an understanding of culture in new surroundings. It can be helpful to recognize cultural differences such as **universals**, or rule-based cultural concepts, and **particulars**, or situation-specific cultural concepts. Shaules (2007, p. 80) argues that rather than using the terms *prejudice* or *ethnocentrism* when referring to negative reactions to cultural differences, we should use the term **resistance**:

> Resistance is seen as a negative reaction accompanied by a negative value judgment, whereas dislike is seen as a negative reaction without a negative value judgment. This distinction is necessary because we may accept the value of what we find in a new environment without necessarily wanting to adopt it ourselves.

In other words, not every negative reaction to a cultural difference implies a lack of intercultural sensitivity.

When we are traveling or living abroad, we develop a sense of security if we are able to rely on our stereotypes. Barna (1988, p. 181) defines **stereotypes** as "overgeneralized, secondhand beliefs that provide conceptual bases from which we make sense out of what goes on around us, whether or not they are accurate or fit the circumstances." When we interact with people whose behavior does not fit with our experience, we develop stereotypes to help us explain the situation. Stereotypes are not easily overcome or corrected because they rationalize our biases and prejudices.

When we assume that all the members of a particular group or culture have the same attributes, we are stereotyping them. These can be positive or negative stereotypes, yet both types are problematic. Stereotypes not only create a false impression, but they also feed into our inaccurate observations and confirm our **cultural biases.** Of course, we do make cultural generalizations on some level because members of a culture often share certain characteristics. For example, it may be appropriate to generalize that people from the United States are individualistic and that Japanese are collectivistic; however, we must still admit that not every individual in each of those cultures falls into the dominant category.

Stereotypes can be barriers to successful cross-cultural communication. The bottom line is that when we form stereotypes, we see what we want to see and we refute any interpretations that do not fit into our worldview. How can we overcome this barrier? Hofstede et al. (2002) argue that the answer is through awareness, knowledge, and better communication skills. In other words, we need to be aware of the preconceptions and stereotypes that we direct toward other cultures; we need to learn as much as we can about the other culture; and we need to "reinterpret their behavior from their cultural perspective, adapting [our] own stereotypes to fit [our] new experiences" (p. 19).

 Voices from the Classroom

In my advanced ESL class at a college in Boston, Massachusetts, students were discussing an essay written by a graduate student from China. In the essay, she describes visiting a college advisor at his home. Although she was thirsty, she declined an offer of a drink out of politeness, but was then surprised when the advisor got something to drink just for himself. She was confused and didn't understand why her advisor hadn't continued to ask if she would like something to drink. She had expected him to insist several times. This would be the norm in China.

On reading this story, Avi, an Israeli student, exclaimed, "But that's crazy! In Israel, if we want something, we say yes, and if we don't, we say no. We don't beat around the bush."

Shota, a Japanese student, remarked that in Japan his response would have been similar to that of the Chinese student and that he often felt uncomfortable in his college classes in Boston, where U.S. students expressed personal opinions loudly, disagreed with classmates and teachers, and behaved in a manner that would seem selfish and rude in Japan.

This led to a discussion about direct vs. indirect communication styles. At the end of the class, Avi turned to Shota and jokingly said, "Maybe I'm the one who's crazy!" The class laughed at Avi's remark, but he and the other students left the room with a new appreciation of how they viewed cultural differences, negative value judgments, and stereotypes.

— Peter Gardner
Berklee College of Music

What the teacher can do

Teachers can help reduce cultural conflict by exposing students to situations that allow them to explore different cultural biases and stereotypes. Students are then able to better understand how the experiences of their classmates relate to how they view the world and how they might solve different cultural conflicts.

Teachers can use Activity 5.5 to encourage students to contemplate causes of cultural misunderstandings caused by biases and stereotypes. This practice can help them reduce cultural conflicts in future encounters.

Activity 5.5	*Avoiding cultural bias and stereotypes*
Level	High beginner – Advanced
Handouts	Pages 213 – 214
Tip	Reduce cultural conflict.

Steps:

1. Make copies of the two handouts for Activity 5.5.
2. Review with students that a critical incident is a cross-cultural problematic situation. The incidents are concerned with various dimensions of culture. Inform the students that there are no right or wrong answers but that there are solutions.
3. Ask students to work in groups of 3 or 4. Pass out the handouts for Activity 5.5. Assign each group one critical incident. Have students read the critical incident and questions and discuss what they think caused the conflict.
4. If a group finishes early, assign another critical incident.
5. As a class, discuss each critical incident, the solutions from each group, and the area of cultural conflict manifested. See page 191 for possible interpretations and share them with the class if none of the groups suggest them.

Teaching notes:

- Each critical incident presents an area of conflict designed to stimulate discussion about the situation described and to make students aware of and sensitive to cultural differences.
- *Alternative:* If necessary, simplify the vocabulary used to describe the critical incidents.

Conclusion

In this chapter we discussed cultural conflict and cultural adjustment, looking especially at culture shock. We presented the causes and stages of culture shock and explored its symptoms and effects. We highlighted different strategies to adjust to a new culture and emphasized the importance of knowing one's cultural style. Finally, we addressed the issue of cultural bias and stereotypes and examined how cultural conflict could be reduced.

When referring to culture shock, the terms *homesickness* and *uprooting* are sometimes used. We need to remember that we ourselves determine the extent of the culture shock we experience in our lives, and we ourselves must develop a sense of awareness about how to avoid cultural conflict and expedite cultural adjustment.

We have helped students cope with culture shock by inviting them to share their own cultural experiences, explore the symptoms of culture shock, and identify the stages of culture shock. We have also used critical incidents, helped students explore their cultural style, and invited them to share coping strategies.

Check your understanding

After reading this chapter and using the activities with your class, check your comfort level with the following:

- ❏ I can help my students recognize the causes of culture shock.
- ❏ I can help my students identify the stages of culture shock.
- ❏ I have helped my students identify and understand the symptoms of culture shock.
- ❏ I have shared ideas with my students on how to counter the effects of culture shock.
- ❏ I can guide my students to become aware of their own cultural style.
- ❏ I have given my students some basic tools for reducing cultural conflict.

CHAPTER 6

TRADITIONAL WAYS OF TEACHING CULTURE

Consider these questions:
- How do you usually learn about another country or culture?
- When you think of traditional ways used to teach culture, what comes to mind?
- Have you ever tried teaching about culture? What techniques or activities did you use? Describe how the class reacted.

Over the decades, teachers have been helping students learn new languages with traditional techniques focusing on the sound system, grammar, and vocabulary of the new language. The inclusion of a focus on intercultural communication and teaching about the target culture is a relatively recent development in language teaching

English teaching professionals in different parts of the world have diverse views about teaching the culture of the target language. Teachers who prepare nonnative-speaking students to live, work, and study in countries where English is the dominant language generally feel it makes sense to help those students learn about the culture as well. Teachers who prepare new immigrants in English-speaking countries usually think it is important to inform them about the traditions and culture of the new country in which they are living as well as see it as a preliminary step toward possible citizenship. It is also the case that school and university students in non-English-speaking countries often learn about life in the countries where English is spoken at the same time that they learn the language. So courses in English may include aspects of history, social life, and literature in addition to the fundamentals of the language.

In the 1990s and beyond, proponents of the emerging concept of world Englishes and of English as an international language have suggested that the English language does not belong only to those countries where English originated. Along with this point of view comes the perspective that it may not be necessary for students to learn about cultures of the traditionally English-speaking countries. In the tips for teaching culture that follow, we do not intend to suggest that the culture of one country is more worthy of study than the culture of another but simply want to recognize that in many teaching situations, teaching the target language goes hand in hand with teaching about the target culture.

TIPS FOR TRADITIONAL WAYS OF TEACHING CULTURE

In this chapter, we explore teaching techniques that focus on sharing the basics of the target culture. The eight tips offer teachers various ideas and ways for teaching culture in their language classrooms. Throughout the chapter we provide a summary of the research related to each of these tips and offer practical suggestions for what teachers can do in the classroom. Some of the activities include photocopiable handouts. These are located in Appendix A on pages 215–219.

TIPS

1. Use literature to explore culture.
2. Use the arts to explore culture.
3. Surround students with stimuli from the target culture.
4. Assign students to present research on the target culture.
5. Include problem-solving skills to help discover culture.
6. Engage students in role plays, dramas, and simulations.
7. Get students involved through experiential learning and contact assignments.
8. Introduce holidays, festivals, and religious traditions.

In this chapter we examine various ways of teaching culture. We explore how literature, the visual arts, film, and music can be used, and we consider the function of cultural artifacts. We look at how to engage students in research about culture and everyday life. The activities promote the active engagement of students in cultural learning, make use of their problem-solving skills, and involve students in role plays, dramas, and simulations. Finally, we look at ways that teachers can make use of holidays, festivals, and religious traditions to teach culture in the classroom.

Use literature to explore culture.

In Chapter 1 we explored the concept of little *c* culture and big *C* culture. Peterson (2004) suggested that big *C* culture consists of grand themes that are often readily visible, whereas little *c* culture consists of minor themes that are often invisible. Throughout much of this book, we have focused on the less visible aspects of culture such as behavior, attitudes, and values. In this chapter, our emphasis turns to the more traditional themes of big *C* culture.

Many of these themes can be found in the literature of the target culture. Literature, after all, offers authentic language, and for many teachers it provides an excellent source of available language. Indeed, up through the 1970s and beyond, many foreign language courses had the primary goal of helping students become sufficiently fluent to read literature in the target language.

Literature can be used to teach culture at all levels. In elementary school language classes, children's books in English can be found for each language level. For young adults and older students, both simplified and authentic versions of literature are available. Many teachers are curious about which literary genres they should use to help students learn about a new culture.

What the research says

Valdes (1986) suggests that English language teachers primarily make use of poetry, short stories, and short novels in the teaching of literature. She encourages teachers to "make clear the values that underlie the behavior of characters and points of view of the authors" (p. 139) with the goal of helping students grasp key elements of the target culture.

Christison (1982, pp. 5-11) provides numerous examples of simple ways of using poetry with even low-level learners. She also highlights suggested criteria for the selection of poetry and tips for teachers on how to prepare and then present the poetry.

CRITERIA FOR THE SELECTION OF POETRY
High student interest
Short and simple
Fun-filled and rhythmic

SUGGESTIONS FOR PRESENTING POETRY IN THE CLASSROOM

Study the poem and practice reading it ahead of time.

Follow the natural rhythm of the poem. Pause where it makes sense to pause.

Speak in a natural voice.

Be quiet when you are finished to give students time to absorb the poem's sound and meaning.

Further ideas for the use of prose, poetry, and drama are available in Whiteson (1996) and Collie and Slater (1987). Whiteson's edited volume provides a number of ready-made "recipes" for the use of literature. Collie and Slater outline the "why, what, and how" of the teaching of literature and recommend the following aims:

- Maintain interest and involvement by using a variety of student-centered activities
- Supplement the printed page by appealing to a variety of learning styles
- Tap the resources of knowledge and experience within the group by encouraging shared activities, including group and pair work
- Help students explore their own responses to literature
- Use the target language
- Integrate language and literature

Useful resources for an overview of literature are the outline of English literature by Thornley and Roberts (1984) and the similar outline of American literature by High (1986). These contain the essential histories of these literary traditions from their origins through the mid-twentieth century.

 Voices from the Classroom

I was teaching a course called English Language and Culture to student teachers in Uruguay. As part of their reading, I assigned one chapter of a novel by W. H. Hudson called The Purple Land. *Hudson was born in America, raised in Buenos Aires, and spent his last years in London. He traveled in Uruguay during the civil wars of the nineteenth century.* The Purple Land *describes the people and places he encountered during this period.*

Most of my students came from the same lands that Hudson visited. The novel is rich in its description of rivers, hills, flowers, and places that my students knew well. I was amazed when I realized that despite Hudson's meticulous care in describing with absolute faithfulness my students' very own country, they did not recognize that the novel was set in Uruguay. They simply couldn't believe that the River Yi described in the text could be their own. If the novel was written in English and was introduced to them by a teacher who taught a foreign language and culture, how could it possibly be about Uruguay?

— *Gabriela Kaplan*

What the teacher can do

Using literature can provide valuable cultural insights for students and can also tap into the desire of many teachers to make use of authentic materials in the classroom. It is important, however, to be sure that students are capable of handling the level of language that is found in the texts that you present to them. Several publishers offer versions of classic novels that are simplified for various levels of reading ability. Many English language teaching presses have also published textbooks containing selected short stories, poems, and dramas that may be suitable for your students. These books usually include activities to promote vocabulary acquisition, reading comprehension, and discussion. You can supplement these activities with your own ideas to help students grasp cultural concepts.

You may wish to take a poem or story and prepare it for your students. To do this, divide the activity into three parts. First, consider what you want your students to think about before they begin to read. How can you best activate their **schema** or background knowledge about the subject of the reading? You may also wish to preteach difficult vocabulary words or provide glosses for them. Next, think of how you wish students to engage with the text. Prepare some questions for them to think about while reading and then some comprehension questions at the end. Finally, consider what you want students to do after they have read the passage. What values, issues, or cultural questions are raised? Write discussion questions to help students come to grips with these cultural issues.

Students can develop awareness of poetry if teachers carefully expose them to this genre. By reading a poem, students can enter the world and culture of the poem and look at their own experiences in light of what they have read. Teachers can use the tremendous variety of poetry in English available through publishers and online sources to introduce students to poets and other cultural icons of the target culture.

Teachers can use Activity 6.1 to help students gain insight into the target culture through literature. If teachers choose an accessible poem that exemplifies a typical aspect of the target culture, students can have their eyes opened to another way of seeing, exploring, and understanding the new culture.

Activity 6.1	*Unscrambling a poem*
Level	High-beginning – Advanced
Handout	None
Tip	Use literature to explore culture.

Steps:

1. Find a poem that exemplifies a typical aspect of the target culture or is representative of the literature of the target culture. Be sure to select a poem of suitable length, interest, and language level for your students.
2. Type or print out the poem; then cut the poem into pieces so that each line is on a single strip of paper. If the poem is broken into separate verses, write the number of the verse on the back of each slip to identify which verse it was taken from.
3. Give each student one slip of paper. Distribute any extra slips of paper as evenly as possible. Then ask the class to form groups based on the verse number on the back of their strips of paper.
4. Tell the groups that their task is to try and recreate their verse of the poem. Encourage students to read their line out loud as they work. Students should stand in a line in the order they think is correct.
5. Walk around and help as needed. If students are having difficulty, you may want to read the first line of each verse out loud or let students look at each other's papers.
6. To check the work of each group, read their verse out loud. Have each group listen and rearrange themselves if necessary. The rest of the class can help.
7. Read the complete poem out loud. Lead a discussion about the poem. Ask: "What do you think the poet is saying? What are some symbols in the poem? What are some of the cultural implications in this poem?"

Teaching notes:

- You may want to distribute printed copies of the poem to your students.
- Give students some biographical information about the poet.
- You may want to select a poem that has an easy rhythm as well as obvious images and cultural implications. If students do the activity successfully and enjoy it, select poems with less evident images and implications for next time.
- Questions for more advanced speakers could include: "What emotions emerged when you read this poem? What abstract ideas surfaced from the poem's details?"

2 │ Use the arts to explore culture.

Although literature and the written word provide many clues to culture, there are other art forms that can expose the language learner to the new culture as well. The visual arts, films, and music are all valuable means of connecting students with the target culture. We now know that students have different learning styles and multiple intelligences. Including the arts helps us tap into the artistic, visual, and musical learning styles of our students.

What the research says

Using popular songs is a traditional way of introducing students to language and culture. It is important to think about the steps necessary to introduce and teach songs successfully. Murphey (1992) provides excellent caveats and ideas for working with songs.

- What is the pedagogical value of the song? What do you hope that students will learn? Are there specific aspects of language and culture that you hope your students will learn?
- Be sure that the song is enjoyable for the students. They may not share your musical taste.
- Are the lyrics easily accessible and understandable to the students?
- Do the lyrics have some degree of repetition? A chorus that repeats helps to reinforce language and makes comprehension easier.
- Be sure that you have obtained an accurate copy of the lyrics. Some of the online versions of popular songs are not always accurate.
- If you plan to have students sing, is the tune simple and easy to learn?
- Do the lyrics of the song contain language or ideas that might be objectionable to some students, parents, or your school administration?

Movies are another powerful medium to learn about cultural values. The visceral power of film with moving images, music, and spoken language provides a rich source of cultural information. Some films deal specifically with intercultural conflict. Others present historical information. Most films deal with relationships between people, which is always interesting to observe. Practically any movie can be treated as a text and used for language and culture study.

RECOMMENDED MOVIES BY GENRE AND CULTURAL TOPICS[1]

Family relationships	• *Dead Poets Society* • *The Graduate* • *A River Runs Through It*
Race relations	• *Boyz n the Hood* • *The Color Purple* • *Trading Places* • *Gran Torino* • *Crash*
Feminist films and the role of women	• *9 to 5* • *Thelma and Louise* • *Tootsie*
Religion	• *Gandhi* • *Malcolm X* • *Witness*
Short-story adaptations	• *The Story of an Hour* by Kate Chopin • *A Rose for Emily* by William Faulkner • *A White Heron* by Sara Orne Jewett
American history	• *An American Tail* • *Butch Cassidy and the Sundance Kid* • *The Last of the Mohicans*
Cultural conflict	• *The Gods Must Be Crazy* • *Gung Ho!* • *E.T.—The Extra-Terrestrial*
Novel adaptations	• *Jurassic Park* by Michael Crichton • *The Client, The Firm,* or *The Pelican Brief,* all by John Grisham • *The Grapes of Wrath* by John Steinbeck
Biography	• *Bugsy* • *The Cotton Club* • *JFK*
Problems in American society	• *Cocoon* • *Moscow on the Hudson* • *The Long Walk Home*

[1] Adapted from Mejia, Kennedy Xiao, and Kennedy (1994) and Williamson and Vincent (1996).

What the teacher can do

Teachers can find song lyrics in books and from online sources. When presenting songs to students, prepare students ahead of time. For example, introduce the singer or musical group, show images that illustrate the content of the song, or introduce difficult vocabulary words. A copy of the lyrics or a fill-in-the-blanks version of the lyrics can help students understand the meaning. After students have had a chance to listen, discuss the song, its language, and its cultural meaning.

When studying a movie in depth, it can be very helpful to have a copy of the screenplay. In this way, the dialogue of the movie becomes the "text" on which the lessons are based. Teachers can find screenplays for many movies in books and online, but be careful: What is published as a screenplay may be the dialogue in a final draft of the script submitted by the writer, and the screenplay as written often changes significantly by the time the film appears in theaters. The "shooting script" or transcript of the film provides word-by-word dialogue, although this may be more difficult to locate. If you do have a shooting script or transcript, review the text for vocabulary words, idiomatic expressions, and cultural observations to include in your lessons.

Teachers can use a movie with Activity 6.2 to teach students about elements of culture.

Activity 6.2	***Movie study***
Level	Intermediate – Advanced
Handout	Page 215
Tip	Use the arts to explore culture.

Steps:

1. Make copies of the handout for Activity 6.2.
2. Select a movie that you believe appropriate for your students that is readily available. See the list on page 126 for suggestions.
3. If possible, obtain a transcript for the dialogue in the movie. Review the transcript to be sure that it is accurate. Note any potentially challenging vocabulary and expressions and be prepared to explain them to students.
4. Prepare students for the film by explaining the background. You may wish to prepare students for any plot complexities if you can do so without giving away important plot points.
5. Pass out the handout for Activity 6.2. Go over the directions and the questions with the class.

(continued on next page)

6. View the movie with students. You may wish to break it up into digestible sections so that you can pause for explanation and discussion.
7. After students watch the film, have them answer the questions on the handout. Then have students discuss their answers in pairs or small groups.
8. To finish this activity, discuss the answers with the class.

Teaching notes:

- Make sure to preview the movie for content that might be inappropriate for your students such as language, violence, or sexual situations.
- *Alternative:* If you don't have enough class time to watch the entire film, choose specific scenes that focus on cultural elements and pertain to the questions on the handout.

3 Surround students with stimuli from the target culture.

If your students are in a learning environment where the target language is not spoken outside the classroom, it is particularly valuable to surround the students with stimuli from the target culture. These may take a variety of forms and can be prepared by you or brought to class by the students.

What the research says

What can you do to help immerse your students in the target language and culture? First, remember that your students may have different **learning styles**—"preferred or habitual patterns of mental functioning and dealing with new information" (Ehrman and Oxford 1990, p. 311). For example, not all of your students may be terrific readers. Research in learning styles suggests that some learners may comprehend better through aural (listening) presentation or kinesthetic (active movement) involvement rather than through reading a text. Similarly, Gardner (1983, p. 62) has examined the area of **multiple intelligences,** which he defines as "a human intellectual competence that entails a set of skills of problem solving—enabling the individual to resolve genuine problems or difficulties that he or she encounters." He suggests that learners have eight intelligences and that students have different strengths and weaknesses within these intelligences. Some students, for instance, learn better visually. An awareness of these differences can help you focus your efforts when you surround your students with stimuli from the target culture.

With this in mind, how can you help your students learn more about culture? First, consider the ways in which posters, paintings, photographs, or realia can add to the student learning experience. Maley, Duff, and Grellet (1981) have a number of intriguing ideas for working with visual art, including paintings, photographs, drawings, and cartoons. They suggest that the surreal paintings of Magritte and the interlaced drawings of Escher can provide a useful stimulus for discussion. Another proponent of art and pictures is Wright (1987), who offers suggestions to help students and teachers explore many aspects of art, including color, lines, perspective, and movement, which are often used differently by artists with different cultural backgrounds.

Photographs and drawings can also produce useful cultural content. In his book, Wright (1989, p. vii) lists the following types of pictures that can be useful in teaching and learning the target language and culture:

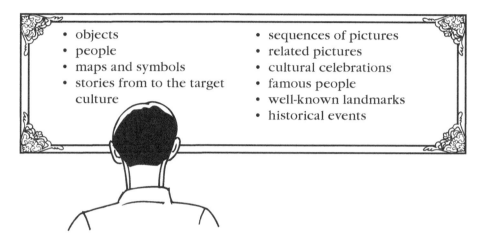

- objects
- people
- maps and symbols
- stories from to the target culture
- sequences of pictures
- related pictures
- cultural celebrations
- famous people
- well-known landmarks
- historical events

Goldstein (2008) notes the possibilities of describing, interpreting, and creating images. He suggests dozens of activities for classroom use and also provides useful sources of images that can be used to provide cultural insights.

Other stimuli that may help give students a sense of the new culture include newspapers and magazines, radio and television broadcasts, films, popular songs, and food. Newspapers and magazines provide stories of current events and photos of popular figures from politics, athletics, and entertainment, and they can give a real flavor of the new culture. Radio and television broadcasts can expose students to popular culture. Food taps into the visceral and real sense of taste and smell.

What the teacher can do

Consider the space in which you teach. If you are permitted to decorate the walls in your classroom, this is a good place to begin. Put up posters showing various pictures of the new culture, bring in objects, provide a corner with resource materials in the target language such as newspapers and magazines, or offer DVDs that students can take to practice listening and speaking at home. You can also organize a special day when students have the opportunity to try preparing and sampling typical or traditional food and drink of the target culture.

Teachers can use Activity 6.3 to focus their students' attention on aspects of culture through visual stimulation. By bringing in pictures or photographs from the target culture, teachers can extend students' awareness of the wealth of cultural elements outside the classroom.

Activity 6.3	***A picture is worth a thousand words***
Level	Beginning – Advanced
Handout	None
Tip	Surround students with stimuli from the target culture.

Steps:

1. Bring to class a set of large pictures or posters that are big enough for the entire class to see. You might select travel posters, pictures of everyday life, or advertisements that show the target culture.
2. Begin by asking simple questions about the pictures and have students answer.
3. Then have students take turns asking questions of each other.
4. Focus the students' attention on any elements of the pictures that are culturally significant. Can the students explain them? Add cultural explanations as needed.
5. Ask students to choose their favorite picture and then write a brief descriptive essay. If possible, encourage them to go beyond surface description to talk about what is hidden in the picture as well as what is easily seen.

Teaching notes:

- *Alternative:* Bring in a number of small pictures and have students study and discuss them in small groups.

 Assign students to present research on the target culture.

An excellent way to involve students in learning about a culture is to give them the responsibility of first learning about the culture and then presenting their knowledge to their peers. By conducting research on their own, students gain a deeper knowledge of a subject than they do if the information is passed on to them by an instructor. Students often take a greater interest in a topic that they can research and develop themselves.

What the research says

Fruitful topics for research include a country's history, government, and geography. Alternately, historical or currently popular heroes in the realms of sports, music, politics, or military history are suitable subjects. You and your students can easily find information about all of these subjects in libraries, reference books, and online sources.

Seelye (1993) cites Taylor and Sorenson (1961) as the first to describe one form of student research known as a **culture capsule**. Students are assigned to present information about the target culture in a short report. The teacher helps students choose suitable subject matter for the reports. The capsule consists of a brief two- to four-paragraph oral report that students deliver to the class. Each presentation is followed by a series of comprehension questions, also prepared by the students. Ideally, the presentation is combined with audio-visual reinforcement that may involve projecting images or introducing realia into the classroom. This is yet another way to help students share the responsibility for their culture-learning.

What the teacher can do

Consider the linguistic abilities of your students and construct suitable assignments for them. Beginners might be able to give a one- or two-minute summary of a passage that you provide. Advanced students might be capable of taking on a research project that results in a term paper or an extensive oral presentation. Use your judgment as to what is appropriate for your students. Be sure that their research is on topics that are sufficiently narrow to be handled in the allotted time and that the expectations of the assignment are clear.

Tailor your assignment to the available resources. If a nearby library is not accessible or if Internet searches are not available or practical in your setting, you may need to assist students in obtaining the basic materials for their research. You can readily obtain primers on Australian, British, Canadian, and United States culture from English as a second language (ESL) publishers. One excellent resource for low-level students is *The ESL Miscellany* by, Clark, Moran, and Burrows (2007). It contains a great deal of useful cultural and linguistic information about the United States that is accessible to students at beginning levels.

Teachers can use Activity 6.4 to help their students investigate culture in greater depth. In this activity, students conduct research on a particular topic within a country or culture. Teachers can choose the level of research required and assign either written or spoken reports. This activity can also give students a sense of what might be expected of them in future academic coursework. (See next page.)

Activity 6.4	*Country expert*
Level	Low intermediate – Advanced
Handout	None
Tip	Assign students to present research on the target culture.

Steps:

1. Identify a country or countries that your students want to learn more about.
2. Assign students research topics or allow them to choose their topic with your guidance. Topics about the country might include government or political structures, history, geography, a famous person, a particular industry or cultural group, or something about sports or the arts.
3. Based on the language ability of your students and the time available, define the scope of the assignment.
   - How much time will students have to complete the assignment?
   - How much research do you expect them to do?
   - How much help will they receive?
   - Do you want them to present the results of their research in writing, in an oral presentation, or both?
   - Do you expect them to prepare a handout for the class?
4. Offer help as needed for students to do their research and complete their projects.
5. Have students present the results of their research to the class.
6. You may want to take notes on the presentations and then provide feedback to students either orally or in writing. Comment on the content of the presentation as well as on the language used.

Teaching notes:

- Be sure to assist students in limiting the scope of their research.
- Provide clear criterion so that students know how they will be evaluated.
- You may wish to involve students in the evaluation process by giving them a numbered form to comment on delivery, language skills, content, etc.

5 Include problem-solving skills to help discover culture.

Nothing is as intriguing as an unsolved mystery. When we tell students something directly, they may just shrug their shoulders and think, "So what?" But when presented with an information gap or a problem-solving task, students are more likely to rise to the occasion and participate in learning. By taking advantage of students' natural curiosity and desire to solve problems, we can motivate them to learn more about culture.

What the research says

Common culture-learning techniques that take advantage of students' problem-solving abilities include information gaps, research projects, problem-solving activities, and critical incidents. Another classic technique is the **culture assimilator.** As presented in Seelye (1993, p. 162), the culture assimilator

> describes a "critical incident" of cross-cultural interaction that is usually a common occurrence in which a [foreign visitor] and a host national interact, a situation one or both find puzzling or conflictual or that they are likely to misinterpret, and a situation that can be interpreted in a fairly unequivocal manner, given sufficient knowledge about the other's culture.

After the students read about the incident (a paragraph or two), they are asked an interpretive question: "Why do you think the man behaved the way he did?" or something similar. The students are then presented with four possible answers. Only one of the answers is correct. After the students have selected an answer, they are directed to the feedback for that answer. If they chose an incorrect answer, they are redirected and asked to reread the passage and choose another answer. When they answer correctly, they are given a more detailed description of why their answer is correct.

Culture assimilators are difficult to write correctly. The writer must take care to ensure the following:

- The incident must be reasonably natural rather than too artificially contrived. Ask yourself, "Would a real person from the culture described really do this?"
- The incorrect answers or distractors must be sufficiently plausible so that they are not rejected out of hand, but at the same time they cannot be too similar to the correct answer.
- The explanations offered for the distractors should also lead to learning.
- The correct answer needs to be such that a typical native speaker would answer correctly without any difficulty. You may wish to test your questions on a native speaker.

What the teacher can do

Teachers can use Activity 6.5 to involve their students in a problem-solving activity by having them search for the correct answer to the cultural dilemma presented. This experience allows students to learn more about the ways in which different cultures view time. Teachers can also use this activity as a model on which to base their own culture assimilators about topics of their choice. (See next page.)

Activity 6.5	***Time differs culturally***
Level	Intermediate – Advanced
Handouts	Pages 216 – 217
Tip	Include problem-solving skills to help discover culture.

Steps:
1. Make copies of the two handouts for Activity 6.5. Pass Handout 6.5A out to the class.
2. Form pairs. Instruct students to read the incident and answer the question.
3. Direct each pair to decide together which answer they think is correct. Then pass out Handout 6.5B and have them read the explanations.
4. Discuss the answer and the situation with the class.

Teaching notes:
- You may wish to have students underline any new vocabulary words. You can review the words with the class.
- If you have time, talk with students about the role of expectations in cultural encounters. What are their expected norms of sharing space with others?

6 Engage students in role plays, dramas, and simulations about cultural issues.

It is important to include a variety of activities in the language classroom. Engaging students with different learning styles—for example by getting students up and moving around the classroom—helps create a new and vibrant energy in the class. Just as some students benefit more from visual learning, other learners have a preference for **kinesthetic learning** (involving movement). By engaging learners in role plays, dramas, and simulations, teachers can help students more fully grasp concepts and ideas about the new culture.

What the research says

Wintergerst and DeCapua (2001) investigated the learning styles of international students studying in the United States. They found that Russian-speaking students preferred a kinesthetic learning style over auditory, visual, and tactile styles. In a later study, Wintergerst et al. (2003, p. 92) found that both Russian English as a foreign language (EFL) students and Asian ESL students also preferred a kinesthetic learning style or what researchers called "project orientation," defined as "a student's preference of learning best when he or she is involved in 'hands-on' activities or when working with materials in a learning situation." So too, Spanish-speaking ESL students and native-speaking English composition students preferred project orientation, as reported in Wintergerst et al.'s review of related studies. Ryffel

(1997) noted that when selecting, adapting, and using culture-learning activities, teachers should vary tasks in an effort to acknowledge the different learning style preferences of students. She also cautioned that role plays and simulations "are naturally high risk due to the uncertainty involved and the possibility of failure or exposure" (p. 31). Involving students as a group rather than as individuals reduces this risk.

Simulation and role play have been a part of intercultural training for many years. Two of the best-known published simulations are *BaFá BaFá* and *Barnga*. In *BaFá BaFá* (Shirts, 1994), participants are divided into two groups and separated. They are given instructions on how to form two very different cultures. One is a relationship-oriented, high-context culture; the other culture has different values and is highly competitive. Then, in small groups, students exchange both visitors and observers. In between the visits they discuss what they have found with their own group. The resulting stereotyping, misperception, and misunderstanding form the basis for a final debriefing at the end of the simulation when everyone gathers together to discuss their experiences.

Barnga (Thiagarajan and Steinwachs, 1994) is a card game. Participants sit at different tables and learn how to play the game. They then move to new tables and continue playing.

The participants do not know that they have learned slightly different forms of the rules of the game, which leads to misunderstandings. Participants experience the shock of realizing that despite their good intentions and the many similarities among them, people interpret things in profoundly different ways, especially people from different cultures. Players learn that they must understand and reconcile these differences if they want to function effectively in a cross-cultural group.

Both of these simulations attempt to mimic some of the emotions and experiences that are found in cross-cultural communication. Teachers wishing to use simulations such as *BaFá BaFá* or *Barnga* first need to obtain copies of the games. They then need to be sure that they will have sufficient time to complete the simulation. Each one takes about three hours, and these need to be continuous hours.

Another method of recognizing miscommunication caused by cultural differences is through role play. Role play is another method of helping students experience the miscommunication that can be caused by cultural differences. Students take on the role of a visitor to a new culture or the role of a native of that culture and then act out a scene in which miscommunication occurs. Brown (2001, p. 183) notes that "role-play minimally involves (a) giving a role to one or more members of a group and (b) assigning an objective or purpose that participants must accomplish." Following the role play, offer a debriefing or a series of questions for discussion to help the participants understand what happened. Storti (1994) put together an entire book of short role plays and cross-cultural dialogues. These can be either read or acted out. Each one illustrates a different aspect of the challenges of cross-cultural communication.

What the teacher can do

Teachers can make sure role-play activities are successful by giving clear instructions and making sure students are equipped with the necessary language to complete their tasks. Role plays can be a useful way to break the ice with a new group of students at the beginning of a term.

Teachers can use Activity 6.6 to help students practice communication in cross-cultural settings. By working through the cultural challenges in the role play, students will be better prepared for similar encounters they may face in the future. Teachers can also use this activity as a model for role plays that they would like to develop focusing on specific cultural issues.

Activity 6.6	*A cultural miscommunication?*
Level	Intermediate – Advanced
Handout	Page 218
Tip	Engage students in role plays, dramas, and simulations.

Steps:

1. Make copies of the handout for Activity 6.6.
2. Divide the class into pairs. Have students select one of the role-play situations and write a dialogue for the characters and the situation.
3. If possible, have at least two pairs create and perform the same role play so that different versions are represented.
4. Have students agree on the part each will play. Give them enough time to write the dialogue and practice.
5. Have students perform their role plays in front of the class.
6. After each role play, ask the students how they felt in their roles and how they felt dealing with miscommunication. Ask the class to suggest appropriate ways to deal with the situations.

Teaching notes:

- *Alternative:* You may wish to assign students to write their role plays as homework rather than having them write during class time.
- *Alternative:* For a lower-level class, you can write the role plays for the students or provide them with a cued dialogue in which some of the lines are scripted and others are left blank for students to complete.
- If you think that your students may be self-conscious about performing their role plays in front of the class, have them sit at their seats instead.

 ## Get students involved through experiential learning and contact assignments.

If you teach in a situation where the target language is spoken in the local community, you have a wonderful opportunity. The world around you can become an extension of your classroom. This can have a very positive effect on students' levels of confidence if they are carefully prepared for the assignment. It also provides a useful way for students to interact with native speakers of English and to absorb aspects of culture as well as language.

What the research says

Experiential learning or contact assignments involve the creation of a task that your students then carry out in the community around your classroom. Common types of contact assignments include interviews of native speakers, opinion surveys, trips to various types of stores, or rides on public transportation. For example, a teacher might put together a scavenger hunt in which students need to visit several different stores in a shopping mall to collect clues to solve a puzzle.

One popular destination for contact assignments is a restaurant, an activity that Jerald and Clark (1983) call "Eating Out." A visit to a restaurant can introduce students to typical foods of the host culture, as well as to the appropriate behaviors in a restaurant setting. The teacher can preteach vocabulary and expressions used for ordering food or speaking with a server. If possible, the teacher should obtain an actual menu from the restaurant in advance and then have students practice role-playing the parts of customer and server.

Another type of contact assignment is for students to interview native speakers. This provides students with excellent language practice as well as introduces them to a **cultural informant.** Gaston (1984), Jerald and Clark (1983) and Tomalin and Stempleski (1993) suggest variations on interview tasks. The latter find it more practical to bring a native speaker to the classroom. The other authors prefer to send the students out to find their own interviewees. Alternately, the teacher can arrange for interviews with prescreened and willing participants. It is best to have a specific topic or list of questions and to give students opportunities to practice these before starting the project. Be sure that they have learned the necessary language to carry out the interview successfully.

What the teacher can do

Gaston (1984, p. 9) suggests that experiential techniques should be carefully presented. She emphasizes the importance of structuring the experience. First, the teacher presents the task and guidelines. Second, the students venture out to complete the task. Finally, the teacher conducts a debriefing session in which students are asked to reflect on their experience in order to synthesize learning.

Teachers can select activities with an eye toward what will be both helpful and accessible for students, their interests, and their language abilities. Students may be shy or nervous about exposing their linguistic inadequacies in front of strangers. Provide plenty of support and **scaffolding** leading up to the activity so that students have sufficient preparation and will be confident and comfortable in their contact with native speakers. It is often preferable to have students complete contact assignments in groups or pairs to provide a greater sense of security.

Teachers can use Activity 6.7 to get students involved in experiential learning and as a way to introduce them to the idea of contact assignments. Through such an activity, students can learn to develop an appreciation of the role that food and shopping play in the target culture. Teachers can create more contact activities modeled on this one.

Activity 6.7	*A trip to the supermarket*
Level	High-beginner – Advanced
Handout	Page 219
Tip	Get students involved through experiential learning and contact assignments.

Steps:
1. This activity exposes students to shopping, food, and community behaviors in the target culture. To prepare your students, teach them the language of food and shopping. Tell them that they will take a trip to a local food market.
2. Make copies of the handout for Activity 6.7. Pass them out to the class.
3. Give students time to discuss questions 1 through 4 in small groups; then review the answers with the class. Read questions 5 through 10 with the class.
4. Go on the trip.
5. At the end of the trip or when you meet again as a class, form small groups and ask them to answer questions 5 through 10 and then 11 through 14.
6. To finish the activity, discuss students' answers as a class.

Teaching notes:

- You may wish to notify a store manager in advance about your trip and its purpose.
- Be sure to inform students before the trip if they are to stay together as a group or if you want them to participate in pairs or small groups. Review any information or rules before you leave the classroom.

8 Introduce holidays, festivals, and religious traditions.

Holidays, festivals, and religious traditions provide rich opportunities for students to learn more about the culture they are studying. Whether the students are in an ESL or an EFL environment, they can still benefit from the study of these traditional cultural events. The source or reason for a holiday and the way that a culture chooses to celebrate it provide valuable insights into the way that a group of people think about themselves.

Particularly when students are newcomers to a country and culture, it can be very helpful for them to understand the origins and practices of the holidays in the new place, whether or not they choose to participate in and celebrate them. Knowing about holidays can also provide important schema or background information for future occasions and interactions.

Joe has vivid memories of his days as a volunteer tutor and of sitting down to a Thanksgiving dinner in the home of Vietnamese refugees to the United States. The dinner was a wonderful amalgam of American and Vietnamese cultures and cuisines. Ann always introduces her students to the holidays and traditions celebrated in the United States during the semester. She finds that often her international and immigrant students are unaware of the circumstances surrounding these holidays, so she shares details including the historical origins and the current traditions. As a follow-up, Ann asks her students if they celebrate similar days in their countries. The result is an interesting exchange of cultural information.

What the research says

A shift in focus from the traditional ways of teaching culture to new ways of looking at intercultural communication deemphasized the teaching of the three Fs: food, fiestas, and famous people. However, these elements of culture have a legitimate place in any language curriculum. Klebanow and Fischer (1985) offer a number of suggestions and resources for teaching about holidays in a U.S. context. They suggest approaching holidays by looking at them in two steps: first by examining current traditions and customs and then by looking into the background, origins, and traditions of the holiday. In addition to simplified readings, they suggest a list of appropriate gifts to give on holidays as well as traditional songs and readings of historical and political significance.

Kohls (1996, p. 63) suggests identifying the nation's heroes and heroines as a key part of "knowing thy host country." Kohls further suggests that it is helpful to learn about the predominant religion or religions, the sacred writings, and important religious observations, including ceremonies and forms of marriage celebrations.

What the teacher can do

Teachers can introduce their students to major holidays, such as, in the Western English-speaking world, Christmas, Easter, and national holidays. New Year is a cross-cultural holiday that most students celebrate. In autumn there are harvest or Thanksgiving festivals. Holidays such as Christmas come with an abundance of traditional stories, both sacred and secular, as well as music and gift-giving traditions. Seasonal music can add atmosphere as can special holiday food items you can share with students. Decorating the classroom appropriately and bringing in visual reminders of the holiday can add to the celebration.

Teachers can use Activity 6.8 to explore a holiday in greater depth and create an awareness of how a holiday fits into the new culture. The research component of the activity helps students develop their academic and presentation skills.

Activity 6.8	*Celebrating a holiday*
Level	Beginner – Advanced
Handout	None
Tip	Introduce holidays, festivals, and religious traditions.

Steps:

1. In advance of an upcoming holiday, bring in information to help students understand its origins, significance, and forms of celebration. You might include:
   - short readings or articles about the holiday
   - photographs of people celebrating
   - any appropriate realia or foods (candy canes, Easter eggs)
   - movies or television episodes that focus on the holiday
2. Assign students the readings for homework. Prepare comprehension questions to be sure that they understand the key aspects.

3. Ask students about their own experiences with the holiday: Is it celebrated only in the target culture, or are they familiar with a version from their first culture? How do the celebrations differ? Note that some cultures do not see January 1 as the new year and celebrate at different times (for example, the Chinese and Vietnamese lunar new year, the Tibetan new year Losar, the Iranian new year Nowruz, etc.).
4. You and your students may want to plan a classroom celebration with food, costumes, and ceremonies.

Teaching notes:

- *Alternative:* As a follow-up assignment, students can do a search online to find additional information on the holiday.
- *Alternative:* If all of your students speak the same first language, have them do the online research ahead of time; then have them present information about the holiday to the class.
- *Alternative:* Ask students to share the names of holidays from their respective countries and then to explain the significance of each and when it is celebrated. They can be asked to bring in pictures as well.
- *Alternative:* If you have students from different religious backgrounds in your class, you can support efforts to promote religious tolerance by having students of the same religion work together to find photos and content about their religious holidays. Then ask them to share their information with the class. Encourage students to ask each other questions about their religions in a peaceful, positive manner.

Conclusion

This chapter examined some traditional ways of teaching culture through literature, the visual arts, film, and music as well as through cultural artifacts. It offered suggestions on engaging students in conducting research about culture and about everyday life in the United States and other countries. It presented students with opportunities to utilize their problem-solving skills and surround themselves with stimuli to immerse them in the new culture.

Teachers were encouraged to help students be active participants in cultural learning through involvement in role plays, dramas, and simulations. Through experiential learning and contact assignments, students were exposed to culture outside of the classroom. Local holidays, festivals, and religious traditions were emphasized to students who have a kinesthetic learning style.

Check your understanding

After reading this chapter and using the activities with your class, check your comfort level with the following:

- ❑ I know how to use literature to help students explore culture.
- ❑ I use the arts to help my students explore culture.
- ❑ I surround students with stimuli from the target culture.
- ❑ I assign my students to present research on the target culture.
- ❑ I include problem-solving skills to help discover culture.
- ❑ I try to engage my students in role plays, dramas, and simulations about cultural issues.
- ❑ I involve students through experiential learning and contact assignments.
- ❑ I introduce students to holidays, festivals, and religious traditions.

CHAPTER 7

CULTURE AND EDUCATION

Consider these questions:

- What are the characteristics of a good student? a good teacher? Does this vary from culture to culture? How?
- Imagine you are a parent of young children and you move to a different country. What challenges might you face regarding your child's education in a new culture?
- What are some ways colleges and universities can support international students on their campuses?

Throughout this book we introduce ideas and concepts about intercultural communication in a wide variety of contexts. In this chapter, we focus on the implications of those concepts for educational settings. We look at issues relating to interaction in the classroom, larger issues of multiculturalism, and working effectively with parents.

Educational settings—and classrooms in particular—offer wonderful opportunities for learning and teaching about cultural differences. However, the classroom is also a place where cultural differences can cause difficulties. If you are teaching a class with students from different cultures, you may find yourself with a variety of challenging issues ranging from the appropriate behavior of students in the classroom to acceptable types of class participation to attitudes toward test-taking.

Joe, one of the authors, finds that when he tells people that he teaches English to speakers of other languages, the first question is always: "What other languages do you speak?" After he talks a bit about his high school knowledge of French and his rudimentary Chinese, he tries to explain that the important thing is not so much knowing how to speak many other languages but rather knowing enough about them that you can predict where students will have difficulty. In pronunciation, for instance, the informed teacher will anticipate that Korean students will be challenged by the difference between /p/ and /k/, whereas Japanese and Chinese students will struggle with /l/ and /r/ and Spanish speakers will have trouble with the difference between the front vowels in *ship* and *sheep*.

One semester Joe taught in an intensive English program and had students from fifteen different countries in the same classroom! Clearly it would take quite a linguist to master that many languages. But in the same way that teachers can learn what aspects of the structure of English will cause difficulty for students, they can also become familiar with the challenges that students from different cultures are most likely to face in the classroom in a new culture. Some of the tips in this chapter are more applicable to those living and working in English-speaking countries than to those teaching in an EFL context.

TIPS FOR EXPLORING CULTURE AND EDUCATION

The six tips in this chapter provide concrete suggestions about how teachers can address cultural differences in educational settings. With each tip, we provide a summary of the research and offer practical ideas for what teachers can do in the classroom. Some of the activities include photocopiable handouts. These are located in Appendix A on pages 220–224.

TIPS

1. Investigate how teacher and learner expectations vary across cultures.
2. Understand the characteristics of a multicultural classroom.
3. Address differences in communication styles in the classroom.
4. Connect with parents from different cultural backgrounds.
5. Help students adapt to life on a college or university campus.
6. Become familiar with different views of testing across cultures.

In this chapter we look at ways of enhancing intercultural communication in the language classroom between teachers and students from different cultures. For teachers working with lower grade levels, we discuss ways of improving communication with parents who come from different cultural backgrounds. For teachers working with college and university students, we offer suggestions for helping international students adapt to campus life. Finally, we examine the topic of test bias and different cultural attitudes toward testing.

 ## Investigate how teacher and learner expectations vary across cultures.

What does the behavior of a "good" teacher include? What about the behavior of a "good" student? By now you can probably anticipate our response: It depends on the perceptions of individuals within their own cultural context. It is this context that sets the tone for how teachers and students relate to and identify with each other in the classroom. It is helpful to look at the expectations that teachers have of students and vice-versa. These expectations change with a new cultural lens or perspective.

What the research says

Although we hope to promote intercultural communication and understanding, there are times when it is necessary for a guest in a new culture to adapt to the cultural norms of the host country. For instance, it is unlikely that a university will change its ways to accommodate cultural differences among visiting international students. For this reason, it is important for instructors working with international students to help them understand the cultural assumptions and norms of the educational setting in which they are studying. On the other hand, in an English as a foreign language (EFL) setting where a native English teacher is a guest, it is the task of the teacher to adapt to local customs. Differing cultural expectations may come into conflict over issues such as the definition of appropriate classroom behavior, the relative importance of the group versus that of the individual, and the behavior of the teacher inside and outside the classroom.

Teachers find that one of the first areas of intercultural disagreement is in the varying expectations surrounding appropriate classroom behavior. Snow (1996, p. 256) notes that some classroom behaviors considered improper in the teacher's home country may be considered normal or at least less serious in the host country. Issues such as the importance of class attendance, the appropriate level of effort for a student, and the expectations of silence by students vary from culture to culture. Snow further points out that nonverbal behavior such as burping may vary in its appropriacy in the classroom. He advises finding out how any unexpected behavior is normally dealt with in the culture before taking action.

 Voices from the Classroom

As a young teacher from the United States, I was feeling a bit insecure before my first English class in France. I was teaching a special test-preparation course to high school age students. As I entered the classroom for the first time, I was startled when the students all noisily stood up. I thought they must be trying to play a trick on me. "Sit down, immediately, all of you!" I shouted. "What is the meaning of all this?" After a long silence, finally, one lone voice explained, ". . . a sign of respect?" It turns out that in many European countries, students routinely stand when the teacher enters the room. I was accustomed to the United States, where students just remain seated, so I hadn't understood the meaning of their behavior.
— Judy L. Miller
American Language Program, Columbia University

Cultural expectations may also differ in the expected level of formality and informality in the classroom between teachers and students. As seen in Judy Miller's story, it is common for students in some countries to stand out of respect for teachers. Many U.S. and Canadian teachers would be surprised by this student behavior. Questions of formality and informality raise similar concerns: Is the teacher expected to be distant and somewhat authoritarian, or a friendly helper to students? Is it more appropriate for students to call teachers by their last name or by their first name?

A second source of potential conflict is that of teacher behavior outside the classroom, especially in EFL settings. There are particular pitfalls for Western teachers who teach in countries with a more conservative moral code. As Snow (1996, p. 255) notes, "Cultural sensitivity is also a key part of earning respect—it may well be in the inability to win the respect of a class that a teacher's decisions to flout local norms by doing such apparently irrelevant things as wearing shorts and sandals in class may come back to haunt him or her."

Another area that may require special attention in intercultural settings is different expectations of **academic integrity** or adherence to a code of moral values such as honesty in course work or in the general educational environment.

North American and other Western educational institutions place a high value on the independence of student work. At the same time, collaboration is encouraged. Often when to collaborate and when to work individually is confusing for international students. Of particular concern is the potential for miscommunication and differing intercultural views related to test-taking. This is discussed further in Tip 6 on page 165.

What the teacher can do

Teachers can help students grasp standards of academic honesty by reviewing the essential guidelines that apply to their institutions. The Eberly Center for Teaching Excellence and the Intercultural Communication Center of Carnegie Mellon University (2006, pp. 23–24) suggest the following guidelines:

• Explain the reasons for rules regarding academic integrity. Discuss the reasoning behind citation conventions and explain how correctly citing and building on the work of others can help students establish their credibility as scholars.
• Include definitions of cheating and **plagiarism**, which refers to wrongly using the words or ideas of another or using paraphrasing too similar to the original version without giving due credit to that person in the form of a citation. In your course syllabus, explain institutional policies and clarify what your own response will be to infractions.
• Explain what kinds of collaboration are and are not acceptable in your course.
• Explicitly teach documentation and paraphrasing conventions in the classroom.
• Ask to see assignments and papers at various stages of development (for example, ask for early project proposals, first drafts of papers, and so on). This not only discourages outright plagiarism but can help you discern problems students may have with paraphrasing, citing sources, and so on.
• Use software (for example, Turnitin) that checks for plagiarism. You can use this yourself or you can also have students use it to monitor their own work to see if they have inadvertently borrowed too much of an author's own language to constitute paraphrasing.

Teachers also need to be sensitive to their own roles, particularly if they are teaching in a culture other than their own. Novice teachers from Western backgrounds are often reluctant to take on the kind of authority that is expected of them in many other parts of the world. They may be more familiar with the model of teacher as facilitator and friend, and therefore uneasy at taking on the more authoritarian role of teacher that is expected in some cultures. As Snow (1996, p. 256) points out, "A reality of teaching is that you have a degree of power over students, if only because you determine grades, so the question is not one of

whether or not you should exercise power in class but of how well you exercise it."
Visiting teachers can ask their institutional colleagues about expectations of faculty
members in terms of the appropriate level of formality in the classroom, as well as
the expected levels of interactions with students outside the classroom.

Teachers can use Activity 7.1 to help students understand expectations for
classroom behavior, participation, and academic integrity. It is important for students
to have a clear idea of what constitutes acceptable and unacceptable behavior in an
academic setting.

Activity 7.1	*Classroom behavior*
Level	Beginning – Advanced
Handouts	None
Tip	Investigate how teacher and learner expectations vary across cultures.

Steps:

1. Before you begin this activity, consider carefully your educational context and
   your own ideas about teaching. These will inform the way in which you conduct
   this activity.
2. Based on your own experience and values, make a list of potentially problematic
   student behaviors.
3. Consider the behaviors written below and add to the list. Write down your policy
   and what you intend to do if students fail to adhere to your policy. A few ideas
   help you get started.

Potential Problems and Responses

1. A student consistently arrives late to class.

   *Students are expected to arrive in class on time. A student arriving late
   three times will be counted absent.*

2. A student presents written work that is clearly not his or her own.

   *Students must submit only their own work. Students presenting plagiarized
   work will be dismissed from class.*

3. A student doesn't pay attention during class.

4. A student talks to other students and distracts them instead of paying
   attention.

5. A student fails to complete homework assignments.

6. A student is consistently quiet and does not participate in spoken activities in the classroom.

7.

8.

4. During the first weeks of your course, present students with your written expectations for behavior. Indicate what you will do if students fail to follow the guidelines. Make it clear if any of these behaviors will have an impact on student grades for the course or will result in other disciplinary actions.

Teaching notes:

- *Alternative:* Negotiate expectations for classroom behavior with your students. Ask students what forms of behavior should be acceptable or unacceptable in class. Ask them for suggested consequences for each type of behavior. Write a list of policies based on your class discussion and hand it out to students or post it in your classroom.

2 Understand the characteristics of a multicultural classroom.

In addition to cultural characteristics, all students arrive in class with their own set of linguistic and **sociolinguistic behaviors**. If these behaviors are in harmony with the classroom culture, there should be no problems. However, if students bring linguistic and sociolinguistic behaviors that contrast with the host culture, communication difficulties—and difficulties with graded classroom performance—may result. For instance, the culture of U.S. education encourages students to be active and vocal participants in the classroom, whereas in many educational settings in Asia, students are expected to be more passive.

 Voices from the Classroom

I have taught in a variety of situations where I had students from Asian countries in the same class with students from Arab countries. In general, I found that most of my Arab students have been active members of class and very willing to speak. Most of my East Asian students have been much more reluctant to speak and generally prefer not to voice an opinion in front of the class.

When I was teaching in an intensive English program (IEP) in New York, East Asians made up the majority of the class. They were often unfriendly toward the one or two Arabs in the class and would not include them in activities. I got the impression that the Asians didn't like the way that the Arabs would speak up and comment in the class. They seemed to feel that Arabs were distracting me as the teacher and interrupting the flow of the class.

When I taught in an IEP in the Arabian Gulf, the majority of the students were Arabs, but we had several Chinese. In these classes, Arab students were often willing to share their views and would encourage the small number of Chinese students to participate. But somehow the two cultures did not really get along, and the Chinese students would usually not engage.

I now teach at an IEP in the Mid-Atlantic region of the United States. Here, there is a roughly even split between East Asians and Arabs. Relations are much stronger between the two groups here, with solid friendships being formed. Students cooperate well, with Arabs helping East Asians become more active in class and East Asians modeling disciplined study habits.

— T. Leo Schmitt
Intensive English Communication Program
Pennsylvania State University

What the research says

In U.S. classrooms, students are expected to "speak up for themselves," to compete for the floor in discussions, and to volunteer information. They should make eye contact when spoken to and are encouraged—at least in higher education—to state an opposing view when they disagree with a classmate or a professor. These expectations may come as a surprise to students whose first culture expects a "good" student to sit quietly and attentively, to speak only to answer questions, and to never challenge the authority of the instructor.

Often international students may be reluctant to speak up in the classroom. Reitzel (1986, p. 189) notes that "communication anxiety is a phenomenon which many foreign students experience" and suggests that its "debilitating effects" can be countered by effective classroom practice. To counter communication anxiety, Reitzel recommends teaching students about the concept of culture shock, as well as using modeling, oral interpretation, and drama techniques in the classroom. Reitzel also suggests introducing a communication anxiety hierarchy and teaching students how to work through it. The hierarchy places communication tasks on a continuum from less threatening to more threatening. To help students become less anxious, students first begin to attempt to communicate in less threatening situations, such as ordering food at a fast-food restaurant, and gradually increase the level of difficulty of speech events to something like a speech given in front of the class.

What the teacher can do

Teachers can help students participate more fully in class discussions by explicitly teaching conversational management strategies (Maurice 1986, p. 47).

These strategies were introduced as functions of the speech acts discussed in Chapter 2. The following are some sample conversation strategies with examples.

CONVERSATION STRATEGY	EXAMPLES
Interrupting	*Excuse me ...* *Hold it a minute ...*
Taking the floor	*If I could just jump in here ...* *I think ...*
Rephrasing	*In other words ...* *What you're saying is ...*
Generalizing	*On the whole ...* *All things considered ...*
Persuading	*Wouldn't you agree ...* *Don't you think ...*
Disagreeing	*Not necessarily ...* *On the contrary ...*
Piggy-backing	*And another thing ...* *And what's more ...*
Hesitating	*Well ...* *You know ...* *Let me see ...*
Redirecting	*By the way ...* *Anyway ...*
Ending a discussion	*Well, all I can say is ...*

The Eberly Center for Teaching Excellence and the Intercultural Communication Center of Carnegie Mellon University (2006, pp. 19–28) also offers ideas for enhancing communication in the classroom: Make expectations explicit, model the skills you want students to develop, present and represent the materials in multiple ways, provide ample opportunities for students to practice skills, improve performance over the course of the class, and provide varied opportunities for interaction.

Teachers can use Activity 7.2 to learn more about their students' linguistic and sociolinguistic characteristics and about their level of comfort when communicating in English. This activity encourages students to share their own strengths and weaknesses in communication to see how they differ from their classmates. (See next page.)

Activity 7.2	***Confidence in communication***
Level	High beginner – Advanced
Handouts	Pages 220 – 221
Tip	Understand the characteristics of a multicultural classroom.

Steps:

1. Make copies of the two handouts for Activity 7.2. Pass them out to the class.
2. Review the directions with students for Handout 7.2A. They should first circle their evaluation of their ability in their first language. They should then circle their ability in English.
3. Have students complete Handout 7.2B regarding their communication anxiety. Explain any vocabulary words as needed.
4. Discuss the results with the class as a whole and ask students how they rated themselves on the scales. Discuss the results of the questionnaire and the students' anxiety in communication.
5. Brainstorm with the class about ways to become more confident in speaking and using English. Share some of your own ideas.
6. Conclude the activity with words of encouragement. Many students start out feeling a lack of confidence. Regular practice, exposure to the language, and hard work will help them to improve their language ability as well as their level of confidence.

Teaching notes:

- If the members of the class speak different languages, then there is a chance to see whether a student's culture plays a significant role in this activity. Do students with similar language background have similar responses? Could this be due to culture, or do you think that their personalities are similar?
- *Alternative:* If your students are at a beginning level, you can simplify the questions. You can also designate areas of the classroom as the numbers on the scale and have students move to the number they choose.

3 | Address differences in communication styles in the classroom.

When students from different cultural backgrounds are taking the same course together, differences in their communication styles may lead to classroom management concerns for instructors. This is especially true when one group of students is more talkative than another group. For example, one summer Ann, one of the authors, was teaching a writing course. Her Spanish-speaking students were much more verbal in class than her Chinese- and Korean-speaking students. The Spanish speakers asked more questions, gave lengthier answers, and interacted more with each other and with the teacher than did the Asian students. Ann saw that the Asian students had fewer opportunities to share their ideas, so she implemented a round-robin format of going around the classroom one by one, thus giving everyone an opportunity for class participation.

What the research says

A common challenge for any classroom teacher is balancing speaking opportunities for talkative and less talkative students. Typically, talkative students are eager to answer questions and contribute to discussions, whereas quieter students prefer to sit back and take in what is going on around them. This classroom management issue can become more difficult to respond to when teachers are dealing with a mixed classroom of students from contrasting cultural backgrounds. In intensive English programs in English-speaking countries, it is not uncommon to have students from five to ten different countries in the same course. Generally speaking, students from Latin American countries and Middle Eastern countries are eager to participate in class. They are not inhibited by concerns about accuracy of grammar or pronunciation but are eager to join in and make their point. In contrast, students from many Asian countries are more reluctant to speak in class. Their culture has suggested that it is important to be correct when you speak. If they

can't be certain of getting things right, they prefer not to speak; they do not want to be in a position that might embarrass them or cause them to lose face.

When confronted with the talkative student, Snow (1996, p. 258) notes that "the problem is how to control the behavior without discouraging the student; the student who participates frequently is, after all, doing what we wish most students would." Snow recommends speaking to talkative students individually, praising their willingness to participate, and asking them to give other students a chance to talk. He notes that the goal is ultimately to get the other students to participate more, rather than to get the talkative student to speak less.

Another difficulty is how to encourage quieter students to participate more. Snow suggests that "it may be counterproductive to pressure students to participate unwillingly in all-class settings," which he refers to as "trial by questioning." However, says Snow, "One way in which you can encourage students who tend to speak very little is by providing speaking opportunities that are as nonthreatening as possible" (p. 259).

What the teacher can do

Teachers can help students with different communication styles by getting them to work together. This can be tricky. One challenge with students from different cultures is dividing them into small groups. Students often gravitate toward those from their own cultural groups and then speak in their first languages rather than practice English. Purgason (2007) offers several creative techniques for grouping students. Among her suggestions are:

- Create sets of cards and have students circulate in the room to find others whose cards match theirs. Student A's card might be a picture of a banana, while student B's card has the word written out. Student A's card might have a date or the name of a famous person on it. Student B's card would have the holiday that matched the date, or a list of the accomplishments of the famous person, and so on.
- Mount magazine pictures on cardboard and then cut them up. Students group themselves by describing the photo to others who have similar photos.
- Give students cards with color-coded dots according to their first language and then instruct them to find others with different colored dots.

Teachers can use Activity 7.3 to gently nudge less talkative students out of their quiet comfort zone by encouraging them to participate more actively in class discussions. Left to their own devices, it is likely that they will prefer to remain quiet, which could have an adverse effect on class participation and course grades when they reach mainstream classes.

Activity 7.3	*Conversation tokens*
Level	Beginning – Advanced
Handout	None
Tip	Address differences in communication styles in the classroom.

Steps:

1. Prepare a set of conversation tokens for your students. You can use plastic poker chips, checkers, tiddly-winks, or buttons. Alternatively, you can make them from cardboard. Make 5-10 tokens for each student in your class.
2. Talk with your students about turn-taking in conversations. Tell them that the goal of this activity is to have everyone participate more equally in class. Inform them about your institution's and culture's expectations of normal class participation.
3. Put your students into small groups; then distribute an equal number of tokens to each student.

4. Provide your students with a set of questions for discussion. Tell them that each time they speak they must put one of their conversation tokens in the middle of the table. When they run out of tokens, they may no longer contribute to the discussion.
5. After the students have talked, debrief them on their experience. Ask them about their thoughts on this experience of using the tokens to monitor turn-taking, as opposed to no monitoring.

Teaching notes:

- This activity can also be used in whole class discussions, with fewer tokens.
- Students who are normally extremely enthusiastic participants may have difficulty limiting their contributions even after their tokens have run out. Circulate around the room and remind them of the rules of the game.

 Connect with parents from different cultural backgrounds.

If you work in an English-speaking country and you teach in elementary, junior high, or high school settings, there's a good chance that you will also have interactions with the parents of your students. Immigrant and refugee parents may not have a clear understanding of the educational system in their new country. As a teacher of English to speakers of other languages (ESOL), you are in a unique position to help parents understand more about how schools work and to help them assist their children in succeeding at school. For example, many immigrant parents do not have the English language ability needed to understand the papers and forms that their children bring home for their signatures. Parents must rely on their children's translation and on the teacher's help in such situations. Teachers can help by bringing in an aide who speaks their first language and by arranging a meeting with the child and the parents to help them understand the expectations of the school and the teacher.

What the research says

Trumbull et al. (2001, pp. xviii–xix) propose a framework called Bridging Cultures. They suggest that home-school relationships and thus parent and family involvement can be improved by the following:

- understanding differences between home cultures and school culture
- enhancing cross-cultural communication
- organizing parent-teacher conferences that work
- using strategies that increase parent involvement in schooling
- supporting teachers to become researchers
- using ethnographic techniques to learn about home cultures

First, determine the parent's own ability to function in English. Many written communications from the school are sent home in an effort to inform parents about what is going on at school, but if these are written in English and the parents' abilities in English are minimal, then that communication is not going to take place. In addition, numerous forms, permission slips, and the like are required to be completed and returned by parents. Teachers in a California school district with high numbers of immigrant students from China, Vietnam, and Latin America reported that "written forms go home for one service or another, forms that are often hard to read, invasive, or potentially insulting—a 'communication' strategy that seems designed to increase the distance between home and school" (Dyson et al. 1997, p. 38).

Difficulty with English can also present a barrier to the amount of assistance that parents can offer their children. Trumbull et al. (2001, p. 39) point out that "parents limited in formal literacy skills or with little experience in schools cannot be assumed to be helping children with schoolwork in the way teachers expect . . . parents may not believe it is necessarily their role to help with academics because that is the domain of the professional teacher."

Trumbull et al. further observe that cultural conflicts can occur when the host culture, such as the United States, has a strongly individualistic orientation while the culture of the parents, such as those of Latin American students, has a strongly collectivistic orientation. Parents and teachers may have differing expectations of what constitutes appropriate behavior for students in the classroom.

What the teacher can do

School administrators and teachers can take the following steps to improve connections with parents (Banks 2001, pp. 409, 411–415).

STEPS TO INCREASE PARENT AND FAMILY INVOLVEMENT
• Establish two-way communication between the school and home.
• Enlist the support of other staff members and students.
• Enlist support from the community.
• Develop learning resources for parents to use at home.

WORKING WITH SINGLE-PARENT FAMILIES

- Provide flexible times for conferences such as early mornings, evening, and weekends.

- Provide baby-sitting service when activities are held at the school.

- Work out procedures for acknowledging and communicating with noncustodial parents.

- Use the parent's correct surname. Students will sometimes have different names from their parents. Different cultures may also have different protocols for the order of first and last names.

In addition, it may sometimes fall to the ESOL teacher to serve as a cultural bridge to mainstream teachers. Do your best to help your colleagues understand the special roles and needs of your students and advocate for them when necessary. In public schools in the United States, be mindful of any policies that regulate how English as a second language (ESL) teachers in schools need to connect with classroom teachers or with parents.

A common way of communicating how things are going at school is through the parent-teacher conference. In a typical conference, one or both of the student's parents come to the school to talk with the teacher about the progress of their child. The child may or may not be present for the discussion, depending on the policies of the school.

Teachers can use Activity 7.4 (adapted from Trumbull et al. 2001, pp. 55–73) to help set up an effective cross-cultural parent-teacher conference. Parents play an integral role in the education of their children. Clear and frequent communication between teacher and parents can contribute to better classroom performance and learning for students.

Activity 7.4	***The cross-cultural parent-teacher conference***
Level	Beginner – Advanced
Handout	None
Tip	Connect with parents from different cultural backgrounds.
Note	Most of the activities in this book are designed for teachers to use in the classroom with ESL/EFL students. This activity is designed for the teacher to use with the *parents* of school-age children. It may not be appropriate for all teachers in all circumstances.

Steps:

1. Arrange to meet with the parents of your students. In advance of the meeting, learn all you can about their home countries and cultures.
2. If you know that some parents do not speak English and you cannot speak their language, arrange for an interpreter.
3. Prepare written reports on the students' progress. Having a report in writing can reinforce what you have to say when you speak to the parents.
4. As you work with the parents, write the main points of your conversations. Then prepare a summary to send home with the parents.
5. Use the following guidelines when meeting with parents:
   - Foster a comfortable and respectful conversational tone
   - Use indirect comments and questions, rather than being too direct
   - Recognize that many cultures have collective rather than individual values
   - Communicate a message of caring
   - Cultivate empathy
   - Discuss your class in general and their child in particular
   - Ask about their support and understanding of the child's work
   - Together set goals for progress and commit them to writing
6. Be sure to answer any questions that parents may have.

Teaching notes:

- If possible, prepare a list of the agreed-upon goals to send home that day with parents.
- *Alternative:* Some teachers find group conferences with parents from the same cultural background successful. The presence of others increases the parents' confidence, and often issues that relate to one child are also relevant to others.
- *Alternative:* Some teachers also travel to the students' homes.

Help students adapt to life on a college or university campus.

There are a variety of ways to help international students encounter university life for the first time. For example, simply making students aware of the existence of an international student services office on campus or a guidance counselor who specializes in working with foreign students in the schools is a good start in making students feel comfortable and reassured that someone is there for them if and when they need help.

What the research says

Most institutions that have high numbers of international students or that house an ESL program hold an orientation session to help new students become familiar with their surroundings and with new ways of doing things. Barnes (1986) suggests that in such orientation programs, it isn't particularly helpful to simply bombard students with information. Although students in his study found campus tours to be useful in general, he found that the most important feature of a successful orientation program was opportunities for interaction between new students and continuing students, who served as experts. The second key feature, according to Barnes, is that the content of the orientation program should have immediate relevance for international students, such as pointing out where to go for food or other basic items and explaining how the registration process works. Finally, Barnes found that a useful orientation program helps students think about how they will structure their daily lives in the new institution.

Althen (1994) provides an extremely useful guide for foreigners, applicable to international students, in the United States. In it he shares insights into many of the topics discussed earlier in this book, such as nonverbal communication and social relationships. He suggests a number of places on a university campus that provide opportunities for communicative interaction such as the classroom, dormitory, cafeteria, library, playing fields, and health and counseling centers.

Althen (1994, p. 62) further notes several unwritten rules of behavior that international students should know about the United States and Canada:

- People should be able to walk or stand in public places without having physical contact with strangers.
- When they settle themselves in a public place, such as a study table in the library, Americans assume that they have staked out a territory that others should enter only by invitation.
- People in public places should keep the level of noise they make by talking or playing music below a certain level so as not to disturb others.
- In a situation where a number of people want attention or service from someone, people should line up and wait their turn. There is an understood first-come, first-served policy in place.

Althen goes on to catalog specific behaviors that are appropriate for roommates in dormitories, for neighbors, in offices, at work places, and when talking with doctors or health care personnel. For example, when dealing with roommates, he offers the following tips (p. 63):

- There is an imaginary line down the middle of the room, separating one person's territory from the other's.
- One person is not supposed to use the other's possessions without permission.
- One person should be quiet and dim the lights when the other wishes to sleep.
- Complaints or personal preferences should be expressed directly and openly.

What the teacher can do

Teachers can encourage school administrators and counselors to help international students get off to a good start at a university by providing a solid orientation program that helps students learn the basics about the culture of the university and how it is operated. Such an orientation can be carried out by members of the ESL teaching faculty or by an office for international students. It is essential, however, that the orientation include information about cultural differences and that it be carried out by professionals knowledgeable about cross-cultural communication and familiar with all of the cultures involved. Opportunities for interaction with current students should also be provided.

Teachers can make use of classroom activities such as role plays. These are ideal for sorting out the boundaries of appropriate behavior for roommates, classmates, and colleagues. It is also useful to include activities or offer some tips on appropriate and inappropriate behavior between the sexes. For instance, what sort of eye contact and other nonverbal communication might be considered offensive? Short readings about cultural communications issues are also helpful. Readings about university life can include topics such as appropriate personal hygiene, expectations about dress, and other social aspects of life in addition to more academic concerns.

Teachers can use Activity 7.5 to help students analyze an incident of cross-cultural miscommunication and discuss and understand why the miscommunication occurred. This activity introduces a tool known as the **culture assimilator**. Multiple-choice answers are provided and the students choose the answer they think is best. Explanations are given for each answer choice.

Activity 7.5	*Living with roommates*
Level	Intermediate – Advanced
Handouts	Pages 222 – 223
Tip	Help students adapt to life on a college or university campus.

Steps:

1. Make copies of the two handouts for Activity 7.5. Pass out Handout 7.5A to the class.
2. Form pairs. Instruct students to read the incident and then answer the question, "Why do you think Marco was confused by this situation?"
3. Direct each pair to decide together which answer they think is correct. Then pass out Handout 7.5B and have them read the explanations.
4. Discuss the answer and the situation with the class. Have any students had difficulties with roommates?

Teaching notes:

- You may wish to have students underline any new vocabulary words. You can then elicit the vocabulary and give definitions.
- If you have time, talk with students about the role of expectations in cultural encounters. What are their expected norms of sharing space with others?
- If students enjoyed the culture assimilator, challenge them to write one for themselves with their partner.

6 Become familiar with different views of testing across cultures.

In any educational setting, tests, quizzes, or examinations can cause stress to students. However, students from varying cultural backgrounds may arrive in class with different ideas about testing. In particular, students may have different concepts of what constitutes academic integrity, including plagiarism and cheating on tests. Also, there may be different ideas about grades from one culture to another. As a gatekeeper to further educational opportunities for students, teachers need to be sensitive to cultural differences to help students deal successfully with tests in the ESOL classroom.

What the research says

H.D. Brown (2004, p. 292) addresses the question of cultural expectations in grading. English-language learners from different cultures may arrive with their own philosophies of grading that stem from their educational background in their native countries. These views may be quite different from that of an English-speaking culture. Such cross-cultural differences may affect a teacher teaching in countries where the educational traditions are at odds with his or her own. Likewise, a teacher teaching at home must demonstrate an awareness of students' differing cultural expectations.

Studies have found differences in test performance across cultural, linguistic, or ethnic groups (e.g., Chen and Henning, 1985, Zeidner, 1986) pointing to the effect that test-taker characteristics have on test performance. At times, however, cultural bias in testing may be found. Cultural bias in testing can be minimized in several ways. According to Garcia and Pearson (1994), one way is by devising a variety of assessment forms and including different assessment types, such as oral or written, group or individual, subjective or objective, hands-on tasks or paper-and-pencil tests. Using testing and evaluation procedures that mirror diverse cultural content and values is also helpful.

The pressures of tests on students can create considerable anxiety, and this anxiety may in turn lead to inappropriate behavior. Snow (1996, p. 63) notes that

> Many problems with tests derive from the fact that they judge the work of several weeks or months on the basis of a single, brief performance. One undesirable result of this is considerable pressure and anxiety for students, often more than is productive. Because of the unusual amount of pressure that tests generate, they are especially likely to have negative backwash effects, one of which is that they tend to encourage students to engage in short intense periods of cramming rather than regular study and practice.

Another observation about testing across cultures is offered by the Eberly Center for Teaching Excellence and the Intercultural Communication Center of Carnegie Mellon University (2006, p. 14), which notes the following: In cultures where a strong emphasis is placed on interdependence, "helping" your classmates do well in a course may be more important than competing with them. In some other cultures, a certain amount of cheating on exams may be expected, particularly if students perceive those exams to be arbitrarily and impossibly difficult. In these contexts, actions that are considered cheating in the United States might be considered just good common sense and may perhaps not even be described as cheating. Students from cultures with different orientations toward cheating and plagiarism may not realize that the sanctions for such behaviors in the United States are harsh and are shocked to find themselves facing severe penalties for actions that were considered minor in their home cultures.

What the teacher can do

Teachers can help students deal with anxiety about tests and assessment by varying their test-giving procedures and policies. If the institution is amenable, one of the best ways to do this is through portfolio assessment. In portfolio assessment, students receive regular feedback on their work throughout the academic term. Their grade is an assessment of all of the work that they have done over the course of a term, rather than on one or two significant tests or exams. By having a number of assignments that count in lesser amounts, students are likely to be less anxious about any one particular assignment.

Teachers can help students by using sound practices in test administration. Clear and uniform policies make tests fairer for all. Coombe et al. (2007, p. 147) recommend the following:

- Require all students to keep their belongings at the front of the room or under their desks.
- Develop regular policies for latecomers and those who are absent, and stick to them.
- Number all test papers and require students to sign them out.
- With multiskills tests, begin with the listening so that part of the test begins and ends at the same time.
- Give students information about the remaining time.

Teachers can give multiple forms of the same test to prevent any cheating. Computers make it easy to move questions or multiple-choice answers around, thus making cheating more difficult. When possible, varying seating patterns can also be effective.

To help students from other cultures feel more at ease during testing, Coombe et al. (2007, p. 155) offer the following advice:

- Create a positive attitude towards testing.
- Be transparent.
- Follow proctoring instructions or instructions in the test manual to the letter.
- Prepare policies and procedures well in advance.

- Explain to students the distinction between teaching and testing.
- Refrain from helping students who are having difficulty.
- Note unexpected events that might interfere with assessments.
- Adopt a special-needs assessment policy.
- Inform students of the consequences of academic dishonesty.
- Minimize the opportunities for cheating and plagiarism.

 Voices from the Classroom

I was teaching an advanced ESL course in a U. S. university to a group of twenty-five students from China who were starting a specialized graduate program. The day I gave our first vocabulary quiz, I was surprised to see that several of the students attempted to look at one another's papers or talk during the quiz. Because of this incident, and other similar incidents in their other ESL courses, I developed a unit on academic integrity. As part of our discussion comparing policies in China and the United States, one insightful student offered a possible explanation for their behavior on the quiz.

In China, course grades are almost entirely based on final exams, whereas in the United States, course grades are calculated by including the scores of many assignments, quizzes, and exams. Chinese students take final exams seriously and generally conform to a strict honesty policy. However, because quizzes and other assignments don't have an impact on grades in China, they are viewed as much less important. It doesn't really matter if you study for them or do your own work. Therefore, what Chinese students need to learn is not how to have integrity but rather how grades are determined in the United States. That is, everything done in and for their courses contributes to their grades and requires their own effort.

— *Kristen E. Hiller*
University of Utah

Teachers can use Activity 7.6 to help students learn about appropriate test-taking behavior. Teachers may be reluctant to take on issues of plagiarism and cheating directly, but as cultural informants, it makes sense for teachers to help students understand the importance of issues of academic integrity and make sure that they understand them. This activity provides a structured way to do that.

Activity 7.6	*Appropriate test-taking behavior*
Level	High-beginner – Advanced
Handout	Page 224
Tip	Become familiar with different views of testing across cultures.

Steps:

1. Make copies of the handout for Activity 7.6. Pass them out to the class.
2. Go over the directions with students. Have them answer the questions on their own.
3. Discuss the answers with students. Be sure that they are aware of your institution's penalties for those who are found to have violated standards of academic integrity.

Teaching notes:

- You can adapt these questions as needed to suit your own institution's policies on academic integrity.
- An Internet search for "honor code" will provide numerous examples of campus policies on academic integrity if your institution does not have its own. You can perform such a search and bring examples to class or assign students to look for them.

Conclusion

In this chapter we have examined issues relating to culture in educational settings. We have looked at ways in which teacher and learner expectations may vary across cultures and have examined the effects of different linguistic and sociolinguistic backgrounds in the classroom. We considered how differences in communication style can be important and how they are viewed in different ways by teachers of school-age children attempting to connect with parents of different cultural backgrounds. We then looked at helping international students adapt to life on a university campus and finally at issues relating to culture and testing in the language classroom.

Check your understanding

After reading this chapter and using the activities with your class, check your comfort level with the following:

- ❑ I understand how teacher and learner expectations vary across cultures.
- ❑ I understand the characteristics of a multicultural classroom.
- ❑ I know how to address differences in communication styles in the classroom.
- ❑ I know how to connect with parents from different cultural backgrounds.
- ❑ I know how to help students adapt to life on a college or university campus.
- ❑ I am familiar with different views of testing across cultures.

CHAPTER 8

CULTURE AND SOCIAL RESPONSIBILITY

Consider these questions:

- How can language educators promote tolerance between people of different cultures?
- As teachers, should we share our values, beliefs, and hopes in the classroom? Or should we keep our opinions to ourselves?
- Would you feel comfortable using controversial issues to create discussions in the classroom? Why or why not?

Teaching culture in our English classrooms can mean different things to different teachers, but as we have already discussed in this book, it is important for teachers to create a safe place for students to share their opinions and cultural differences respectfully. Because English is the target—and therefore dominant—language in our classes, we need to be careful to avoid creating an atmosphere in our classrooms where the target culture is seen as better than some other culture. For example, when we teach about a part of the culture or tradition of an English-speaking country, such as the Independence Day holiday of July fourth in the United States, we can expand the focus to include students describing their own national day and national heroes.

As teachers, however, we are faced with another issue, which Brown (2007) has identified as one of a series of moral dilemmas. This has to do with our identities in the classroom and our true purpose as language-teaching professionals.

> Somewhere in those deep recesses of your mind and emotion you are guided by a sense of mission, of purpose, and of dedication to a profession in which you believe you can make a difference. Your sense of social responsibility directs you to be an agent for change. You're driven by convictions about what this world should look like, how its people should behave, how its governments should control that behavior, and how its inhabitants should be partners in the stewardship of the planet. (Brown 2007b, p. 512)

Somewhere in our hearts we desire more for our students than simply that they learn to distinguish between the simple present and the present progressive. We want our teaching to make a difference in our students' lives. As teachers, should we hold back our own values, beliefs, and hopes? We rather think that these can serve as strengths to help our students become responsible citizens of the world.

Ann, one of the authors, teaches an ESL advanced writing class. She involves students in prewriting discussions about controversial ideas. The topic of social responsibility has emerged as an interesting one for her students. Writing about various issues encourages them to take a stand and present their viewpoint on whether or not social responsibility should be encouraged. Their essays have shown that students have varying degrees of optimism about the role that social responsibility plays in their lives and in the lives of others.

TIPS FOR EXPLORING CULTURE AND SOCIAL RESPONSIBILITY

The six tips in this chapter offer specific suggestions about how teachers can explore culture in connection with social responsibility. The tips encourage you as the teacher to do more than simply introduce language and talk about cultural differences. They challenge you to work with your students to include social responsibility in their lives and help make the world a better place. With each tip we provide a summary of the research related to the tip and offer practical ideas for what teachers can do in the classroom. Some of the activities include photocopiable handouts. These are located in Appendix A on pages 225–227.

TIPS

1. Include critical pedagogy in your approach to teaching culture.
2. Incorporate principles of multicultural education in your classroom.
3. Create respect for diversity and ethnic differences in the classroom.
4. Explore issues of power balance and the roles of teacher and learners.
5. Manage controversial issues in the classroom with respect.
6. Introduce the concepts of social responsibility, ethics, and human rights.

In this chapter we tap into the heart of culture as it relates to social responsibility. We look at the principles of critical pedagogy and multicultural education. We consider how to create respect for diversity and ethnic differences in the classroom and explore issues of power balance and the roles of teacher and learners. We discuss how to manage controversial issues in the classroom with respect and how to introduce our students to concepts of social responsibility, ethics, and human rights. The activities presented help students and teachers become more aware of key issues of social responsibility. Our goal is to sensitize our students to ethical issues and help them realize their own roles in promoting harmony between cultures. Some of these tips may be more applicable to teachers in English-speaking countries than to those working in an EFL context.

1 Include critical pedagogy in your approach to teaching culture.

A fairly recent development in the history of education has been the notion of **critical pedagogy**. The ideas and perspectives of critical pedagogy are most often attributed to the Brazilian educator Paulo Freire, whose book *Pedagogy of the Oppressed* (1970) forms an essential introduction to the topic. In this text, Freire leads teachers to a self-examination of their motives and their methods of teaching. He points out the extent to which teachers and the dominant culture impose their ideas on students and encourages teachers to create learning spaces in which information is exchanged between students and teacher, rather than simply having the teacher pour knowledge into the students.

What the research says

Much has been written on critical pedagogy and theory in general, but its application to the teaching of ESL and culture is comparatively recent. Pennycook (1999) addresses three areas of critical pedagogy in teaching English to students of other languages (TESOL): critical domains, transformative pedagogy, and a self-reflexive stance on critical theory.

Pennycook suggests that some of the key elements to examine are power and inequality, especially the relationships between men and women and between native and nonnative speakers. He also notes that sexual orientation and the way it is understood in different ethnic and cultural backgrounds are interesting subjects for inquiry. He highlights the issue of power, in particular the power of the English language to subjugate others, and cautions against attempting to divorce teaching from a political stance—a central idea of critical pedagogy.

Pennycook proposes that the power of critical teaching is to transform the individual—both teacher and student. An initial step toward this should be to create an awareness, not only of the self but also of language and especially of issues that require change. A next step is one of transformative pedagogy— putting the curriculum in the hands of the students. To truly reach transformation requires "an engagement

with people's investment in particular discourses, that is, in questions of desire" (Pennycook 1999, p. 340.) This "leads to what might be called a *pedagogy of engagement*: an approach to TESOL that sees such issues as gender, race, class, sexuality, and postcolonialism as so fundamental to identity and language that they need to form the basis of curricular organization and pedagogy" (p. 340).

Finally, Pennycook states that critical teachers must always be willing to challenge even their own ideas and must take care not to let their own personal beliefs become stagnant. He even recommends that teachers be skeptical of their own stances toward critical theory.

What the teacher can do

Teachers can help students implement critical pedagogy into their classrooms by taking the following steps. Wink (2005, p. 123) quotes Freire as to how teachers to "do" critical pedagogy.

How to "do" critical pedagogy
- Name the problem or difficulty
- Reflect critically on the problem or difficulty
- Act to solve the problem or difficulty

Wink notes (p. 125) that when teachers and learners make use of the following principles, they are empowered to solve problems.

Principles of problem posing
Teachers and learners . . .
- Trust each other
- Believe that their involvement will matter
- Understand resistance and institutional barriers to change
- Are aware of their own power and knowledge

She further notes that teachers have a key role in problem posing. They can be most successful when they create a safe place for it to happen, are willing to ask challenging questions that make students think, and assist students with codification, which is a Freirean method of using a visual representation of one thing for another (p. 125).

Teachers can use Activity 8.1 (adapted from Wink 2005; used by permission) to help students by asking them what they think about the way the class is run. This allows teachers to give learners more power by offering students an opportunity for input and the chance to voice their opinions about the course.

Activity 8.1	*Four corners*
Level	Beginner – Advanced
Handout	None
Tip	Include critical pedagogy in your approach to teaching culture.

Steps:
1. Tape a large piece of paper to the wall in each of the four corners of the room.
2. Write each question on one of the pieces of paper.
   - What has been the most valuable or most important thing that you have learned in this course so far?
   - What have we discussed that you do not really understand?
   - What can the students do to make this a better class?
   - What can the teacher do to make this a better class?
3. Divide the class into four groups. Give each group a different colored marker. They should use only this color when writing their answers.
4. Tell students that each group will have a chance to answer each question by moving in a circle around the room. They will have 4-5 minutes for each question.
5. Ask each group to stand in front of a piece of paper, discuss the question, and write down some of their ideas. After approximately five minutes, ask groups to move clockwise to the next piece of paper and question. Repeat this until each group has answered all of the questions.

(continued on next page)

6. To finish the activity, review each piece of paper with the class. Ask students to clarify their ideas and give examples, as well as edit any information that is not clear.

Teaching notes:
- You can either have students agree on their answer or have different students in the group share their own ideas.

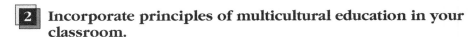 **Incorporate principles of multicultural education in your classroom.**

For many North American **mainstream teachers**, the idea of teaching culture brings to mind the concept of **multicultural education**. Multicultural education should not be confused with the concept of cross-cultural or intercultural education that we have been discussing in this book. Rather, it looks at education from the point of view of those individuals who are different from the mainstream and asks how they can be better included in the educational process.

What the research says

The multicultural education theorist Sonia Nieto (2000) connects multicultural education to critical pedagogy. Her definition of multicultural education is comprised of seven characteristics:

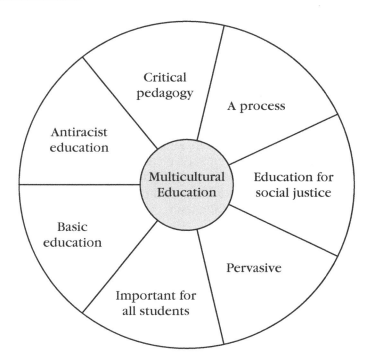

She identifies critical pedagogy as the "underlying philosophy" of multicultural education. Gay (1995) sees critical pedagogy and multicultural education as "mirror images" of each other that work together.

Banks and Banks (2001, p. 3) state that multicultural education can be thought of as an idea or concept, an education reform movement, and a process. As an idea or concept, the movement toward multicultural education has been prompted by tension among diverse groups and by extensive immigration movements in many countries around the world. The civil rights movement in the United States, the movement for women's rights, and the desire of other marginalized groups to reach equality have all moved this concept forward.

As an educational reform movement, one of the aims of multicultural education is that all social class, gender, racial, language, and cultural groups have an equal opportunity to learn. Such a goal requires changes in the school or educational environment and not only curricular changes. For that reason, a major goal is to improve academic achievement for all students. Finally, multicultural education is a process or an ideal because its goals will never be fully and completely realized (Banks and Banks 2001, p. 4).

Part of the challenge of defining and designing multicultural education involves setting out the values of the core culture. In the United States, the core values include the following:

VALUES OF THE CORE CULTURE IN THE UNITED STATES[1]		
The importance of individual freedom and self reliance	Equality of opportunity and competition	The importance of material wealth and hard work
A strong sense of individualism as opposed to group orientation	The idea of expansionism and manifest destiny	The importance of privacy
Belief in the future, change, and the inevitability of progress	A belief in the general goodness of humanity	Directness and assertiveness
An orientation to action	Informality	Cooperation and fair play
Pragmatism	The distinction between work and play	The need to be liked

[1] From Althen (1988); Banks and Banks (2001); Kearney et al. (2005); Stewart and Bennett (1991).

In addition to the core culture and its values, there are subcultures consisting of a number of different groups. Although these groups may hold similar values to the core culture, they have their own values as well. It is particularly these values of the subculture that multicultural education seeks to address. Banks and Banks

(2001, p. 14) note that a number of groups may be thought of in terms of multicultural education. For that matter, it is quite possible for a person to belong to more than one of these groups at the same time, something previously discussed in Chapter 4 on culture and identity. Possible types of group membership in subcultures are

- Nationality
- Race/ethnicity
- Religion
- Exceptionality/nonexceptionality[1]
- Social class
- Gender
- Sexual orientation

Several of these categories interact with each other. The teacher must "remember that individual students are members of several of these groups at the same time" (Banks and Banks 2001, p. 15). Any one student, for instance, belongs to several subgroups, including race, class, and gender.

What the teacher can do

Teachers can help implement multicultural education in their schools and classrooms by addressing several dimensions (Banks and Banks 2001, p. 23).

DIMENSION	APPLICATION
Content integration	Teachers use examples and content from a variety of cultures in their teaching.
Knowledge construction	Teachers become aware of how implicit cultural assumptions, frames of reference, perspectives, and biases within a discipline influence the ways that knowledge is constructed.
Prejudice reduction	Teachers make use of teaching methods and materials to modify students' racial attitudes and consequential behaviors.
An equity pedagogy	Teachers modify their teaching in ways that facilitate the academic achievement of students from diverse racial, cultural, gender, and social-class groups.
An empowering school culture	Teachers examine grouping and labeling practices, sports participation, disproportionality in achievement, and interaction of staff and students across ethnic and racial lines to create a school culture that empowers students from diverse racial, ethnic, and gender groups.

---

[1] *Exceptionality* refers to the following broad characteristics of learners: developmental disabilities; learning disabilities; speech communication disorders; emotional and behavioral disorders; sensory, physical, and health impairments; and giftedness. *Nonexceptionality* is the characteristic of not possessing any of the characteristics mentioned above (Bennett 2003, p. 226).

Another way that teachers can help both themselves and their students is by identifying the groups and subgroups to which their students belong. Once students are aware of the groups to which they belong, they can develop a sense of their own identities and how membership in those groups plays a role in the make-up of who they are.

Teachers can use Activity 8.2 to help students share their identities. This activity can also provide the teacher with useful information about student subgroups and identity to help inform the teacher's approach to multicultural education in the classroom.

Activity 8.2	*Sharing identities*
Level	Beginning – Advanced
Handout	Page 225
Tip	Incorporate principles of multicultural education in your classroom.

Steps:
1. Make copies of the handout for Activity 8.2. Pass them out to the class.
2. Have students write their answers. Then put students in pairs and have them discuss their answers.
3. After students have shared their answers, write the following questions on the board. Then discuss them as a class:
   a. How do you define your identity?
   b. What parts of your identity are most important to you?
   c. What parts of your identity have you chosen yourself? What parts do you have no control over?
   d. How does your identity reflect your culture?

Teaching notes:
- Be aware that this exercise requires self-disclosure on the part of students and that some students may not be completely comfortable with it. Be sure to stress to students that they do not need to answer any questions that they don't want to. Also, take care to group students in pairs where they will feel comfortable sharing their answers.

3 Create respect for diversity and ethnic differences in the classroom.

One of the most important goals of multicultural education is to end discrimination by valuing diversity and ethnic differences. The term *diversity* refers to differences between people. In the United States this term is used especially to mean racial and ethnic differences. Other types of diversity may include differences in gender, sexual orientation, or religious background. Some institutions, such as colleges and universities, celebrate that they have a diverse student population. For example, when Joe moved to the state of Vermont, he found that Middlebury College was proud of the diversity of its student body. Seventy percent of the student body was white, with about 15 percent African American, Asian, or Hispanic American, and about 15 percent international students. In comparison, Joe had previously worked at California State University at Los Angeles, where white students made up less than 15 percent of the student population and 60 percent of the students were Hispanic or Asian. At that school, diversity was taken for granted and barely mentioned.

People are concerned about diversity because historically, in most countries, the ethnic or racial majority tends to dominate in many fields, including education. It is one of our goals as teachers to ensure that there is equal respect for people of all backgrounds in our classrooms. However, there are significant barriers to this goal.

What the research says

One challenge to harmony in the language classroom is ethnocentrism. **Ethnocentrism** is the tendency of a culture to view its own assumptions, values, and beliefs as normal and those of another culture as odd, different, or wrong. Indeed, "most peoples in the world regard their own culture as superior" (Nanda and Warms 1996, p. 7). Even if we acknowledge this reality and make it explicit for our students, we may still find that some of them maintain stereotypical views of other students in the classroom. Teachers need strategies in the classroom to encourage students to value differences in culture, race, and ethnicity. Bennett (2003, p. 370) points out:

- It is worthwhile for educators to focus on the reduction of racial/ethnic prejudice and discrimination even though powerful sectors of the society and the world do not presently value this goal.
- It is appropriate for schools to teach certain humanistic and democratic values, such as the negative effects of racism and sexism.
- A reduction of racial/ethnic prejudice and discrimination is possible through appropriate educational experiences.

Ethnocentrism taken to extremes can result in **prejudice**, which can have an even more serious impact on classroom dynamics and student learning.

> Prejudice refers to the emotional component of people's reactions to other groups. It involves not only a set of beliefs about others, which are captured in stereotypes, but it is also a deeply felt set of feelings about what is good and bad, right and wrong, moral and immoral, and so forth. (Brislin 2000, p. 209)

Unspoken prejudices can exist in the language classroom, particularly when the class is composed of students from a variety of cultures. If this prejudice is not addressed, it can lead to conflicts between students and a disruption of instruction. Within society, there are several levels of the expression of prejudice (Samovar and Porter 2004, p. 290):

EXPRESSIONS OF PREJUDICE

LEVEL OF EXPRESSION	EXAMPLES
Talking about a member of the target group in negative and stereotypical terms	"Those people just can't be trusted."
Avoiding or withdrawing from contact with the disliked group	Not attending an event because you know that someone from the group will be there
Discrimination: excluding members of the group from certain types of employment, housing, educational opportunities, or other type of social institution	Refusing a job, a house, etc. to someone because of the group that he or she belongs to
Physical attacks	Attacking minorities or their property physically

On a similar plane is **cultural bias.** Cultural bias is the effect of social categorizing, or making sense of the world by imposing meaning and structure on it; stereotyping, or generalizing about a group of people; showing negative attitudes toward others based on incorrect stereotypes; or stirring up emotional reactions by categorizing people whose physical or other ethnic traits make them appear culturally different from the majority group (Lustig and Koester, 2003). In the realm of education, cultural bias can be seen in the creation of tests that assume that everyone who takes the test shares the same background knowledge.

"Students are exposed to a wide variety and quality of content about ethnic and cultural diversity" according to Gay (2000, p. 145). Whether the images conveyed are positive or negative, they affect students both in and out of the classroom. When a student's ethnic group is portrayed negatively or when racially biased instructional materials are used, it can affect the student's self-value and also have a negative impact on academic performance. To change this, curriculum content and materials need to be accurate and inclusive when representing cultural diversity. This component is essential for culturally responsive teaching and for improving student achievement.

What the teacher can do

Teachers can help students learn to value diversity and ethnic differences by creating a real sense of community in the classroom. Samovar and Porter (2004, p. 251) quote Palmer (1993) who says that "real learning does not happen until students are brought into a relationship with the teacher, and with each other, and with the subject" (p. 5). Such relationships may be forged by adhering to the six characteristics of a "true community" offered by Orbe (1995, pp. 3–5).

- The community must be inclusive.
- The members of the community must have a strong sense of commitment.
- The community must recognize the necessity of consensus.
- Members of a community must have an awareness of both themselves and others.
- Members of the community must feel secure enough to be vulnerable to one another.
- The community must be able to resolve differences.

Teachers can use Activity 8.3 to help build community in their classrooms. The activity builds students' awareness of their own actions and behaviors and helps them connect this awareness to how they treat other people.

Activity 8.3	*Respecting others*
Level	Intermediate – Advanced
Handout	Page 226
Tip	Create respect for diversity and ethnic differences in the classroom.

Steps:
1. Make copies of the handout for Activity 8.3. Pass them out to the class.
2. The purpose of this activity is to help students think about how they work together with others—especially those who are different from themselves.
3. Tell students that you will be having a discussion about tolerance and prejudice. Write these words on the board and define them: tolerance, the willingness to

accept others and their behaviors even if you do not like them; prejudice, an unfair feeling of dislike against someone who is different from you.

4. Discuss the questions with the class. See if students can provide examples of their behavior.

5. Lead students in a discussion about differences and responding to those who are different from us. Try to elicit from students ways in which we all might be more sensitive, tolerant, and helpful to others.

Teaching notes:

- You may prefer to have students complete the handout on their own for homework.

- A good entry into this topic is to describe Jane Elliot's famous brown eyes/ blue eyes experiment. Elliot divided students in her third-grade class into two groups according to their eye color. Then she began to treat one group favorably and discriminate against the other. A documentary about the impact of this experiment can be viewed at http://www.pbs.org/wgbh/pages/frontline/shows/divided/.

 Explore issues of power balance and the roles of teacher and learners.

One of the key questions raised by critical pedagogy is the issue of power and especially power in the classroom. Because teachers set the agenda, choose the curriculum, lead the class instruction, create the tests, and grade the students, clearly they have the upper hand in terms of power in the classroom. For many teachers, this is fine; however, to be socially responsible teachers, we need to explore this power balance and consider what would happen if we were to find ways of sharing this power with our students. What might be the impact of such a change?

What the research says

Cummins (1996, p. 1) notes that "human relationships are at the heart of schooling." If Cummins is correct, Wink (2005, p. 115) suggests that the negotiation of identity in the classroom is essential to the sense of self of students and teachers alike. Wink further comments on her own experiences of Cummins's concept of collaborative and coercive relations of power. In collaborative power relationships, power is shared, but in coercive power relations, power is concentrated at the top. Wink notes that when teaching in a coercive environment, she is less productive and more likely to be angry about the limited amount of work that she produces. However, in an environment of collaborative relations of power, she finds herself more productive. "The trick for teachers is to have the courage to negotiate their own power even when they are within the context of coercive relations of power"

(Wink 2005, p. 115). So we can see that power relations may be significant for us in our roles as teachers in the classroom, where we are the ones holding the power, and also significant for us in our roles as employees in our workplaces, where we may not be the ones holding the power.

Freire (1970) describes the one-sidedness of many educational systems as "the banking concept of education." As he puts it, "Education thus becomes an act of depositing, in which the students are the depositories and the teacher is the depositor. Instead of communicating, the teacher issues communiqués and makes deposits which the students patiently receive, memorize, and repeat" (p. 58). Freire (p. 59) describes what happens in the banking method of education:

- The teacher teaches and the students are taught.
- The teacher knows everything and the students know nothing.
- The teacher thinks and the students are thought about.
- The teacher talks and the students listen—meekly.
- The teacher disciplines and the students are disciplined.
- The teacher chooses and enforces his choice and the students comply.

In contrast to the banking concept of education, Freire proposes "problem-posing education," in which teacher and student jointly seek answers and power is shared collaboratively in the classroom. It is through dialogue, Freire suggests, that true knowledge is found. He further recommends "thematic investigation," whereby investigators portray their results through "codification" or translating them into visual terms.

What the teacher can do

Teachers can explore their own feelings about balancing power by using the classroom as a laboratory of power relations. Students consciously or unconsciously experience how power functions. Teachers can also reflect on their own role as a powerful figure in the classroom and in the lives of their students. Some teachers may focus on their role as the teacher who is in charge, whereas others may focus on the role of the students as followers of the teacher's delegated classroom instructions and classroom management. Perhaps you can even try to take on both of these roles at once.

Teachers can use Activity 8.4 to help put this balance of power in perspective and to gradually share power with students in the classroom. In this way, students may not only be more accepting of the rules of the classroom, but also of the way in which power is distributed.

Activity 8.4	*Balancing power in the classroom*
Level	Intermediate – Advanced
Handout	None
Tip	Explore issues of power balance and the roles of teacher and learners.

Steps:

Part 1

1. Think about the balance of power in your classroom. Write a list of decisions you make and actions you take when managing the class. These might include common administrative tasks, choices about the syllabus, the correction of papers, or the delegation of turns when speaking. Then write a list of decisions students make and actions they take during class time.

2. Think about which decisions and actions could be shared with or delegated to students.

Part 2

1. Gradually begin experimenting with letting your students take on some of these roles.

2. Share your ideas with your students and see what tasks they are willing to take on.

3. Periodically reflect on the effect of having students take on more roles in the classroom. What is the effect on you? on the students?

Teaching notes:

- Some tasks that students might take on could include:
  - taking attendance or roll
  - writing notes or comments on the board
  - leading discussions
  - correcting each other's written work
  - reading a dictation
  - collaborating on the grading process
  - establishing ground rules for classroom behavior
  - helping to choose the topics for the course syllabus
  - deciding when the next test should be and what it should cover
- You may wish to keep a reflective journal to note your own reaction as well as student reactions to these changes. How do you feel about giving up this power? Does it feel scary? liberating? What is the trade-off? How did your students respond?

5 **Manage controversial issues in the classroom with respect.**

Depending on our own personalities and the context in which we teach, we may shy away from controversial issues in the classroom. As responsible teachers, it is important for us to consider the institution where we teach, as well as the age and level of maturity of our students. Obviously there are topics that may not be appropriate or productive for discussion with your students. However, "complex issues . . . can become the focus of intrinsically motivating content-based language learning" (Brown 2007b, p. 515). Controversial topics on which students are likely to have diverse opinions can be a catalyst for language and culture learning and provide valuable opportunities for students to learn more about the opinions of others and broaden their ideas about the world.

What the research says

Published textbooks for students of English as a second language generally avoid controversial materials. Publishers hope to sell the largest possible number of textbooks, and they know from experience that some subjects are taboo. Major markets—entire countries, even—may spurn a book that addresses certain subjects. Textbook authors are generally discouraged from raising such issues as religion, politics, sexuality, race, abortion, and discrimination. Publishers hoping to sell books in some parts of the world must avoid textbook characters that drink alcohol and photographs of people baring too much skin.

There are a few rare exceptions to these policies. Books that are clearly intended for the higher education market in the United States may be able to raise more controversial topics. One book that does so is *In Our Own Words* by Mlynarczyk and Haber (2005). This text, intended for students at community colleges, includes examples of student writing that address issues such as interracial marriage and sample essays on the subject of gay marriage and parenting. Another is Shulman's *Cultures in Contrast* (1998), which addresses controversial issues such as cheating, plagiarism, sexual harassment, sexual orientation, drug abuse, racism, and discrimination based on religious beliefs. Folse's *Discussion Starters* (1996) also provides controversial topics for discussion.

Brown (2007b, p. 515) believes that "teachers are responsible for creating an atmosphere of respect for each other's opinions, beliefs, and ethnic/cultural diversity." In other words, if teachers are going to introduce controversial topics in the classroom, they need to be sure that the voice of the minority is heard and respected and that students are encouraged to interact with each other and with the ideas presented in a respectful way.

What the teacher can do

Teachers can deal respectfully with controversial issues in a number of ways. First, teachers should select topics for discussion with care, considering their own students and what will work best with them. Second, teachers can introduce controversial topics in an even-handed manner so that any student with strong views will not be offended. Third, teachers can ensure that everyone has an equal voice in the discussion and can monitor turn-taking in the classroom to be certain that alternative points of view are presented. Finally, teachers need to be able to sense when it is time to end the discussion and move on, either because things are becoming too heated or because the topic has been exhausted.

Discussion of controversial topics will be more free-flowing if teachers can be even-handed in their management of the discussion, rather than revealing their own biases. Approaching these topics from a neutral perspective gives students permission to state their own point of view freely. Of course, teachers do reveal their own point of view, to some extent, in the selection of topics. Teachers may also wish to state their own views, but this is better done after students have had the opportunity to share their ideas.

Teachers can use Activity 8.5 to introduce students to words and expressions to utilize when they disagree with one another. The activity encourages students to engage each other in a controversial debate while treating each other's ideas with respect.

Activity 8.5	*Controversial debate*
Level	Intermediate – Advanced
Handout	Page 227
Tip	Manage controversial issues in the classroom with respect.

Steps:

1. Make copies of the handout for Activity 8.5. Pass them out to the class.
2. Choose a controversial topic for debate that is suitable for your students and institutional context. You might find a controversial topic in the news or develop a question in one of the following areas: faith or religion, politics, sexuality, gender roles or differences, war and conflict, abortion and respect for life. An ideal topic is one to which your class has already had some preliminary exposure.
3. Frame the debate by writing down a key question and then some follow-up questions. For example:

   Do you believe that suicide should be a crime? If a person is very ill or is unhappy in life, shouldn't he or she be permitted to end it? Why do you think so?

4. Before beginning the exercise, teach your students the expressions and phrases on the handout for Activity 8.5. You may have students repeat the phrases after you or read them to each other as partners.

(continued on next page)

5. Write the topic on the board. Ask students what they know about the topic. Teach students any vocabulary that might be useful in the discussion.

6. Break students into small teams. Tell each team if they are debating for or against an issue. Give them twenty minutes to discuss the topic and frame their arguments. While they are talking, circulate around the class. Help with any linguistic needs and other issues that may come up.

7. Group two opposing teams together. Give each team five minutes to argue their point of view.

8. Bring the class back together for a debriefing and general discussion of the topic.

Teaching notes:

- The careful selection of the particular topic for debate is essential. The teacher must choose the topic with an awareness of his or her students and the institutional context.
- This activity may be extended in the classroom by providing students with readings of alternate points of view about a topic.
- Debates can become heated. Act quickly to defuse any situations in which students seem not to be treating the opinions of others with respect.
- You can follow up this activity with a writing assignment, particularly one that focuses on persuasive argumentation.

6   Introduce the concepts of social responsibility, ethics, and human rights.

As suggested in the introduction to this chapter, we hope that, as teachers, we do more than just help our students with verb tenses and the interpretation of nonverbal behavior. We hope that by helping students learn a language and function cross-culturally, we are ultimately improving communication and thus relationships between people from different national, ethnic, and cultural groups. Can we do more in the classroom? Perhaps we can.

 Voices from the Classroom

I was teaching advanced English in a private language school in Jamaica. The school had students from a number of different countries in the region. On the first day of school, Jean, a student from Haiti, recognized a former Haitian soldier, part of the previous oppressive government, sitting in the classroom, and so she refused to enter. I wondered if other Haitian students would have the same reaction. But the next student to enter the room was a Catholic priest, also from Haiti. He had been sent to learn English to help refugees in the Bahamas, who had fled from the same oppressive government that the soldier had supported. The priest sat down at

the opposite end of the table from the soldier, making clear that he was on the other side of the political fence.

As the students introduced themselves, the stories of soldier and priest emerged. Both were gifted sons of large families from neighboring communities. Each had felt the need to leave home early to lighten the family burden—one was offered a military career, the other a religious one. They discovered that they had common acquaintances. Later, each explained to the class in English, without judgment, the reasons for their life choices and political positions. The priest invited the soldier to his home for dinner, and the tension in the classroom dissolved.

I like to think that speaking another language and the neutral ground of the classroom helped make this reconciliation possible.

— Mary Hills Kuck
United Theological College of the West Indies

What the research says

Nieto (2002) notes that scholars have finally started to connect language, literacy, and culture in a substantive manner, whereas before these areas were thought to exist independently from one another. Whereas once educators thought of culture as distinct from language and from reading and writing, the connection is now evident. It is vital that teachers become knowledgeable in how these areas affect students at all levels of schooling.

One part of this connection is the role of ethnic differences which until recently have not become visible topics for serious discussions in the classroom or in teacher education courses. Nieto (2002, p. 1) cautions that "questions about equity and social justice are at the core of education." She comments that once people realize that education is not neutral, then issues relating to power and privilege come to the forefront. This can be frightening to many people.

If we want to help improve communication and international relations, we must go above and beyond the basics of language and culture. We need to help our students become aware of the realities of prejudice and race relations. We can help our students become bridge-builders between cultures. We can help students learn to respect each other in spite of their differences. "It is one thing to develop knowledge and awareness of human similarities and another to develop empathy. Knowledge is a necessary but an insufficient ingredient" (Bennett 2003, p. 349).

What the teacher can do

Teachers can address these issues directly but sensitively by first raising students' awareness of the issues and then gently leading them into discussions or exercises that help them explore their own ideas and opinions. Christine Bennett (2003), whose work is largely intended for teachers of schoolchildren, presents lesson plans that develop intercultural competence, seek to reduce prejudice, and attempt to help students make peace in the world. She suggests that teachers push students beyond mere reflection to develop empathy with others.

Teachers can use Activity 8.6 (adapted from Ochoa-Becker in Bennett 2003, pp. 386–392 and used by permission) to help students develop empathy. Empathy is a quality not everyone possesses to the same degree. It is best to approach this topic cautiously and to nurture students in the direction of empathy, rather than to force it on them.

Activity 8.6	***Thinking peace / doing peace***
Level	Intermediate – Advanced
Handout	None
Tip	Introduce the concepts of social responsibility, ethics, and human rights.

Steps:

1. Select 4 or 5 photographs that depict war and violence from magazines and newspapers. Allow students time to examine them carefully and then discuss the following questions:
   - Why do you think this violence is taking place?
   - Could these problems have been settled in other ways? How?
   - What are the ways we can help prevent war?
2. With the students, brainstorm the ideas that come to mind when hearing the word "peace."
3. Place students in small groups and have them discuss the following questions:
   - How would you define "peace"?
   - Think about a time you experienced peace. What was the situation? Why did you find it peaceful? Explain why you found it peaceful. Give an authentic example of your own to begin the sharing.
   - Can you think of a place where you feel more peaceful than in other places?
   - What can you do to contribute to peace at a local level among your friends, in the classroom, and in your family?

Teaching notes:

- You may shorten this activity by omitting one or more of the questions in Step 3 or by doing only one of the steps.
- You may want to simplify the language for the questions in Step 1.
- You may extend this activity as a writing assignment by asking students to research and write about a person they think has contributed to peace in the world.

Conclusion

In this chapter we have explored the concept of critical pedagogy and how we can incorporate it into our teaching as well as looked at principles of multicultural education and how those principles can be integrated into the classroom. We examined ways of creating respect for diversity and ethnic differences in the classroom. After looking at the issue of power balance between students and teachers, we considered various methods of discussing controversial issues. Finally, we analyzed issues of social responsibility, ethics, and human rights to see how we could introduce our students to these ideas.

As teachers we are constantly growing and developing both personally and professionally. We aspire to be socially responsible in our actions, including in our teaching, and to inspire our students to do the same. By fostering intercultural communication and understanding between peoples, we hope to bring about a more peaceful world.

Check your understanding

After reading this chapter and using the activities with your class, check your comfort level with the following:

- ❏ I include critical pedagogy in my approach to teaching culture.
- ❏ I incorporate principles of multicultural education in my classroom.
- ❏ I create respect for diversity and ethnic differences in my classroom.
- ❏ I explore issues of power balance and the roles of teacher and learners.
- ❏ I deal respectfully with controversial issues in the classroom.
- ❏ I introduce the concepts of social responsibility, ethics, and human rights into my classroom.

The following pages provide possible answers for the critical incident activities used in *Tips for Teaching Culture*. Handouts for those activities that require them follow the possible interpretations.

Activity 1.5 possible interpretations:

Critical Incident 1. *Individual vs. group.* Vladimir and Evgeniy are Russian. Russia is a collectivistic society where the good of the group prevails. In a collectivistic society everything is shared. As Russian students, they were accustomed to sharing with each other. They were unaware of the American educational practice in which sharing answers to an assignment violates the practice of an individual having to demonstrate knowledge. In the U.S. educational system, there can be serious consequences if students help each other when they are supposed to work individually.

Critical Incident 2. *Large power distance vs. small power distance.* In Asian cultures, age is a sign of wisdom, experience, and respect. Young people are taught this viewpoint from birth. The older person occupies first place, has first choice, and commands respect, while the younger person defers. Makoto thought that because he was older, Miguel should defer to him.

Critical Incident 3. *Feminine vs. masculine.* In José's country, the traditional roles of men and women suggest that cooking in the kitchen was work for women. José found that the idea of cooking compromised his sense of the type of behavior that was appropriate for a man in his culture.

Critical Incident 4. *Long-term planning vs. short-term planning.* Walter lives for the present, whereas Liming lives for the future. Some cultures have long-term plans in their worldview, and others have short-term plans.

In the case of money, for example, there are both spenders and savers. Understanding that there may be an alternate point of view helps us better understand individuals and cultures that have different points of view.

Activity 2.5 possible interpretations:

Critical Incident 1. Appropriate forms of address in one culture may not be considered acceptable in another. These variations in modes of address across cultures may confuse language students. For example, second-language students sometimes make the mistake of addressing the English instructor as "teacher." This is acceptable in the United States only at the elementary school level and is rare even then. At high school and university levels, teachers generally expect to be addressed by their last name, preceded by their title such as Mr., Mrs., Dr., or Professor. Some instructors may invite students to use their first names. This can be uncomfortable for some students who may feel that it is inappropriately informal.

Critical Incident 2. Antonella didn't do anything wrong at all except for misinterpreting her professor's remark. In English, some expressions are not to be taken literally. "How are you?", for instance, does not invite a detailed explanation of the well-being of the person greeted. A vague expression such as "Let's get together sometime" or "Let's do lunch" is not an actual invitation to a meeting unless a definite time and date are fixed. These expressions are sometimes used to end a conversation without making any definite plans to get together in the future. Antonella made the mistake of thinking that her professor had issued an invitation when he had not.

Critical Incident 3. When two speakers do not speak the same language with comparable proficiency, misunderstandings can occur. Cultural differences can make these misunderstandings even worse. In this case an innocent request for help by the speaker was misinterpreted by the listener as a suggestion that he was doing an inadequate job or that he was expected to show preference. In many cultures, such a request of a teacher would be perfectly normal and would have been taken in stride by the teacher. Perhaps the only way to have avoided this misunderstanding would have been if the speaker had more clearly conveyed his intent, had been sensitive to the concerns of the listener, and had phrased the request differently.

Critical Incident 4. Although Aya wanted to get her money back, her own cultural background made her reluctant to put another person in a difficult position. Even though Aya may have thought Erica rude for not returning the money, she wanted to be sure that her friend did not lose face.

Activity 3.1 possible interpretations:

Critical Incident 1. *Eye contact.* The use and meaning of eye contact varies from culture to culture. In Japan individuals are taught at an early age to avoid eye contact with superiors and elders. In Canada it is considered impolite to avoid eye contact with someone who is talking to you, regardless of age and position. Katsushi is a product of his Japanese culture and upbringing, which brought him into conflict with the Canadian cultural norm where eye contact is expected.

Critical Incident 2. *Touching.* In some cultures touching another person, male or female, is unacceptable. However, in Turkey, Greece, Latin American countries, and Arab countries, among others, touching is a common cultural practice between those of the same gender. This, however, is often viewed as sexual in the United States, Canada, northern European countries, and some Asian countries. Unless touching is clear cross-culturally, the parties involved could wind up in a cross-cultural misunderstanding.

Critical Incident 3. *Signs of respect.* Bowing is a form of respect practiced in Asian cultures, especially by the Koreans and Japanese. When Haesik encountered an older person who was helpful, he acknowledged this by bowing. Americans are not accustomed to this behavior and may not know how to react or interpret this gesture. Cultural awareness of which behaviors are common and which are not acceptable in a new culture is important.

Critical Incident 4. *Time.* Time is typically viewed in a rather flexible manner in Spanish-speaking countries. Swiss culture, on the other hand, espouses punctuality and time awareness. When two culture types—the linear Swiss and the cyclical Latin American—get together, there are likely to be misunderstandings unless the parties are very cross-culturally aware. An added complication is the way in which time is valued in the country where this incident takes place, the United States.

Activity 4.4 possible interpretations:

Critical Incident 1. Mike was experiencing one of the variables in cultural identity: the strength of the connection with the home culture. While he was in Australia, Mike didn't feel particularly attached to his home culture. However, when he was traveling abroad, he found himself feeling much more patriotic and attached himself more closely to the identity of his home culture.

Critical Incident 2. Cultural identity includes social distance or any dissimilarity existing between two cultures. The social distance between Canadians and U.S. Americans is closer than the social distance between U.S. Americans and Chinese. In this case, Marilyn and Jane's social distance is quite similar, and so they found themselves in agreement, whereas Ying's culture had greater social distance from Jane's and Marilyn's.

Critical Incident 3. What generally represents a cultural identity and its values can vary. People are influenced by their culture being individualistic or collectivistic. U.S. American culture is seen as individualistic, where individuals are proud of their accomplishments and it is appropriate to "toot your own horn." Japanese culture, on the other hand, is seen as collectivistic. Eleonora's and Maki's behaviors reflect their cultural identities.

Critical Incident 4. Nguyen was experiencing extreme social distance between the culture of Vietnam and that of Canada. The two cultures are so different that it was probably affecting Nguyen's progress in English and his feeling comfortable in the new culture in general. For Pierre, on the other hand, the cultures of France and Canada have little social distance, creating a more comfortable and successful learning experience.

Activity 5.5 possible interpretations:

Critical Incident 1. We are often quick to stereotype cultural groups as a result of a negative experience or even because of our upbringing. Was the taxi driver taking the long way to make some easy money? Was he lost? Susanne's final comment gives the impression that she considers all Africans to be stupid, revealing her prejudices.

Critical Incident 2. People from Mexico and other Latin American countries are sometimes stereotyped as being lazy or slow. This stems, in part, from the Latin American sense of time, where strict punctuality is not considered very important. In this incident, cultural bias reinforced the other student's stereotype of Mexicans being lazy, but in fact Manuel didn't have time to do homework and was exhausted in the evening because he worked twelve-hour days.

Critical Incident 3. We often stereotype other cultures based on generalizations that have been made about them or on experiences we may have had. These stereotypes can sometimes be perceived as positive or negative, depending on one's personal point of view, and may hurt others unintentionally.

Critical Incident 4. People are accustomed to the foods they grow up with in their own country. Foods that may be perfectly natural in some settings appear to be odd in another cultural setting. If one group decides that a certain type of food is "strange" or unusual, this could lead to cultural insensitivity and conflict.

Handout 1.4   Cultural values clarification

Directions: Look at the values on each side of the chart. Which value is most important to you? Circle the number that most closely represents your point of view.

1	It is important to maintain harmony (not talk about subjects where there is disagreement).	1	2	3	4	5	It is important to talk about and resolve differences.
2	The needs of the group are more important than the needs of the individual.	1	2	3	4	5	The needs of the individual are more important than the needs of the group.
3	It is good to spend money now to get what is needed, so don't worry about tomorrow.	1	2	3	4	5	It is important to save money now, rather than spend it, so that there will be enough in the future.
4	A person's importance is based on family or connections.	1	2	3	4	5	A person's importance is based on what he or she has done.
5	We should recognize and emphasize differences in power and status between people.	1	2	3	4	5	We shouldn't focus too much on power differences between people.
6	I prefer indirect communication.	1	2	3	4	5	I prefer direct communication.
7	I have flexible and open views about time, so we get there when we get there.	1	2	3	4	5	Being on time and keeping to schedules is important.

Adapted from Gardenswartz and Rowe (1994, p. 58), *The Managing Diversity Survival Guide: A Complete Collection of Checklists, Activities, and Tips* (Chicago: Irwin Professional Publishing).

Handout 1.5A   Culture in action

Directions: Form small groups. Read the incidents below. Think about the different cultural backgrounds of the participants. Discuss each story. What do you think happened? Why? How could the misunderstanding have been prevented?

Critical Incident 1

Vladimir and Evgeniy, exchange students from Russia, are studying in a high school in the United States. They are in Mrs. Tomitz's class working on a reading assignment. The students are sitting in rows and are all working individually. During the task, Vladimir asks his twin brother, Evgeniy, who is sitting next to him, for the answer to the third reading question. Evgeniy allows his brother to copy his answer. The teacher sees what is taking place and takes away both papers. She tells both students that they will get a failing grade for the assignment. Vladimir and Evgeniy don't understand why the teacher is reacting this way.

Critical Incident 2

Makoto and Miguel go to the library together to research their term paper for their ESL writing class. Makoto, a mature Japanese graduate student, and Miguel, a young Ecuadorian undergraduate freshman, share the same library book that Makoto takes from the library stacks for their use. As they are looking at the book and taking notes, Makoto keeps looking at his watch. He has a meeting and needs to leave. He stands up, takes the book they are using, and leaves. Miguel calls after him to stop and bring back the book, but Makoto ignores him.

Handout 1.5B   Culture in action

Directions: Form small groups. Read the incidents below. Think about the different cultural backgrounds of the participants. Discuss each story. What do you think happened? Why? How could the misunderstanding have been prevented?

Critical Incident 3

In José's adult English class in Chicago, students are learning about different names for food. To make things more realistic, the teacher makes a plan to use the school's kitchen and have the students prepare some food. When the day comes for the kitchen assignment, José and two other men from Mexico do not go into the kitchen with the other students but remain outside in the hall. His teacher cannot understand why José and the other men do not want to participate.

Critical Incident 4

When Walter has money in his pocket, he spends it immediately. He can't seem to hold onto a dollar. Before he even gets any money, he already has it spent! His Chinese friend, Liming, however, always has money in his wallet. He does not spend it on useless and unnecessary things like Walter. At the end of the month, Walter is always out of money and then goes to Liming to borrow a couple of dollars.

Handout 2.2   The language of meetings

Directions: Choose a meeting to attend. Listen as people talk. Listen for topics, expressions, and how information is presented. Listen to how attendees speak and what communication styles they use. Write your notes on the lines below and in the chart.

Your name: _____

Organization/ meeting you attended: _____

Date: _____ Time: _____ Location: _____

How many people were at the meeting? _____

Who spoke at the meeting? _____

What major topics were discussed? _____

Vocabulary	Expressions
What were some words you heard that seemed specific to this group?	Did you hear any expressions used regularly? Write them down.

Grammar	Culture
Did you notice any unusual grammar patterns? Write them down.	What did you notice about the "culture" of the meeting and the people who attended? What seemed to be interesting or different?

Handout 2.4   Writing vs. speaking

Directions: Your teacher will give you a transcript or written text. Compare the characteristics of the spoken and written language. Put a check mark [✓] in the column of the type of language that is most like the statement.

Characteristic	Spoken Language	Written Language
1. Doesn't last; has no record		
2. Builds on what has been said before		
3. Doesn't repeat very much		
4. Is grammatically looser		
5. Permits "filler words" with no particular meaning		
6. Is less likely to use informal language		

Handout 2.5A   Language in context

Directions: Form small groups. Read the incidents below. Think about the different cultural backgrounds of the participants. Discuss each story. What do you think happened? Why? How could the misunderstanding have been prevented?

Critical Incident 1

Dr. Charlotte Denk, a new teacher at a U.S. college, was teaching different techniques for writing introductions to an ESL writing class. After reviewing seven techniques, the professor asked the class for examples of each technique. Sangram, a student from India, raised his hand and called out "Ma'am" to get the professor's attention. Miguel, a student from Ecuador, excitedly yelled "Teacher, teacher!" in an attempt to be recognized. Erman from Turkey called out "Miss" to be noticed, and Rafael from El Salvador used "Miss Charlotte." Dr. Denk was surprised by the many different forms of address that her students were using.

Critical Incident 2

On her way to class, Antonella, an Italian student studying in the United States, ran into Professor Manetta, her art professor. She had become friendly with him since, as an art major, she had recently exhibited some of her work at his studio in New York. Eager to discuss some of her newest paintings but late for class, Professor Manetta said, "We should talk more over lunch one day." A week went by and Antonella had still not heard from him. He did not follow up on his invitation, and she was uncertain as to what she might have done wrong.

Handout 2.5B   Language in context

Directions: Form small groups. Read the incidents below. Think about the different cultural backgrounds of the participants. Discuss each story. What do you think happened? Why? How could the misunderstanding have been prevented?

Critical Incident 3

An immigrant parent approached a high school teacher and asked, "Please do everything you can to help my daughter in your class." The teacher was offended by this request. To the teacher the request implied that he was not doing his best for the parent's daughter. What was the parent thinking?

Critical Incident 4

Aya, a Japanese student studying in the United States, and Erica, her American friend, were meeting in the school cafeteria to have a cup of coffee together after class. At the register, Erica realized that she did not have enough money with her. Aya lent her five dollars, but Erica forgot to pay the money back. Although she wanted to have her money returned, Aya never spoke of the matter to Erica.

Handout 2.6   Language functions

Directions: Write two examples for each language function.

Definition: A language *function* is the purpose for which language is used. For example, when you tell someone at the end of a party, "I had a wonderful time," the purpose or function is *thanking* someone.

Function	Example
1. Thanking	*I had a wonderful time.* *I love it! It's the most beautiful necklace I've ever seen!*
2. Requesting	
3. Concluding	
4. Complimenting	
5. Apologizing	
6. Ordering	

Handout 2.7   Maintaining face

Directions: Complete the chart according to what would be acceptable in your native culture. Put a check mark [✓] under "Culturally Acceptable" if a statement or action would be okay. Put a check mark [✓] under "Culturally Unacceptable" if the statement or action would not be okay in your culture.

Is it acceptable in your culture?	Culturally Acceptable	Culturally Unacceptable
1. To call your professors by their first names		
2. To interrupt people when they are speaking		
3. To say "no" to a request		
4. To insist that your doctor sign a document for you		
5. To call someone a liar in front of others		
6. To tell a "white lie" to save face		
7. To not issue orders but only hint at what's to be done		
8. To speak before your elders speak		
9. To talk negatively about a religious leader		
10. To tell the professor that he or she made a mistake		

Handout 3.1A   Nonverbal communication dimensions

Directions: Form small groups. Read the incidents below. Think about the different cultural backgrounds of the participants. Discuss each story. What do you think happened? Why? How could the misunderstanding have been prevented?

Critical Incident 1

Katsushi, a high school freshman in Canada, recently arrived from Japan. One day in class, his teacher, Mrs. Campbell, called on him to answer a homework question. Katsushi did not answer her, a behavior that she had noticed before. Mrs. Campbell moved on to ask another student, who answered. Mrs. Campbell spoke with Katsushi after class and asked why he wasn't even trying to answer her questions. He stared at the floor and did not respond. Mrs. Campbell asked him to put his head up and look at her while they were speaking. Katsushi felt confused and frightened.

Critical Incident 2

Frank is from the United States and Umit is from Turkey. On the first day of their sociology class at an American university, the professor had students work in pairs on an interview. As Frank asked Umit the questions on the activity handout, Umit patted Frank's hand and then his back to show he understood the questions. Frank was annoyed that Umit was touching him and finally asked him to stop. Umit didn't understand why Frank was annoyed.

Handout 3.1B   Nonverbal Communication Dimensions

Directions: Form small groups. Read the incidents below. Think about the different cultural backgrounds of the participants. Discuss each story. What do you think happened? Why? How could the misunderstanding have been prevented?

Critical Incident 3

Haesik, a student from Korea, came to the United States to study English. He arrived at his new school to take his English as a second language placement test. Although he carried a map with the location of the ESL office with him, he was unable to find the right building. As he passed a maintenance worker fixing a jammed door, Haesik asked for directions. The worker told him how to get to the ESL office. Haesik bowed and left. The janitor wondered why the stranger had bowed to him.

Critical Incident 4

Rafael, a student from El Salvador, agreed to meet Leo, a student from Switzerland, in the university cafeteria at 10:00 A.M. to work on their project for a political science class. Both students needed the extra credit they would get for this project. Leo arrived before 10:00 and got himself a cup of coffee and spread out his materials on the table. He continued to look around for Rafael, who still had not appeared. At 10:15 there was still no Rafael in sight. Leo became discouraged and at 10:30 packed up his belongings. Suddenly, Rafael arrived with no apology and an eagerness to get started. Leo said, "Hey Rafael, you're 30 minutes late. I'm not sure if this is going to work out!"

Handout 3.5   Take your time

Directions:

1. Look at the answer choices and the information in the chart.

2. Imagine that you are attending the events listed. According to your culture, what is an appropriate time to arrive at each event? For each event, write A, B, or C.

3. What is an appropriate time to arrive at each event in the United States, Canada, the United Kingdom, and Australia? For each event, write A, B, or C.

4. Conduct an interview. Find someone who is not from your country. Ask: "How is time viewed in your culture? What is an appropriate time to arrive at each event?" For each event, write A, B, or C.

Answer Choices

A   Arrive fifteen minutes early

B   Arrive exactly on time

C   Arrive fifteen minutes after the start time

Events	Your country	The United States, Canada, the United Kingdom, and Australia	A third country
1. Evening dinner party at someone's home			
2. Business meeting at an office			
3. Lunch date with friends at a café			
4. A class at the university			

Handout 3.6A   Can't you take a hint?

Directions:

1. You are Student A. Work with Student B. Do not share the information on your handouts.

2. Your job is to convince Student B to do something or to give you some information. Use all of the English that you know. Be sure to tell your partner directly what it is that you want him or her to do.

3. After you have finished, Student B will try to get you to do something or give some information. Listen carefully and then respond.

Ask your partner to . . .

1. lend you a pen.

2. tell you the time.

3. tell you his or her age.

4. say your teacher's middle name.

5. tell you the brand of the shirt (or other clothing item) he or she is wearing.

Handout 3.6B   Can't you take a hint?

Directions:

1. You are Student B. Work with Student A. Do not share the information on your handouts.

2. Student A will try to get you to do something or give some information. Listen carefully and then respond.

3. After Student A is finished, it is your turn. Your job is to convince Student A to do something or to give you some information. Use all of the English that you know. When you talk to your partner, do not say directly what you want. Instead give your partner small hints or ideas. You can use body language.

Ask your partner to . . .

1. lend you a book.

2. tell you how long until the class ends.

3. lend you some money.

4. look out the window of the classroom.

5. explain a vocabulary word to you.

Handout 4.3A   Who are you?

Directions:

1. Find a partner.
2. Decide who will be Character A and who will be Character B.
3. Read your parts. Practice acting out your role play.
4. Perform your role play for the class.

Role Play 1	
Character A	**Character B**
You are a doctor and a professional expert in your field. You need to see many patients each day, so you are in a hurry. You think that your patient just has a cold.	You are an elementary school teacher. Your throat has been bothering you for many days and you think it might be serious. You would like to have a closer examination. The doctor seems to be in a hurry and doesn't seem to want to give you more time.

Role Play 2	
Character A	**Character B**
You are a teenage boy or girl. You have stayed out later than you were supposed to, and you are a bit afraid that your parents will be upset. You have just arrived home.	You are the father. You have been worried about your son or daughter, and you are upset by his or her disrespect of your rules about what time to come home.

Handout 4.3B   Who are you?

Directions:

1. Find a partner.
2. Decide who will be Character A and who will be Character B.
3. Read your parts. Practice acting out your role play.
4. Perform your role play for the class.

Role Play 3	
Character A	**Character B**
You are an American business executive. You like to get directly to the point. You want to finish this deal today.	You are a business executive from Saudi Arabia. You feel it is important to build a relationship with people before you do business with them. You invite the American businessman to dinner for the next night.

Role Play 4	
Character A	**Character B**
You are a business manager from Japan. You have many years of experience in business, and you believe that the traditional ways of doing things work well. For example, you expect to be treated with respect by the younger and more junior employees.	You are a young consultant from Australia. You have been hired to help improve the company's business standing. You think your ideas are good ones and want them to be put into action and tested right away.

Handout 4.4A   Culture and me

Directions: Form small groups. Read the incidents below. Think about the different cultural backgrounds of the participants. Discuss each story. What do you think happened? Why? How could the misunderstanding have been prevented?

Critical Incident 1

Mike, an Australian, was traveling in Asia. Although he wasn't usually a very patriotic person, he often found himself defending the actions and attitudes of his country and government. At one point, in Indonesia, he became quite upset when he felt that his new friend, Pom, had wrongly criticized Australia. Mike found his own actions and feelings confusing.

Critical Incident 2

A study reports that women in Germany earn 22 percent less than men. Jane, an American citizen, says she is not surprised by this finding, but she says that people who do the same work should be paid the same amount. Marilyn, a Canadian citizen, agrees with Jane. Ying, a Chinese citizen, is not surprised by the results of the study, but Ying says that in China women are paid less than men for the same work because that's the way it is in her culture. Joyce and Marilyn protest that this was unfair, but Ying seems to accept it as normal; she does not want to discuss it any further.

Handout 4.4B   Culture and me

Directions: Form small groups. Read the incidents below. Think about the different cultural backgrounds of the participants. Discuss each story. What do you think happened? Why? How could the misunderstanding have been prevented?

Critical Incident 3

Eleonora, from Italy, was getting an art degree in the United States. One day she was talking to a classmate, Maki, from Japan. Eleonora talked about how her own works of art were already prominent and that she had exhibited various pieces in a Manhattan art gallery. She said she knew she would become a leading artist during her career. Although Maki's artwork and career in Japan were just as successful as Eleonora's, she chose not to say anything about her achievements. Maki thought Eleonora was showing off and felt uncomfortable.

Critical Incident 4

Pierre, from France, and Nguyen, from Vietnam, were studying together at an English language institute in Canada. Both were at an intermediate level, but Pierre seemed to be learning faster. Nguyen felt frustrated and couldn't understand why Pierre seemed to be having an easier time, even though Nguyen worked just as hard.

Handout 4.6   Ethnic identities in film

Directions: Read the questions below <u>before</u> you watch the movie. After the movie, answer the questions. Be prepared to discuss your answers with the class.

1. Describe the main characters. Include their names and ethnic backgrounds.

    _____

    _____

    _____

2. What obstacles do the characters need to overcome?

    _____

    _____

    _____

3. How are these obstacles viewed by members of different ethnic groups in the movie?

    _____

    _____

    _____

4. Did you think that the movie was realistic in its portrayal of ethnic differences?

    _____

    _____

    _____

5. Did the movie end the way you thought it would?

    _____

    _____

    _____

6. What do you think happened to the main characters after the end of the movie?

    _____

    _____

    _____

Handout 5.4A   My cultural styles

Directions: Read the description of the eleven cultural competencies below. If you have any questions, ask your teacher.

Cultural Competency	Description
Cultural self-awareness	Our own experiences with other cultures, maybe from traveling abroad
Cultural awareness of others	Knowledge about the differences among people, countries, and cultures
Cultural sensitivity	Respect and acceptance of other cultures
Cross-cultural communication skills	Verbal and nonverbal behaviors that are necessary to communicate across cultures
Tolerance for ambiguity	The ability to live with uncertainty
Flexibility	The ability to adjust to other ways of doing things based on the new culture's practices
Open-mindedness	Understanding that there may be more than one "right" way of doing things
Humility	The ability to consider the needs of others before our own
Empathy	The ability to put ourselves in the shoes of another to help us understand the other person's point of view
An outgoing personality	Someone who likes to talk with and be with other people
Self-reliance	The ability to depend on ourselves and to act independently

Adapted from Peterson, B. (2004). *Cultural Intelligence: A Guide to Working with People from Other Cultures.* Yarmouth, ME: Intercultural Press, Inc. (pp. 161–166).

Handout 5.4B   **My cultural styles**

Directions:

1. Read the description of these cultural competencies on Handout 5.4A.
2. Circle the number on the chart that shows how well you think this trait describes you. If you think it describes you well, then circle 5. If you think you don't have the trait at all, circle 1.

Trait	Rating				
	Not at all		Occasionally		A lot
Cultural self-awareness	1	2	3	4	5
Cultural awareness of others	1	2	3	4	5
Cultural sensitivity	1	2	3	4	5
Cross-cultural communication skills	1	2	3	4	5
Tolerance for ambiguity	1	2	3	4	5
Flexibility	1	2	3	4	5
Open-mindedness	1	2	3	4	5
Humility	1	2	3	4	5
Empathy	1	2	3	4	5
An outgoing personality	1	2	3	4	5
Self-awareness	1	2	3	4	5

Adapted from Peterson, B. (2004). *Cultural Intelligence: A Guide to Working with People from Other Cultures.* Yarmouth, ME: Intercultural Press, Inc. (pp. 161–166).

Handout 5.5A Avoiding cultural bias and stereotypes

Directions: Form small groups. Read the incidents below. Think about the different cultural backgrounds of the participants. Discuss each story. What do you think happened? Why? How could the misunderstanding have been prevented?

Critical Incident 1

Susanne, originally from New York City, came to Chicago to begin her internship as part of her final year of studies at Stanford University. Upon arriving at O'Hare Airport, she hailed a taxi and gave the driver the address of her aunt's house on Michigan Avenue. Soon Susanne realized that the driver was going the wrong way, and she attempted to give him directions. The taxi driver said that he knew the way and continued in the same direction. After some time, it was clear they were lost. Susanne yelled, "You idiot. You're all alike. Why didn't you listen to me?"

Critical Incident 2

Manuel works from 6 A.M. to 6 P.M. every day to earn money to support his family. Even though he is tired at night, he signs up for classes to improve his English. There are students from many different countries in his class. Manuel rarely has time to do homework and often falls asleep in class. One evening, a student from France comments to a classmate, "Those Mexicans are so lazy."

Handout 5.5B   Avoiding cultural bias and stereotypes

Directions: Form small groups. Read the incidents below. Think about the different cultural backgrounds of the participants. Discuss each story. What do you think happened? Why? How could the misunderstanding have been prevented?

Critical Incident 3

Dieter, an international student from Germany, was studying at an American university. When he arrived, he found he had been assigned an American roommate, Paul. On the first day, Dieter immediately arranged his books in the bookshelf, his shirts in the drawers, and his clothes in the closet. Paul, on the other hand, did not. His clothes and books were strewn around on his side of the room. Paul commented to Dieter, "You're a typical German with all that organization!" Dieter replied, "And you're a typical American!"

Critical Incident 4

Duc, originally from Vietnam, was a student in a high school in Texas. The first time he went to lunch in the cafeteria, he was surprised by all of the new foods he didn't recognize. The food didn't look very healthy or appetizing to him, so he brought his own lunch from home. When the other students looked at the foods Duc brought, they started to make fun of him.

Handout 6.2   Movie study

Directions:

1. Study the questions before you watch the movie.
2. After the movie, write the answers to the questions on a separate sheet of paper.
3. Form pairs or small groups. Share your answers. Be prepared to present the final answers to the class.

Questions:

1. Write a short description of the story. What happened in the beginning, middle, and end of the movie?

2. Who were the major characters in the film? Name each one and give a description.

3. What were the key elements of the plot or story of the film? Was there conflict at any point?

4. Were there any parts of the movie that you didn't understand? Describe.

5. What new language did you learn from this movie?

6. What do you know about the local culture in the movie that you didn't know before?

7. Did you enjoy the movie? What made you like it or dislike it?

Handout 6.5A   Time differs culturally

Directions:

1. Read the story below and the question that follows.
2. Choose the answer you think is correct.
3. Discuss your answer with a partner.

Helmut, a businessman from Germany, flew to Rome for the day to attend a meeting with Alberto, an Italian partner. The meeting with Alberto was scheduled for 10:00 a.m. Helmut and Alberto needed to make important decisions that would affect Helmut's later meetings. His next meeting was at 11:00 a.m.

Helmut arrived at 9:45 and drank a cup of coffee in the conference room as he waited for Alberto. At 10:00, no one had yet appeared. Then it was 10:15, and Helmut still sat alone. Finally at 10:30, Alberto strolled in. Helmut was angry. Alberto asked his German colleague, "Why are you so angry?" Helmut replied that the meeting was scheduled for 10:00 in his appointment book. Alberto quickly responded, "Simply replace 10:00 with 10:30, and we'll both be content. After all, time is irrelevant. It's our business arrangement and our relationship that matters." Helmut was furious.

Why do you think Alberto did not seem upset by his late arrival and Helmut was furious?

A. Alberto had other things to attend to and did not care about being on time.

B. Meetings can easily be rearranged for both parties involved.

C. Germans are more interested in schedules and punctuality than in the content of the meeting.

D. Italians organize their time in a different way from that of Germans.

Handout 6.5B   Time differs culturally

If you chose A: It is unlikely that Alberto had more important things to do than to be on time at a meeting with a business colleague who flew in from Germany just to conduct business.

If you chose B: This is unlikely because Helmut had a tight schedule and Alberto's lateness reduced the amount of time they were able to discuss their business ventures.

If you chose C: This could be partially true because Germans are concerned about punctuality. But Helmut's later meetings were dependent on decisions made in his meeting with Alberto, so Helmut would have been concerned about the content, too.

If you chose D: This is the correct answer. Southern Europeans, including Italians, organize their time and lives in a different way from that of Germans and Americans. Living in the moment is more important than a schedule or punctuality to Alberto. In other words, his priority as an Italian is the event and not the time.

Handout 6.6   A cultural miscommunication?

Directions:

1. Form pairs.
2. Choose a role play. Write a dialogue for the characters and the situation.
3. Perform your role play in front of the class.

Role Play 1

You are a medical doctor who is just arriving in a new country. You left your own country for political reasons. The quota for admission of immigrants from your country is close to being reached. At the border, the immigration officer doesn't agree that you need to enter the new country. Give a good argument for why you should be allowed to enter.

Role Play 2

You are a psychologist who is doing research in another country. You are eager to mix with the locals, but they are suspicious of you. The head of the psychology department at the visiting university is giving you a hard time because of your extroverted personality.

Role Play 3

You are a European businessman who has been assigned to travel to an Asian country in order to close a business deal. The culture is very different from yours, and you are unfamiliar with the business practices of your local counterpart. You meet with him to discuss your deal.

Role Play 4

As a native speaker of English, you have an English language teaching job for a year in a non-English-speaking country. You hope to be accepted in your new school and to have many opportunities to get to know your students. The local teachers at your school are happy to teach just during regular class hours. They are not enthusiastic about your desire to start an after-school drama club because they do not have the time to give to an unpaid extracurricular activity. They go and complain to the director about you. The director calls you into her office to discuss the matter.

Handout 6.7   A trip to the supermarket

Before the trip

1. What are the rules of good behavior in a supermarket?

2. What food is okay to pick up and squeeze or smell before buying?

3. What is not okay to open or look at?

4. Do you need to bring your own bag to put your food in?

During the trip

5. How is the store organized? What foods are located next to each other?

6. What foods can you pick up directly? What foods do you need to ask for?

7. What kind of people do you see shopping in the store?

8. Look at the people coming in the store. Do most people begin to shop on the same side of the store, or does their behavior vary?

9. What foods do you find expensive? inexpensive?

10. What forms of payment do people use at the check-out counter?

After the trip

11. How was the food available in this store different from that in your country or culture?

12. How was the behavior of the people in the store different from that in your country or culture?

13. Did anything surprise you in the store?

14. What was your general reaction to the trip?

Handout 7.2A   Confidence in communication

Directions: How would you rate your abilities in your first language? Circle your answers.

My first language is _____.

a. Reading in my first language   excellent — very good — good — average —poor
       Reading in English   excellent — very good — good — average —poor

b. Writing in my first language   excellent — very good —good — average — poor
       Writing in English   excellent — very good —good — average — poor

c. Listening in my first language   excellent —very good — good — average — poor
       Listening in English   excellent — very good —good — average — poor

d. Speaking in my first language   excellent — very good — good —average — poor
       Speaking in English   excellent — very good — good —average — poor

e. Grammar in my first language   excellent — very good —good — average — poor
       Grammar in English   excellent — very good —good — average — poor

Handout 7.2B   Confidence in communication

Directions: Check [✓] the answer that best describes your communication skills in class.

		100% Always	75% Usually	50% Half time	25% Sometimes	0% Never
1. I am not afraid of asking a question.	My first language					
	English					
2. I am nervous when I have to answer a question.	My first language					
	English					
3. I try to avoid speaking in front of others.	My first language					
	English					
4. I feel nervous when I have to talk to others.	My first language					
	English					
5. I feel tense when I am participating in a group discussion.	My first language					
	English					
6. I don't like to be called on because I am shy.	My first language					
	English					
7. I feel that my language skills are not strong.	My first language					
	English					
8. I feel comfortable when I am speaking.	My first language					
	English					
9. I feel self-conscious when compared to others.	My first language					
	English					
10. I communicate with my friends without a problem.	My first language					
	English					

Handout 7.5A   Living with roommates

Directions:

1. Read the story below and the question that follows.

2. Choose the answer you think is correct.

3. Discuss your answer with a partner.

Marco, a student from Italy, was about to begin his first semester abroad at a university in the United States. He was looking forward to settling in and meeting his new roommates. Because he was the first one to arrive, he started to familiarize himself with the dormitory arrangements and the campus. He discovered that there were two bedrooms, which each had two beds. The bedrooms shared a common living room and kitchen area.

Soon his new roommates arrived: Bandish was from India, Junehyoung was from Korea, and Babak was from Iran. Babak and Marco were to share one of the bedrooms. As soon as Babak arrived, he immediately told Marco that he wanted the upper of the two beds. He also told Marco that it was important to him to have privacy and not to be interrupted with friends and parties in their shared bedroom. He didn't mind having friends in the living room but not in the room they shared together privately for sleeping and studying. Marco was puzzled by Babak's comments, especially since Bandish and Junehyoung also came from different cultures but hadn't set such rules with each other.

Why do you think Marco was confused by this situation?

A. Marco wasn't used to being told what he could and couldn't do.

B. Marco expected his new roommate to feel the same way he felt about their living arrangements.

C. Marco thought that Babak must think that Italians are only interested in partying and having a good time.

D. Marco was not aware that for Iranians keeping their distance from others and having a lot of personal space is a basic part of their culture's nonverbal communication pattern and that education is very important to them.

Handout 7.5B   Living with roommates

If you chose A: It is unlikely that Marco wasn't used to being told what he could and couldn't do. Certainly his parents in Italy would have put restrictions on his actions and behavior at some point.

If you chose B: This is unlikely because Marco must realize that not everyone in the world has the same worldview and mindset as he does. Even if he was an only child, Marco most likely learned in his early schooling that people feel and react differently to different situations in life.

If you chose C: It is possible that Babak held this idea; however, this stereotype of Italians does not hold true. Italians tend to be more demonstrative and nonverbal than the French, Spanish, or Germans. However, Italians are far from being party animals, something that is more typical of American college students.

If you chose D: This is the correct answer. Marco had no way of knowing that Iranians like to keep their distance and that they attach great importance to education.

Handout 7.6   Appropriate test-taking behavior

Directions:

1. Look at each statement. Think about your school and the class you are presently in.
2. Write a check mark [✓] to show your answer. Be ready to share your reasons with the class.

	True	False	It depends
1. *Cheating* means to have an unfair advantage.			
2. It is cheating to get help from your friend (unless your teacher says it is okay).			
3. It is cheating to write down the answers ahead of time.			
4. It is cheating to look in your book (unless your teacher says it is okay).			
5. It is cheating to learn about the questions ahead of time.			
6. It is okay to use your book during an open-book test.			
7. It is okay to work with a friend on a test if a teacher says you can "collaborate."			
8. At this school if you are caught cheating, you might fail this class.			
9. At this school if you are caught cheating, you might be expelled.			
10. Cheating is not considered acceptable in this academic culture.			

Handout 8.2   **Sharing identities**

Directions:

1. Write your answers to each question.
2. Share your answers with a partner.

What country are you from?	What is your religion?	What is your ethnic heritage?
What is your gender? Are you male or female?	How would you describe your social class?	What is your level of education?
Do you belong to any clubs or organizations? What are they?	What other groups are you a part of?	Who are your best friends?

Handout 8.3   **Respecting others**

Directions: Read the statements below. Circle the response that best describes your behavior.

1. I am concerned when someone is threatened by another classmate.

    strongly agree   *agree*   *disagree*   *strongly disagree*

2. I am willing to be friendly toward others from a different culture even if their point of view differs from mine.

    strongly agree   *agree*   *disagree*   *strongly disagree*

3. I try to understand the actions of others when they are different from my culture.

    strongly agree   *agree*   *disagree*   *strongly disagree*

4. I support my classmates when they are unfairly blamed for doing something wrong.

    strongly agree   *agree*   *disagree*   *strongly disagree*

5. I accept a variety of cultures and demonstrate this by my approval of others who have been known to speak badly against my own culture.

    strongly agree   *agree*   *disagree*   *strongly disagree*

6. I don't refuse to work with another student because of differences in culture or tradition.

    strongly agree   *agree*   *disagree*   *strongly disagree*

7. I have never insulted members of other cultures or groups out loud.

    strongly agree   *agree*   *disagree*   *strongly disagree*

8. I am kind to students whose religion is different from mine.

    strongly agree   *agree*   *disagree*   *strongly disagree*

9. I do not make fun or joke about students who are different from me.

    strongly agree   *agree*   *disagree*   *strongly disagree*

10. I listen carefully to ideas that are different from mine.

    strongly agree   *agree*   *disagree*   *strongly disagree*

Handout 8.5   Controversial debate

Agreeing

- I see your point.
- I think you're right.
- No doubt about it.

Disagreeing politely

- I'm not so sure about that.
- I disagree because . . .
- That's one way of looking at it. But I think . . .

Showing respect and sympathy for another's point of view

- I know what you mean.
- I understand your point.
- I see where you're coming from.

Asserting your own point of view

- However, in my opinion . . .
- I think that . . .
- Don't you think it might be possible that . . .

Dealing with anger

- Take it easy.
- Settle down.
- Don't take it personally.

APPENDIX B

RECOMMENDED MOVIES FOR INTERCULTURAL COMMUNICATION

Documentaries focusing on intercultural communication

A Different Place: The Intercultural Classroom

Going International series

My Brown Eyes

Writing Across Borders

Documentaries focusing on aspects of American culture

Married in America series (marriage and relationships)

Maxed Out (money and credit)

Supersize Me (food and diet)

Feature films with intercultural content

A Fond Kiss	House of Sand and Fog	Shower
Almost a Woman	Lost in Translation	Smoke Signals
Amistad	Monsoon Wedding	The Color Purple
Arranged	My Big Fat Greek Wedding	The Joy Luck Club
Babel	Nowhere in Africa	The Kite Runner
Bend it Like Beckham	Persepolis	Under the Same Moon
Brooklyn Lobster	Picture Bride	The Last Samurai
Dances with Wolves	Rabbit Proof Fence	The Milagro Beanfield War
East is East	Rain Man	The Notebook
El Norte	Relative Stranger	The Squid and the Whale
Good Bye Lenin!	Remember the Titans	The Syrian Bride
Gracie	Selena	The Whale Rider
Hotel Rwanda	Shall We Dance?	

Thanks to the following members of TESOL's Intercultural Communication Interest Section for contributing their ideas: Cem Balcikanli, Joshua Borden, Cheryl Brenner, Holly Dilatush, Heidi Faust, Karen Lapuk, James H. Robinson, Sharon Van Houte, Polina Vinogradova, Kay Westerfield, and especially Diana Trebing.

Academic integrity	a code of moral values such as honesty in coursework or in the general educational environment
Acculturation	the process of adapting to a new culture while not giving up one's existing cultural identity
Adjustment stage	a stage of acculturation or culture shock that involves a gradual adaptation to a new culture
Assimilation	a process in which a new culture and its beliefs and values replace the original culture
Attitudes	mental stances that we take in regard to a fact or a state of something
Attribution	explanation of the behavior of others through one's own cultural lens
Backchannel behavior	conversational feedback including sounds such as *uh huh* to show that listeners are attentive to what is being said
Beliefs	convictions of the truth of something or the reality of some phenomena based on an examination of the evidence
Big C culture	objective culture or something that is accepted by the larger group, such as music, literature, architecture, etc.
Chronemics	the study of the use of time, such as M-time, P-time, and synchrony
Collectivism	a cultural orientation which gives primary importance to the group rather than to the individual and the self
Collectivistic society	a community in which the good of the group prevails over that of the individual
Communication style	incorporates individual's word choice, discourse patterns, and nonverbal cues
Critical incident	a brief story or vignette of cultural miscommunication used to sensitize individuals to cultural differences
Critical pedagogy	Brazilian educator Paolo Freire's philosophy that a teacher who learns and a learner who teaches should be the model of basic roles of classroom participation
Cultural bias	the effect of social categorizing, or making sense of the world by imposing meaning and structure on it from a subjective point of view
Cultural competence	part of the socio-cultural aspect of language, including knowing what to say, how to say it, when and where to say it, and why it is said
Cultural empathy	the use of the imagination to intellectually and emotionally participate in an unfamiliar cultural experience.

229

Cultural identity	that part of identity determined by one's cultural background or way of life
Cultural informant	a person who supplies cultural information in response to questions asked
Cultural style	behaviors acceptable in one's home culture that may not be acceptable in another culture
Culture assimilator	a learning activity in which students read about an incident of cross-cultural miscommunication and then choose from among possible explanations
Culture capsule	a brief student-prepared report presenting information about a specific culture
Culture shock	a stage of acculturation in which participants experience distress and unhappiness because of cultural differences
Enculturation	the life-long process of learning about one's primary culture and becoming socialized into it
Ethnic identity	identification based on race, nation, tribe, religion, language, and culture
Ethnocentrism	the inclination to view one's own cultural practices as better than those of others
Ethnographer	someone who systematically records the behavior of human cultures
Face	the public perception of a person
Facework	the communication behaviors a person uses to preserve the public perception of speaker and listener
Gender identity	identification based on one's gender, and society's conceptualization of the role of that gender
Haptics	the study of the use of touch using hands, lips, and arms for communication
Hierarchy	the degree to which a culture ranges from large power distance to small power distance
High-context culture	a culture in which people have close connections with each other and in which much of a message is implicit and unsaid in communication
Honeymoon stage	a stage of acculturation or culture shock which is filled with excitement and euphoria about everything new
"I" identity	individual identity which focuses on individual rights, individual needs, and individual goals over the needs of the group
Identity	one's sense of self; a dimension of culture that ranges from collectivism to individualism

Individualism	a cultural orientation which gives primary importance to the individual and the self rather than to the group
In-group	a group in which an individual is included or of which one is a member
Kinesics	the study of body movement, including facial expressions and gestures for communication
Kinesthetic learning	learning achieved through body motions or movements
Learning style	individual tendencies or preferences regarding how one learns
Linguistic politeness	the use of language to carry out social actions in which mutual face is respected
Little c culture	subjective culture, or people's everyday thinking and behavior, such as core values, attitudes, and beliefs or common traditions, practices, and customs
Long-term orientation	the cultural perspective on time held by a society as it relates to long-term outcomes
Low-context culture	a culture in which people lack close connections with each other and in which much of a message is explicit and stated directly in communication
Mainstream teachers	term used in the United States for teachers who teach general education classes from kindergarten through high school
Mores	locally agreed-upon values and behaviors that permit or prohibit certain actions and activities
Multicultural education	the movement in the United States that encourages the inclusion of antiracism, social justice, and critical pedagogy in educational settings and promotes recognition of the identities of people of varied ethnic, linguistic, and cultural backgrounds
Multiple intelligences	the possession by individuals of the capacity to think and learn using different parts of the brain and body, such as learning through body movement, music, or words
Norms	principles of appropriate behavior generally agreed on by and binding upon the members of a culture
Oculesics	eye movements and behaviors including gazing, blinking, winking, glancing, and squinting
Out-group	a group from which an individual is excluded or of which one is a non-member
Paralanguage	vocalized linguistic features other than words that communicate meaning, such as pitch, loudness, and rate of speech
Particulars	situation-specific cultural concepts
Personal identity	the unique individual nature that makes a person different from others in the same cultural and social group

Plagiarism	using the words or ideas of another without giving credit in the form of a citation, or the use of paraphrasing that is overly similar to the original
Power distance	a measure of the distribution of power and control between the more and less powerful members of a culture
Pragmatics	the branch of linguistics that studies language in context, particularly the conveying and interpretation of meaning
Prejudice	negative attitudes or judgments towards others based on stereotypes
Primary identities	identities that affect a person on an ongoing basis, including personal identity, gender identity, cultural identity, and ethnic identity
Principle of linguistic relativity	known as the Sapir-Whorf hypothesis which holds that the language a person normally uses influences that person's thinking and behavior
Proxemics	the use of physical space to maximize speakers' comfort levels through distance and physical positioning of people in relation to one another
Recovery stage	a stage of acculturation or culture shock in which a person successfully integrates the new culture into one's life
Register	the use of language in social contexts depending on the degree of formality of a situation and the relationship between the speakers
Resistance	non-acceptance of or a negative reaction to cultural differences
Sapir-Whorf hypothesis	developed by linguists Edward Sapir and Benjamin Whorf. cf. principle of linguistic relativity
Scaffolding	breaking down materials into smaller chunks so students have sufficient preparation and confidence when attempting a learning activity
Schema	one's background knowledge about a subject
Secondary identities	identities that are not permanent but change from situation to situation; also known as situational identities
Short-term orientation	the cultural perspective on time held by a society as it relates to short-term outcomes
Social class	factors such as income, occupation, education, family background, lifestyle, material possessions, manner of speaking, and attitudes and beliefs that determine an individual's status in the social hierarchy of one's culture
Social distance	the extent to which two cultures are affectively and cognitively close or dissimilar within an individual
Social gender role	a dimension of culture where the degree to which an individual, or one's behaviors, are perceived as feminine or masculine

Social identity	the portion of one's identity defined by associates, group memberships, and roles
Social roles	socially-expected behavior patterns
Socialization	the process by which children view themselves as members of their families and then develop an awareness of belonging to various social groups
Sociolinguistic behaviors	linguistic behaviors determined by a combination of social and cultural factors
Spatial behavior	one's use of space and distance, and the messages that this behavior sends
Speech acts	the utterance(s) made by a speaker, the intent of those words, and the effect of those words on a listener
Stereotypes	overgeneralizations or oversimplifications used to categorize others
Taboos	unacceptable words or actions in a culture
Truth value	a dimension of culture that ranges from strong uncertainty avoidance to weak uncertainty avoidance
Turns in conversation	different speakers taking turns or going back and forth during an interaction
Uncertainty avoidance	the degree to which members of a culture feel threatened by situations that are unknown to them
Universals	cultural concepts that are rule-based
Values	feelings of the worth, usefulness, or importance of something; standards steered by moral guidelines
Virtue	term, first used by Hofstede, for the dimension of culture that ranges from short-term orientation to long-term orientation
Vocalics	voice qualifiers such as accent, pitch, volume, articulation, resolution, and tempo
"We" identity	group identity focuses on group rights and group-oriented needs over the needs of the individual

BIBLIOGRAPHY

Acton, W. (1979). Second language learning and perception of differences in attitude. Unpublished doctoral dissertation, University of Michigan.

Adler, P. (1977). Beyond cultural identity: Reflections upon cultural and multicultural man. In R. Brislin (Ed.), *Culture learning: Concepts, application and research.* Honolulu: University Press of Hawaii.

Agar, M. (1994). *Language shock.* New York: Morrow.

Althen, G. (1988). *American ways: A guide for foreigners in the United States.* Yarmouth: ME: Intercultural Press.

Althen, G. (1994). Cultural differences on campus. In Althen, G. (Ed.), *Learning across cultures.* Alexandria, VA: NAFSA: Association of International Educators.

Atkinson, D. (1999). TESOL and culture. *TESOL Quarterly* 33 (4), 625–654.

Austin, J. (1962). *How to do things with words.* Oxford: Oxford University Press.

Banks, C. A. M. (2001). Families and teachers working together for school improvement. In J. A. Banks & C. A. M. Banks (Eds.). *Multicultural education: Issues and perspectives* (4th ed.). New York: John Wiley & Sons.

Banks, J. A., & Banks, C. A. M. (2001). *Multicultural education: issues and perspectives* (4th ed.). New York: John Wiley & Sons.

Barna, L. (1988). Stumbling blocks in intercultural communication. In L. Samovar & R. Porter (Eds.), *Intercultural communication: A reader* (5th ed.) (pp. 322-330). Belmont, CA: Wadsworth Publishing Co.

Barnes, G. (1986). Toward a model for cross-cultural orientation. In P. Byrd (Ed.), *Teaching across cultures in the university ESL program.* Washington, DC: National Association for Foreign Student Affairs.

Barnlund, D, (1998). Communication in a global village. In M. Bennett (Ed.), *Basic concepts of intercultural communication: Selected readings.* Yarmouth, ME: Intercultural Press.

Bennett, C. I. (2003). *Comprehensive multicultural education: Theory and practice* (5th ed.). Boston: Pearson Education.

Bennett, J. (1998). Transition shock: Putting culture shock in perspective. In M. Bennett (Ed.), *Basic concepts of intercultural communication: Selected readings.* Yarmouth, ME: Intercultural Press.

Bennett, M. (1986). A developmental approach to training for intercultural sensitivity. *International Journal of Intercultural Relations* 10, 179-200.

Bennett, M. (1993). Towards ethnorelativism: A developmental model of intercultural sensitivity. In R. M. Paige (Ed.), *Education for the intercultural experience* (pp. 21-71). Yarmouth, ME: Intercultural Press.

Bennett, M. (1998). Intercultural communication: A current perspective. In M. Bennett (Ed.), *Basic concepts of intercultural communication.* Yarmouth, ME: Intercultural Press.

Birdwhistell, R. (1970). *Kinesics and context.* Philadelphia: University of Pennsylvania Press.

Birdwhistell, R. (1974). The language of the body: The natural environment of words. In A. Silverstein (Ed.), *Human communication: Theoretical explorations* (pp. 203-220). Hillsdale, NJ: Erlbaum.

Brislin, R. R. (2000). *Understanding culture's influence on behavior,* (2nd ed.). New York: Harcourt College Publishers.

Brown, H. D. (1999). Learning a second culture. In J. Valdes (Ed.), *Culture bound* (pp. 33-48). Cambridge: Cambridge University Press.

Brown, H. D. (2001). *Teaching by principles: An interactive approach to language pedagogy.* White Plains, NY: Addison Wesley-Longman, Inc.

Brown, H. D. (2004). *Language assessment: Principles and classroom practices.* White Plains, NY: Pearson Education Inc.

Brown, H. D. (2007a). *Principles of language learning and teaching.* White Plains, NY: Pearson Education, Inc.

Brown, H. D. (2007b). *Teaching by principles: An interactive approach to language pedagogy* (3rd ed.). White Plains, NY: Pearson Education, Inc.

Brown, P., & Levinson, S. C. (1987). *Politeness: Some universals in language usage.* Cambridge: Cambridge University Press.

Brown, S., & Eisterhold, J. (2004). *Topics in language and culture for teachers.* Ann Arbor, MI: University of Michigan Press.

Carnegie Mellon University, Eberley Center for Teaching Excellence / Intercultural Communication Center. (2006). *Recognizing and addressing cultural variations in the classroom.* [Brochure]. Pittsburgh, PA: Author.

Chen, Z., & Henning, G. (1985). Linguistic and cultural bias in language proficiency tests. *Language Testing, 2* (2), 155-163.

Christison, M. A. (1982). *English through poetry.* San Francisco: The Alemany Press.

Clark, R. C., Moran, P. R., & Burrows, A. A., (2007). *The ESL miscellany* (4th ed.). Brattleboro, VT: Pro Lingua Associates.

Collie, J. & Slater, S. (1987). *Literature in the language classroom: A resource book of ideas and activities.* Cambridge: Cambridge University Press.

Coombe, C., Folse, K., & Hubley, N. (2007). *A practical guide to assessing English language learners.* Ann Arbor, MI: University of Michigan Press.

Crystal, D. (1985). *A dictionary of linguistics and phonetics.* Oxford, UK: Blackwell.

Cummins, J. (1979). Cognitive/academic language proficiency, linguistic interdependence, the optimum age question and some other matters. *Working Papers on Bilingualism, 19,* 121-129.

Cummins, J. (1996). *Negotiating identities: Education for empowerment in a diverse society.* Sacramento, CA: California Association for Bilingual Education.

Damen, L. (1987). *Culture learning: The fifth dimension in the language classroom.* Reading, MA: Addison-Wesley.

Davis, L. (1990). Where do we stand. *In Health.* September/October 1990.

DeCapua, A., & Wintergerst, A. C. (2004). *Crossing cultures in the language classroom.* Ann Arbor, MI: University of Michigan Press.

Dyson, A. H. (1997). *What difference does difference make? Teacher reflections on diversity, literacy, and the urban primary school.* Urbana, IL: National Council of Teachers of English.

Ehrman, M. E. & Oxford, R. L. (1990). Adult language learning styles and strategies in an intensive training setting. *Modern Language Journal, 74* (3), 311-327.

Ekman, P. (1982). *Emotion in the human face.* (2nd ed.). Cambridge: Cambridge University Press.

Ekman, P., & Friesen, W. (1969). The repertoire of nonverbal behavior. *Semiotica, 1,* 49-98.

Ekman, P., & Oster, H. (1979). Facial expression of emotion. *Annual Review of Psychology, 30,* 527-554.

Folse, K. S. (1996). *Discussion starters: Speaking fluency activities for advanced ESL/EFL students.* Ann Arbor, MI: University of Michigan Press.

Freire, P. (1970). *Pedagogy of the oppressed.* (M. R. Ramos, Trans.). New York: Continuum.

Gaines, S., Marelich, W., Bledsoe, K., Steers, W., Henderson, M., Granrose, C., et. al. (1997). Links between race/ethnicity and cultural values as mediated by race/ethnic identity and moderated by sender. *Journal of Personality and Social Psychology, 72,* 1460-1476.

Garcia, G., & Pearson, P. D. (1994). Assessment and diversity. *Review of Research in Education, 20,* 337-391).

Gardenswartz, L., & Rowe, A. (1994). *The managing diversity survival guide: A complete collection of checklists, activities, and tips.* Chicago: Irwin Professional Publishing.

Gardner, H. (1983). *Frames of mind: The theory of multiple intelligences.* New York: Basic Books.

Gaston, G. (1984). *Cultural awareness teaching techniques.* Brattleboro, VT: Pro Lingua.

Gay, G. (1995). Mirror images on common issues: Parallels between multicultural education and critical pedagogy. In E. Sleeter & P. McLaren (Eds.), *Multicultural education, critical pedagogy, and the politics of difference* (pg. 155-189). Albany, NY: State University of New York Press.

Gay, G. (2000). *Culturally responsive teaching: theory, research, and practice.* New York: Teachers College, Columbia University.

Goldstein, B. (2008). *Working with images: A resource book for the language classroom.* Cambridge: Cambridge University Press.

Gray, J. (1992). *Men are from Mars, women are from Venus.* New York: HarperCollins.

Gudykunst, W., & Kim, Y. (2003). *Communicating with strangers: An approach to intercultural communication.* (4th ed.). New York: McGraw Hill.

Gudykunst, W., & Nishida, T. (1999). The influence of culture and strength of cultural identity on individual values in Japan and the United States. *Intercultural Communication Studies,* 9 (1), 1-18.

Hall, E. (1959). *The silent language.* New York: Doubleday/Fawcett.

Hall, E. (1966). *The hidden dimension.* New York: Doubleday.

Hall, E. (1983). *The dance of life: The other dimension of time.* New York: Doubleday.

Hall. E. (1998). The power of hidden differences. In M. Bennett (Ed.), *Basic concepts of intercultural communication* (pp. 53-67). Yarmouth, ME: Intercultural Press.

High, P. B. (1986). *An outline of American literature.* Harlow, UK: Longman.

Hofstede, G. (1980). *Culture's consequences.* Beverly Hills, CA: Sage.

Hofstede, G. (1991). *Cultures and organizations: Software of the mind.* London: McGraw Hill.

Hofstede, G. J., Pedersen, P., & Hofstede G. (2002). *Exploring culture: Exercises, stories and synthetic cultures.* Yarmouth, ME: Intercultural Press.

Hofstede, G., & Bond, M. (1984). Hofstede's culture dimensions. *Journal of Cross-cultural Psychology,* 15, 417-433.

Hymes, D. (1974a). Ways of speaking. In R. Bauman & J. Sherzer (Eds.), *Explorations in the ethnography of speaking.* Cambridge, UK: Cambridge University Press.

Hymes, D. (1974b). *Foundations in sociolinguistics: An ethnographic approach.* Philadelphia: University of Pennsylvania Press.

Jerald, M., & Clark, R. C. (1983). *Experiential language teaching techniques: Out-of-class language acquisition and cultural awareness activities.* Brattleboro, VT: Pro Lingua Associates.

Judd, E. (1999). Some issues in the teaching of pragmatic competence. In E. Hinkel (Ed.), *Culture in second language teaching and learning* (pp. 152-166). Cambridge: Cambridge University Press.

Kaplan, R. B. (1966). Cultural thought patterns in inter-cultural education. *Language Learning, 16* (1 and 2), 1-20.

Kasper, G., & Blum-Kulka, S. (Eds.). (1993). *Interlanguage pragmatics.* New York: Oxford University Press.

Kearney Datesman, M. K., Crandall, J., & Kearney, E. N. (2005). *American ways: An introduction to American culture* (3rd ed.). White Plains, NY: Pearson/Longman.

Klebanow, B., & Fischer, S. (1985). *American holidays: Exploring traditions, customs, and backgrounds* (2nd ed.) Brattleboro, VT: Pro Lingua Associates.

Kohls, L. R. (1996). *Survival kit for overseas living* (3rd ed.) Yarmouth, ME: Intercultural Press.

Kramsch, C. (1993). *Context and culture in language teaching.* Oxford: Oxford University Press.

Kramsch, C. (1998). *Language and culture.* Oxford: Oxford University Press.

Kroeber, A., & Kluckhohn, C. (1952). *Culture: A critical review of concepts and definitions* (Pages of the Peabody Museum, Vol. 47). Cambridge, MA: Peabody Museum.

Leki, I. (1991). Twenty-five years of contrastive rhetoric: text analysis and writing pedagogies. *TESOL Quarterly, 25* (1), 123-143

Levine, R. (1997). *A geography of time: The temporal misadventures of a social psychologist, or how every culture keeps time just a little bit differently.* New York: Harper Collins.

Levine, R., & Wolff, E. (1985). Social time: The heartbeat of culture. *Psychology Today* 19. 28-35.

Lewis, R. D. (2000). *When cultures collide: Managing successfully across cultures.* London: Nicholas Brealey Publishing.

LoCastro, V. (2003*). An introduction to pragmatics.* Anne Arbor, MI: The University of Michigan Press.

Lustig, M., & Koester, J. (2003). *Intercultural competence: Interpersonal communication across cultures.* (4th ed.). Boston: Allyn and Bacon.

Maccoby, E., & Jacklin, C. (1974). *The psychology of sex differences*. Stanford: Stanford University Press.

Maley, A., Duff, A., & Grellet, F. (1981). *The mind's eye: Using pictures creatively in language learning.* Cambridge: Cambridge University Press.

Maltz, D. N. & Borker, R. A. (1982). A cultural approach to male–female miscommunication. In J. J. Gumperz (Ed.), *Language and social identity.* Cambridge: Cambridge University Press.

Matsumoto, D., LeRoux, J., Ratzlaffa, C., Tatania, H., Uchida, H., Kima, C., & Anaki, S. (2001). Development and validation of a measure of intercultural adjustment potential in Japanese sojourners: The Intercultural Adjustment Potential Scale (ICAPS). *Intercultural Journal of Intercultural Relations* 25(5), 488-510.

Maurice, K. (1986). Cultural styles of thinking and speaking in the classroom. In P. Byrd (Ed.), *Teaching across cultures in the university ESL program.* Washington, DC: National Association for Foreign Student Affairs.

McCarthy, M. (1991). *Discourse analysis for language teachers*. Cambridge: Cambridge University Press.

Mejia, E., Kennedy Xiao, M., & Kennedy, J. (1994). *102 very teachable films.* Englewood Cliffs, NJ: Prentice-Hall Regents.

Mlynarczyk, R., & Haber, S. B. (2005). *In our own words: Student writers at work.* New York: Cambridge University Press.

Moran, P. (2001). *Teaching culture: Perspectives in practice.* Boston: Heinle & Heinle.

Murphey, T. (1992). *Music and song.* Oxford: Oxford University Press.

Nanda, S., & Warms, R. L. (1998). *Cultural anthropology* (6th ed.). Belmont, CA: Wadsworth.

Nelson, G. (1995). Cultural differences in learning styles. In J. Reid (Ed.), *Learning styles in the ESL/EFL classroom* (pp. 3-18). Boston, MA: Heinle & Heinle Publishers.

Nieto, S. (2000). *Affirming diversity: The sociopolitical context of multicultural education.* (3rd ed.). New York: Addison Wesley Longman, Inc.

Nieto, S. (2002). *Language, culture, and teaching: Critical perspectives for a new century.*

Mahwah, NJ: Lawrence Erlbaum Associates, Inc.

O'Sullivan, K. (1994). *Understanding ways: Communicating between cultures.* Alexandria, NSW, Australia: Hale & Iremonger.

Oberg, K. (1960). Cultural shock: Adjustment to new cultural environments. *Practical Anthropology, 7,* 177-182.

Ochoa-Becker, A. S. (2003). Thinking peace/Doing peace. In Bennett, C. I. *Comprehensive multicultural education: Theory and practice* (5th ed.). Boston: Pearson Education.

Orbe, M. P. (April, 1995). Building community in the diverse classroom: Strategies for communication professors. Paper presented at the annual meeting of the Central States Communication Association, Indianapolis, IN.

Oxford, R. (2001). A synthesis of existing research on gender differences in L2 learning strategy use. In Cochran, E. & Yepez, M. (Eds.). *Issues in gender, language learning, and classroom pedagogy* (p.1-26). New York: NJTESOL-NJBE & Bastos Educational Publications.

Palmer, P. J. (1993). *To know as we are known: Education as a spiritual journey.* San Francisco: Harper.

Patterson, M. (1990). Functions of non-verbal behavior in social interaction. In H. Giles & W. Robinson (Eds.), *Handbook of language and social psychology* (pp. 101-118). New York: Wiley and Son.

Pennycook, A. (1999). "Introduction: Critical approaches to TESOL." *TESOL Quarterly* 33 (3), 329–348.

Peterson, B. (2004). *Cultural intelligence: A guide to working with people from other cultures.* Yarmouth, ME: Intercultural Press, Inc.

Pleck, J. (1977). The psychology of sex roles. *Journal of Communication*, 26, 193-200.

Porter, R. E., & Samovar, L. A. (1988). Approaching intercultural communication. In L. Samovar & R. Porter (Eds.), *Intercultural communication: A reader.* (5th ed.) (pp. 15-30). Belmont, CA: Wadsworth Publishing Co.

Purgason, K. (2007, March). *"Get into groups" made more efficient and effective.* Paper presented at the annual meeting of Teachers of English to Speakers of Other Languages, Seattle, WA.

Reid, J. (1987). The learning style preferences of ESL students. *TESOL Quarterly,* 21 (1), 87-111.

Reitzel, A. (1986). The fear of speaking: Communication anxiety in ESL students. In P. Byrd (Ed.), *Teaching across cultures in the university ESL program.* Washington, DC: National Association for Foreign Student Affairs.

Ryffel, C. (1997). From culture "teaching" to culture "learning": Structures and strategies for increased effectiveness. In A. E. Fantini (Ed.), *New ways in teaching culture* (pp.28-35). Alexandria, VA: TESOL, Inc.

Samovar, L. A., & Porter, R. E. (2004). *Communication between cultures* (5th ed.). Belmont, CA: Wadsworth.

Samovar, L. A., & Porter, R. E. (Eds.). (1988). *Intercultural communication: A reader.* (5th ed.). Belmont, CA: Wadsworth Publishing Co.

Samovar, L. A., & Porter, R. E. (Eds.). (2004). *Communication between cultures.* (5th ed.). Belmont, CA: Wadsworth Publishing Co.

Schumann, J. (1976). Social distance as a factor in second language acquisition. *Language Learning* 26, 135-143.

Searle, J. R. (1969). *Speech acts: An essay in the philosophy of language.* Cambridge: Cambridge University Press.

Seelye, H. N. (1993). *Teaching culture: Strategies for intercultural communication.* (3rd ed.). Lincolnwood, IL: National Textbook Co.

Shaules, J. (2007). *Deep culture: The hidden challenges of global living.* Clevedon, England: Multilingual Matters.

Shirts, R. G. (1994). BaFá BaFá: A cross-cultural simulation. In L. R. Kohls and J. M. Knight. *Developing intercultural awareness: A cross-cultural training handbook* (2nd ed.) (p. 127). Yarmouth, ME: Intercultural Press, Inc.

Shulman, M. A. (1998). *Cultures in contrast.* Ann Arbor, MI: University of Michigan Press.

Snow, D. (1996). *More than a native speaker: An introduction for volunteers teaching abroad.* Alexandria, VA: TESOL.

Stewart, E. C., & Bennett, M. J. (1991). *American cultural patterns: A cross-cultural*

perspective (Rev. ed.). Yarmouth, ME: Intercultural Press,

Storti, C. (1994). *Cross-cultural dialogs: 74 brief encounters with cultural difference.* (2nd ed.). Yarmouth, ME: Intercultural Press.

Storti, C., & Bennhold-Saaman, L. (1997). *Culture matters: The Peace Corps cross-cultural workbook.* Washington, D.C.: U. S. Government Printing Office.

Tajfel, H. (1978). Social categorization, social identity, and social comparisons. In H. Tajfel (Ed.), *Differentiation between social groups.* London: Academic Press.

Tannen, D. (1990). *You just don't understand.* New York: Ballantine.

Tannen, D. (1994). *Talking from 9 to 5 - Women and men in the workplace: Language, sex and power.* New York: Avon Books.

Taylor, H. D., & Sorenson, J. L. (1961). Culture capsules. *Modern Language Journal,* 45, 350-54.

Taylor, H. M. (1974). Japanese kinesics. *Journal of the Association of Teachers of Japanese,* 9, 65-75.

Thiagarajan, S., & Steinwachs, B. (1994). Barnga: A simulation game on culture clashes. In Kohls, L. R., and Knight, J. M., *Developing intercultural awareness: A cross-cultural training* handbook (2nd ed.) (p. 127-128) Yarmouth, ME: Intercultural Pres., Inc.

Thomas, J. (1983). Cross-cultural pragmatic failure. *Applied Linguistics,* 4 (1), 91-112.

Thomas, J. (1984). Cross-cultural discourse as "unequal encounter": Toward a pragmatic analysis. *Applied Linguistics,* 5 (2), 226-235.

Thornley, G. C., & Roberts, G. (1984). *An outline of English literature.* Harlow, UK: Longman.

Ting-Toomey, S. (1999). *Communicating across cultures.* New York: Guilford Press.

Tomalin, B., & Stempleski, S. (1993). *Cultural awareness.* New York: Oxford University Press.

Triandis, H. (1988). Collectivism vs. individualism. In G. Veerma & C. Bagley (Eds.), *Cross-cultural studies of personality, attitudes, and cognition.* London: Macmillan.

Trumbull, E., Rothstein-Fisch, C., Greenfield, P. M., & Quiroz, B. (2001). *Bridging cultures between home and school: A guide for teachers.* Mahwah, NJ: Erlbaum.

Turner, J. (1987). *Rediscovering the social group.* Oxford: Blackwell.

Valdes, J. M. (1986). Culture in literature. In Valdes, J. M. (Ed.), *Culture bound: Bridging the cultural gap in language teaching* (pp. 137-147). New York: Cambridge University Press.

Weaver, G. (1993). Understanding and coping with cross-cultural adjustment stress. In R. M. Paige (Ed.), *Education for the intercultural experience.* Yarmouth, ME: Intercultural Press

Weaver, G. (Ed.) (1994). *Culture, communication, and conflict: Readings in intercultural relations.* Needham Heights, MA: Ginn Press.

Whiteson, V. (Ed.) (1996). *New ways of using drama and literature in language teaching.* Alexandria, VA: Teachers of English to Speakers of Other Languages, Inc.

Williamson, J. A., & Vincent, J. C. (1996). *Film is content: A study guide for the advanced ESL classroom.* Ann Arbor, MI: University of Michigan Press.

Wink, J. (2005). *Critical pedagogy: Notes from the real world* (3rd ed.). Boston: Pearson Allyn & Bacon.

Wintergerst, A., and DeCapua, A. (2001). Exploring the learning styles of Russian-speaking students of English as a second language. *The CATESOL Journal* 31 (1), 23-46.

Wintergerst, A., DeCapua, A., & Verna, M. (2002). An analysis of one learning styles instrument for language students. *TESL Canada Journal,* 20 (1), 16-37.

Wintergerst, A., DeCapua, A., & Verna, M. (2003). Conceptualizing learning style modalities for ESL/EFL students. *System* 31, 85-106.

Wolfson, N. (1989). *Perspectives: Sociolinguistics and TESOL.* New York: Newbury House Publishers.

Wood, J .T. (1994). *Gendered lives: Communication, gender, and culture.* Belmont, CA: Wadsworth.

Wright, A. (1987). *How to enjoy paintings.* Cambridge: Cambridge University Press.

Wright, A. (1989). *Pictures for language learning.* Cambridge: Cambridge University Press.

Zeidner, M. (1986). Are English language aptitude tests biased towards culturally different minority groups? Some Israeli findings. *Language Testing,* 3 (1), 80-95.

■ NAME INDEX

SUBJECT INDEX